Embrace the Wind of the Holy Spirit

Barbara McDonald Golie

TRILOGY CHRISTIAN PUBLISHERS

Tustin, CA

Trilogy Christian Publishers
A Wholly Owned Subsidiary of Trinity Broadcasting Network
2442 Michelle Drive
Tustin, CA 92780

Embrace the Wind of the Holy Spirit

Copyright © 2024 Barbara McDonald Golie

Scripture quotations marked ESV are taken from the ESV® Bible (The Holy Bible, English Standard Version®), copyright © 2001 by Crossway Bibles, a publishing ministry of Good News Publishers. Used by permission. All rights reserved.

Scripture quotations marked NIV are taken from the Holy Bible, New International Version®, NIV®. Copyright © 1973, 1978, 1984, 2011 by Biblica, Inc.™ Used by permission of Zondervan. All rights reserved worldwide. www.zondervan.com. The "NIV" and "New International Version" are trademarks registered in the United States Patent and Trademark Office by Biblica, Inc.™.

Scripture quotations marked NKJV are taken from the New King James Version®. Copyright © 1982 by Thomas Nelson. Used by permission. All rights reserved.

Scripture quotations marked NLT are taken from the Holy Bible, New Living Translation, copyright © 1996, 2004, 2015 by Tyndale House Foundation. Used by permission of Tyndale House Publishers, Inc., Carol Stream, Illinois 60188. All rights reserved.

Scripture quotations marked KJV are taken from the King James Version of the Bible. Public domain.

For information, address Trilogy Christian Publishing.

Rights Department, 2442 Michelle Drive, Tustin, Ca 92780.

Trilogy Christian Publishing/ TBN and colophon are trademarks of Trinity Broadcasting Network.

For information about special discounts for bulk purchases, please contact Trilogy Christian Publishing.

Trilogy Disclaimer: The views and content expressed in this book are those of the author and may not necessarily reflect the views and doctrine of Trilogy Christian Publishing or the Trinity Broadcasting Network.

10 9 8 7 6 5 4 3 2 1

Library of Congress Cataloging-in-Publication Data is available.

ISBN 979-8-89041-756-5

ISBN 979-8-89041-757-2 (ebook)

Dedication

In our fifty-eight years of marriage, the love, confidence, and undaunted faith of my husband, Jack K. Golie, gave me the courage to birth the story of my hillbilly heritage in the Ozark Mountains of Arkansas. Despite the hurdles, the Holy Spirit— *and a husband who loved me unconditionally*—swept me into a life of courage, tragedies, and miracles.

Hunkered down in a US Marine Corps bunker on a Vietnam hillside, Jack wrote my most treasured love letter. He described the Holy Spirit's canopy over our marriage as an "Ocean of Completeness."

Throughout his extensive battle with stage four MDS leukemia, Jack's steadfast, iron-clad faith reignited courage in others, especially me. His memorable and inspirational affirmations below describe his strength, bravery, and role as the *Forever Love of my life*:

- "Angel, we have today." (Yes! Moments are precious!)
- "In your darkest times, *trust* God!" (God is faithful!)
- "You are never alone!" (The Holy Spirit dwells within you!)
- "I've covenanted with God for my family!" (We'll be together again!)

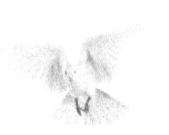

- "Suffering is never for nothing." (Heaven answers all questions!)
- "There is an end to suffering!" (Heaven has no pain! Revelation 21:4, KJV)
- "You are in Christ; I am in Christ!" (We are never far apart!)

Chaplain Jack K. Golie: "I'll catch you down the road, bro!" (1976 US Marine Corps Winter Training in the Sierras)

Acknowledgments

Barbara Golie does not possess the skillfulness of a professional writer. *Embrace the Wind of the Holy Spirit* was birthed by its leading character—the Holy Spirit. He is the "Wind" that *swept over my life* and choreographed tragedies into triumph. The Hebrew word *"Ruach"* means "wind," "breath," or "spirit."

Friends and family have walked with me on my journey. Their influence has been immeasurable. My love and appreciation are expressed to a "few of the many" who have lived special moments alongside me in my pilgrimage:

Jack Golie (husband)—Jack's confidence was consistently greater in me than mine. *His unconditional love and trust lifted my limp wings heavenward.*

Veta McDonald (Mother)—what a legacy her buckboard ride was for our family! As a teen, the Holy Spirit used her to galvanize my faith: *"Barbara, the Bible says God's ways are not grievous. Don't give up on God."*

Chester McDonald (Dad)—you regained consciousness— your family was gone—you were paralyzed! No phone. You got your family to safety! Incredible! You dedicated hours teaching me to sing harmony and alto at age seven. *You piloted my participation in the church.*

Mary McDonald (Granny)—*my tiny grandma—my guardian angel*. She encouraged me in music, education, church, and work ethic. Her words, "Always do more than is expected of you!" *I miss her!*

Freeman McDonald (Papa)—a man of faith, love, and integrity. His joy and appreciation *danced in his eyes* for all his grandchildren. *I miss him!*

DeWayne McDonald (brother)—in my young hillbilly years—a most faithful friend. We walked historical moments together. His singing voice is similar to Dad's. *A precious brother!*

Lonnie McDonald (brother)—twelve years younger, my loyal sidekick and joy in my lonely teenage years. He is our tallest family member! *His PhD thesis was lovingly dedicated to Dad.*

Mary Patterson (aunt)—Aunt Mary gifted me dreamland in "Cinderella's Slippers" as I paraded for hours in her petite shoes! *An amazing wife, mother, grandmother, and great-grandmother!*

Miss Phoebe (neighbor)—horses and iron wagon wheels noisily came up the rocky road. Barefoot, I ran to say it was my birthday! She bought me a toy watch at the store. *"My special friend, happy eighth birthday!"*

Miss Ruby (neighbor)—when youth rallies were miles away, she *walked* to my home and gave me timing details. She and her husband drove me without charge. *She was the invisible arm of God to help me plow through my lonely teenage years.*

Readers

Carolynn McDonald (Batesville, Arkansas)—Kenneth, her husband, my brother, graduated to Heaven at sixty-four. *Carolynn's deep faith and words ignited courage in me!*

Cassandra Marchese (Oak Harbor, Washington)—she and Michael, her husband, triggered my determination to achieve the Holy Spirit's goals for the book. *Their prayers and encouragement helped effectuate its finalization.*

Cliff and Carol Christensen (Burnsville, Minnesota)—since 1960, our "Forever Friends" from college and seminary. They have served others in lifelong ministry. Their valuable expertise was critical to *Embrace the Wind of the Holy Spirit.*

Connie May (Sacramento, California)—Connie, alongside her husband, Chuck, is a full-time counselor. She spurred me on with her effective critiques and inspirational support. Since 1979, Forever Friends!

Jack Gregory Golie (Manteca, California)—Since age twenty, Greg, our son, has suffered the cruel effects of MS, including blindness in one eye and right-side paralysis. *He gave excellent feedback and loved that the book was dedicated to his dad.*

Jana Kay Golie (Chesapeake, Virginia)—Jana, our daughter, has been an effective sounding board. She has been my final reader for each story. *An effective motivator!*

Johnnie Kay Bunch (Berryville, Arkansas)—Johnnie appreciated the insight into our early family history. She was touched to hear details of Nancy Sue's short angelic life. *A sister she never knew! My sister and my friend!*

Lillian Ferris (San Diego, California)—Lillian has been my spiritual and officer-wife mentor for fifty-four years. *Her loving critique and attention to detail were essential.*

Myrna McDonald (Berryville, Arkansas)—Myrna, my brother DeWayne's wife, was the one who read the stories between 2–3 a.m. She was my quickest responder and a great morale-booster—*DeWayne's treasure.*

Rhonda VanZandt (Tok, Alaska)—Rhonda has been an emotional coach since Jack's death. She and her husband, Saber, kept calling, "When will the book be finished?" *Thanks for your push toward the goal!*

Ruthie Hedge (Troy, Montana)—like my husband, a Havre, Montana, native! Ruthie is the pianist at the church Jack formerly pastored. *She was a great encourager!*

Tracy Havens (Chatham, Ontario, Canada)—a loving husband, two college sons, coaching, online courses, and two trips to Israel did not prevent Tracy's crucial feedback and prayers. *Thank you, my Canadian friend!*

Velvet Ivers (Yakutat, Alaska)—a schoolteacher who has a busy life. From her and Wayne's cottage overlooking the Pacific Ocean, *she gave time for the book's success.*

Carol Fairman (Monroe, Georgia)—my professional online coach. Her wisdom and tender words penetrated my broken heart. Tenacity was relit within me to finish the book. *Carol, I'll meet you in Heaven!*

Sarah Holloway (Sussex, England)—her expertise helped finalize the graphics. *Thank you, my UK friend!*

David O'Dell (Virginia Beach, Virginia)—a renowned photographer who captured the perfect moment in an ocean sunrise. David also "resurrected" the *aged photos* inside the book. *Thank you, David!*

Epigraph

More than an autobiography;
orchestrations of the Holy Spirit.
More than problems;
renewal tools of the Holy Spirit.
More than a hillbilly heritage;
a legacy of Holy Spirit choreographed lives.

Reverend Clifford and Carol Christensen
(Friends of Jack and Barbara since 1960)

Contents

January 1939—Ozark Mountains of Arkansas

Chester Earl and Veta Marie (Warren) McDonald
Kenneth Gordon (nineteen months)
and Barbara Earlene (three months)
1930s Depression Aftermath

Divinely Orchestrated Sunday Morning

Indian Creek was a more forceful flow in January 1939.
A slower flow is shown in the July 1973 photo above.

Barefoot, Mother waded Indian Creek on a cold Sunday morning in January 1939. With her shoes in one hand, she lifted her dress and coat above her knees with her other hand to keep them dry. In winter, the waters were more profound and

forceful than in the July picture above—the very location where Mother crossed. The colorful pebbles were brilliantly visible in the cold icy water. Here and there, the small rolling clouds were slowly disappearing. The morning sun reflected the beauty of the feathery, fluffy clouds in the creek's water as they quietly crept over the beautiful Ozark Mountains of Arkansas. The sun's glowing warmth signaled that her journey home would be much more pleasurable.

Unanswered questions filled my twenty-year-old mother's thoughts. Where did she find the courage to make this out-of-the-ordinary solo morning trip? The early spark of her and Dad's marriage appeared to have been extinguished. Their dirt-poor life stressed her husband's usual upbeat personality. Moneyless existence, two children, and a wife had become burdens too heavy for him to bear. Early on, both his brother and his sister had failed marriages. Mother's heart sensed the weight of her secret sorrows—burdens she had been unable to share. The severe impact of her family issues had become an immovable wall—too heavy to budge on her own. Fear and uncertainty overshadowed her young family's future. Early dreams of her and Dad's exciting life together had painfully dimmed. Fear and worry diminished her future hopes. Her self-doubts had depleted her courage and strength to face tomorrow. Perhaps God could rescue what she felt was a downward spiral in her marriage. As a young mother, she longed for a life without uncertainty. Limitations did not have to destroy their marriage.

Thundering across the centuries were the Holy Spirit-inspired words of the apostle Peter. Mother had not read Saint Peter's suggestion to cast all her anxieties upon Jesus because He cared for her. (See 1 Peter 5:6–7, ESV.) Jesus said, "Come to

me, all you who are weary and burdened, and I will give you rest" (Matthew 11:28, NIV).

Scripture described Mother's despair, "Hope deferred makes the heart sick, but a longing fulfilled is a tree of life" (Proverbs 13:12, NIV). The Holy Spirit saw beyond Mother's physical needs. He understood her hopeless heart. Mother needed God to take what she felt was a mess (her life) and turn it into His message. *Isn't that the basic message of the Gospel?*

On Sunday mornings, the Antioch schoolhouse was crowded with farmers whose friendships had ties of substance. Their pledged commitments to God were even more serious. Their handshake was a legal contract. Their family's cornerstone was the inspired command of Hebrews 10:25 (NIV) to meet and encourage one another. Heaven's rain was what the farmers depended on to grow their crops and to keep their life-giving wells from going dry. They revered God's Word, "Remember the Sabbath day by keeping it holy" (Exodus 20:8, NIV).

Painful Wounds of Rejection

Sadly, since childhood, Mother suffered from the silent pains of rejection. That familiar "brushed-off-by-others" feeling tormented her thoughts and dreams. Her hidden emotional scars confronted her each day. Camouflaged hurt, she never voiced.

At birth, her parents viewed her left "adult" eye as a marked eye. Visibly, in contrast to her right eye, her left eyebrow and eyelashes were black. The color of the adult eye was black, and much of the skin tissue around that eye and hairline was darker than the skin around her right eye. Her right eye was a beautiful deep brown. Until she was in her teenage years, the larger eye was prominent. Mother was embarrassed by her abnormal eye. Her heart craved comfort to soften her stressed feelings. She was unable to express her insecurities and rejections. She loved school but hated the stares and the teasing. When her help was needed at home, it was an effortless sacrifice for her to terminate school at the end of the seventh grade.

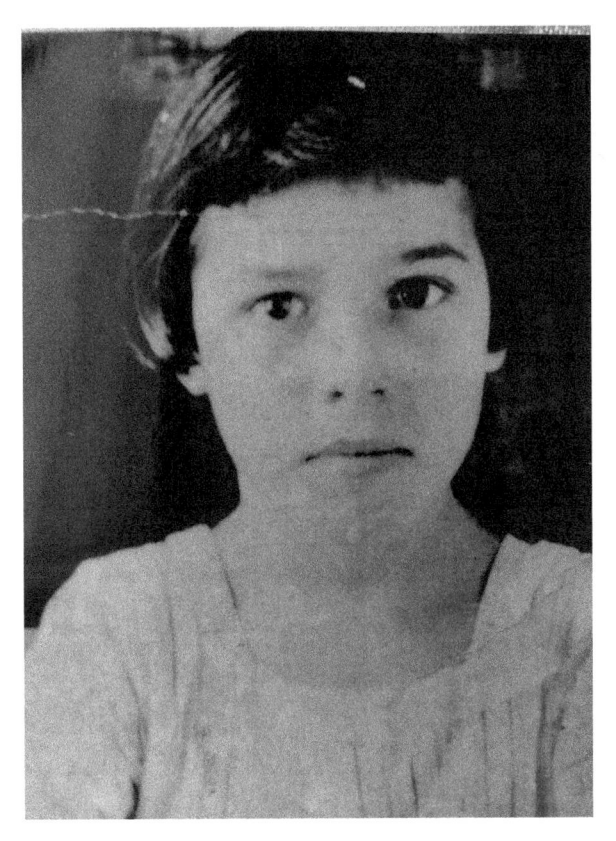

Veta Marie Warren (Eleven Years)

Mother only mentioned the story of her adult eye to me once. When I questioned why her skin was darker on one side of her eye, her unusual story began. "A few months before I was born, my mother built the morning fire in the family's wood stove. The house had to be heated before the children were awakened. Mother opened the stove door only to be shocked by a smoldering rag doll someone had tossed into the stove the prior evening. One of the eyes on the doll was burned and blackened. My mother told me that was why my eye was black and large. She told me that when she looked at the doll's burned eye, it marked my eye. When she saw my marked eye at birth, she said she immediately knew when it had happened."

Emotionally nor intellectually, Mother never understood her hidden pain from the incident.

Once she reached her mid-teen years, her eyes were closer to the same size. When required to assist her grandmother with housework, she ordered the free powder samples offered in her grandmother's magazines. Mother used the samples sparingly to lighten the skin on the abnormal eye, especially when associated with her peers.

She was an attractive teenager but never identified with her true beauty because of her marked eye. Children and teenagers are vulnerable to all types of fear. Most fears can be defined by one definition—false evidence appearing real.

Rejection is God's opportunity for redemption! The Holy Spirit heals hidden or revealed scars of grief and pain. God desires "to give unto them beauty for ashes, the oil of joy for mourning, the garment of praise for the spirit of heaviness" (Isaiah 61:3, KJV). "He heals the brokenhearted and binds up their wounds" (Psalm 147:3, ESV).

As Mother grew older, her olive-skin complexion minimized the darker skin tones. To Dad, she was stunningly beautiful! When she revealed how she felt about herself, I was shocked! Negative childhood remarks dug a deep ditch in her memory. Hurt drove a hammer into her soul. *Unfortunately, Mother had believed the evil taskmaster's deceptive lies.*

The Helper Is Promised

Jesus knew how devastatingly empty our lives would be after His ascension to Heaven. He promised to send us the Holy Spirit, who would indwell every person who loved Him—even little children. In contrast to the limitations of Jesus' earthly body, the Holy Spirit would simultaneously be omnipresent (everywhere present)—throughout the entire world. He would also be omniscient (all-knowing—complete knowledge of the past, present, and future). Limitless!

Jesus left His worried disciples (and us) with His special promise of the Holy Spirit, the Spirit of truth, the advocate, the helper, *who would never leave us!*

> If you love me, keep my commands. And I will ask the Father, and he will give you another advocate to help and be with you forever—the Spirit of truth. The world cannot accept him, because it neither sees him nor knows him. But you know him, for he lives with you and will be in you. I will not leave you as orphans; I will come to you.
>
> John 14:15–18 (NIV)

Jesus' promise to send the Holy Spirit gave His disciples the courage to face His ascension. Jesus instructed the one

hundred and twenty followers—before His departure—to wait in Jerusalem for the descension of the promised Holy Spirit to indwell them. (See Acts 1:4–5, 8, NIV.)

The Holy Spirit opened their hearts to spiritual truths they could never have known or understood without His assistance. He is a gentle, dignified, unimposing member of the Trinity. He is so immersed in Jesus that He is often personally unrecognized for the strong "attraction to Christ" that He produces in the lives of believers. The Holy Spirit becomes so transparent that we only see Jesus Christ.

Jesus' public ministry of miracles began after the Holy Spirit descended upon Him at His baptism. (See Matthew 3:16, ESV.) The Holy Spirit rested upon Him. The Father audibly spoke from Heaven! Visibly, the Father, His Son, Jesus, and the Holy Spirit ministered together at Jesus' baptism. The four Gospels promised that "believers" would be baptized with the Holy Spirit. See Matthew 3:11 (NIV), Mark 1:8 (NIV), Luke 3:16 (NIV), and John 1:33 (NIV).

The Deception of Evil

Evil forces will not be ignored. They will stealthily appear without invitation. "Stealthily" is defined as slow, deliberate, and secret in action or character—*intended to escape observation. Nothing deceptive, however, sneaks past the Holy Spirit!* Even the secrets of our hearts can be disclosed by the Holy Spirit's revelation (1 Corinthians 14:25, ESV). Jesus said, "See that no one leads you astray" (Matthew 24:4, ESV).

There were ouija boards in Mother's community. Mother said, "I was invited to one of the homes. The family decided to entertain the youth with their ouija board. I was terrified when the table began moving. I never went back again." The Holy Spirit guarded Mother's young life against her limited knowledge of spiritual darkness and the subtle inroads that its sinful deceptive poison destructively carves into our souls.

Dad told me how young people gathered at the home of one elderly lady known as the best storyteller of scary ghost stories. Dad said, "By the time we were to leave for home, we would all be too afraid to go alone!" Once minds and hearts are opened to the real or imaginary abode of the dead, it is more dangerous spiritually than can be comprehended. When we permit sin to make inroads into our soul, dark forces will use the opening as an opportunity to take dominion over the sinful areas of our life.

What do the Scriptures say? Regardless of the desperateness of Mother's life—or our lives—*Jesus never runs away from us!* He came from God, His Father—knowing His destiny in this world—and died for our sins so that we would not have to be condemned to die because of our sins. *God sent Jesus to us!* He yearned to give us spiritually abundant living! God has promised He will never leave His children nor forsake them. With confidence, we never have to be afraid of any circumstance! See Hebrews 13:5–6 (NIV).

Through His ministry in our lives, the Holy Spirit enables us to see sin and its deception as He sees sin and deception. A God-shaped cavern exists in every human heart—*a desire to connect with God.* Ecclesiastes 3:11 (NIV) says, "He has made everything beautiful in its time. He has also set eternity in the human heart; yet no man can fathom what God has done from beginning to end." God has always desired to give mankind His love, peace, guidance, and a purpose-driven life, not only for a time (our earthly living) but in preparation for eternity—our life to come!

Our greatest end-of-life fear should be a life that has had remarkable success in things that didn't matter eternally!

Something More

Not surprisingly, Dad saw beauty in Mother that she failed to see in herself. Dad's love gave her validation that she had never known. In the beginning, as an incredibly young lady, she believed her marriage would last forever. When she waded across the ice-cold stone pebbles of Indian Creek that January 1939 Sunday morning, she had no self-assurance about the duration of her marriage. Divorces were an easy way out for many. Would God fill the emptiness in her heart and heal her and Dad's unstable marriage? Why did he spend most days in his parents' home? Was he emotionally divorcing himself from her, Kenneth, and Barbara? Fear resided rent-free in her mind. *Something had to change—soon!*

The Holy Spirit's greatest longing has always been to unite everyone to Jesus—not divide. He is usually the first person of the Trinity we meet because He is designated to draw us to the Father and Jesus Christ, His Son. He administrates the ministry of the Trinity in our world. Inspired by the Holy Spirit, the prophet Isaiah wrote, "Even to your old age and gray hairs I am he, I am he who will sustain you. I have made you and I will carry you; I will sustain you and I will rescue you" (Isaiah 46:4, NIV). Our life-long promise from God!

Throughout her life—though she was unaware—the Holy Spirit had tenderly guarded Mother. He had orchestrated that January Sunday morning church journey when her heart tenaciously grappled for hope. The inspired Scripture tells us in Hebrews 6:19 (NIV), "We have this hope as an anchor for the soul, firm and secure."

Her silent cries for help were limited. She and Dad lived extremely isolated, on the top of a mountain in the woods. She was the first member of the couples with whom they associated to reach out to Christ. The Holy Spirit knew her address in the woods of the Ozark Mountains! He knows no handicaps! Isolation encouraged Mother to "look up" to God. The Holy Spirit can easily redirect and change our trapped and enslaved lives!

Mother wanted to forget her childhood years. She yearned for God to take His erasure and thoroughly clean her heart. She wanted the spark of her and Dad's first two years of marriage to resurface. She loved Dad. She loved her two children. She humbly submitted to personal inner change to salvage her marriage and family.

On her journey to church that Sunday, Mother's heart was burdened, desperate, and lonely. She ached to see the hurts of her life resolved. Her tiniest camouflaged (hidden) scars had become hefty weights. Marital wounds had crept into her and Dad's relationship. She couldn't explain how, but she knew God could open the door of her heart and prevent her silent scars and secret sorrows from inflicting damage on others. In times of difficulty, the small hidden hurts resurfaced and made her vulnerable and unforgiving. Undisclosed scars demand revenge—even to the emotional execution of others. *Sadly, the*

unforgiving person often becomes the one who suffers the most severe and permanent injury. Unforgiveness is part of this world's darkness. It involves payback, revenge, and withholding love from others. Our forgiveness dispenses grace. Whether or not the other person forgives, God forgives us!

For centuries, above the hustle and bustle of this world, the Holy Spirit has nudged hungry hearts to accept Jesus' invitation for peace and eternal life (Revelation 3:20, NIV). The King of kings invites *everyone* to His home forever—Heaven! No exceptions!

In the artist's perfect depiction of Jesus knocking on the door, there is no doorknob outside. The door must be opened from the inside—symbolic of our heart's response to Christ. Jesus tenderly knocks and waits. He doesn't break the door down! The Holy Spirit asks us to open the door. Has your heart heard the Holy Spirit's whisper, "Jesus will never leave you! He will never fail you!" (See Deuteronomy 31:6, NIV, and Hebrews 13:5, NIV.) Jesus wants to justify our hearts—purify them *just as if we had never sinned! Our response opens or closes the door forever to eternal life!*

Sadly, by significant contrast, sin lightly taps its horn or blows its whistle to get our attention!

Dad had no desire to go to church on a Sunday morning. He volunteered to babysit Kenneth, who was nineteen months old, and me (three months). He did not understand the "why" of her out-of-the-ordinary Sunday morning trip. His attitude toward God and the church was casual. In his heart, he was extremely disappointed in their economic lack. Nothing significant ever seemed to materialize into money. He had worked hard to

provide for his family in depressed times. Morally, he had been faithful to Mother. It was difficult to observe his family's needs each day helplessly!

Dad had not yet realized that, from God's perspective, it is much more important to live a life of significance than to live a grandeur and successful life from the world's materialistic point of view. *End-of-life rewards are beyond comparison bounds!*

Mountains of fear and excuses keep us from accepting Jesus' invitation. To follow God's command, Zerubbabel faced a giant mountain. God gave him an unforgettable promise in Zechariah 4:6–7 (ESV), "Not by might, nor by power, but by my Spirit, says the Lord of hosts. Who are you, O great mountain? Before Zerubbabel you shall become a plain."

In His wisdom, the Holy Spirit knew exactly how to reorient Dad's heart—to make him a better husband and father—giving him hope for his family. The Holy Spirit knew how to turn Dad and Mother's marital and economic mountains into a "Zerubbabel plain"! Throughout history, the Holy Spirit has initiated simple, uncomplicated options to enable us to make appropriate life-changing decisions. With great love, He calls us individually. *He graces us with the freedom to accept Him or deny Him.*

Eventually, death comes for each of us. *Our accumulated treasures then go to others.* A well-lived life, with eternal focus, propels us toward our heavenly treasures. We can live both a meaningful and successful life! However, a successful life— *lived only for oneself*—abolishes the spiritually significant "servant" role God ordained us to fulfill. As Christians, we must be focused on God's priorities. In this life, we are "laying up" treasures in Heaven. Jesus said, "But store up for yourselves

treasures in Heaven ...For where your treasure is, there your heart will be also" (Matthew 6:20–21, NIV). Heaven's treasure chests can only be filled during our lifetime. To give away love, hope, encouragement, service, money, or possessions we cannot keep—for what we cannot lose eternally—will fill our treasure chests in Heaven.

Jack, my husband, treasured relationships, not possessions. Generosity was his nature—just like his precious mother. They both died abundantly rich in Heaven's treasures. Jack gave love, encouragement, time, money, and possessions he could not keep—for Heaven's eternal treasures he could not lose! Jack wanted to see and love people as Jesus saw and loved them. Titles and degrees were insufficient for that task. When communicating with anyone, he wanted to treat them like he might never see them again. Only the power of the gospel of Jesus Christ can touch hearts! God is sovereign. Schedules can be created, but nobody owns the next minute of their life. One rarely heard Jack speak about the streets of gold or the mansions in Heaven. His emphasis was on Jesus. His words to me before his death, "Angel, as far as I am concerned, Heaven can be black as long as Jesus is there!" He smiled and said he only wanted to hear five words from Jesus, "Jack, you have been faithful."

Jack knew that I highly treasured every item in our house. After being raised in poverty, it became easy for me to cling to "stuff." In reflection, Jack lay in the bed—extremely ill—when he looked at me and said, *Angel, hold on to material things loosely.*

Since Jack's death, the Holy Spirit has caused those words to reverberate in my memory. Material possessions I have learned to release. Releasing stuff to meet the needs of others,

to encourage and celebrate others, is pure motivation to fill treasure chests in Heaven. Treasures that will never be lost. Blessing others—not only those we are close to—matters to God.

God lovingly takes us beyond our own family to the wounded hearts of our world. The Holy Spirit knows the wounded by name, their address, and how to make our paths intersect. He is the capable manager and administrator of our lives. One caveat—we have to be available to Him.

Mother did not realize that her journey—through the hills and across Indian Creek—would become a predestined spiritual beginning for the succeeding McDonald generations. A new and significant genesis in her and Dad's life together! A divinely choreographed journey! *That is the Holy Spirit at work, and He often begins with one spiritually hungry heart!*

What a difference is made when someone—like Mother— yields to the inner voice of the Holy Spirit. *One right decision can impact succeeding generations for eternity!*

Mother had never read God's promise for her in Isaiah 59:21 (NIV),

"As for me, this is my covenant with them," says the Lord, "My Spirit, who is on you, will not depart from you, and my words that I have put in your mouth will always be on your lips, on the lips of your children and on the lips of their descendants—from this time on and forever," says the Lord.

Wind at Mother's Back

After Mother waded the icy-cold waters of Indian Creek, she leaned against a huge, black walnut tree. The January wind felt bitter cold on her wet feet. She hurriedly put on her long cotton socks. Her feet felt too frozen to walk. The remainder of her trip was primarily uphill—three hills. She worried about how Chester managed the children in her absence. He had never cared for the baby alone. Would she become hungry before she returned? As she began her uphill walk, she wondered if she had made a wise decision.

Suddenly, she heard the sound of horses trotting on the east side of the wagon trail. She looked to her left and thought, *Could it be true for my cold feet?* Yes! A buckboard turned the corner of the hill!

This was a cherished weekly church journey for Mr. and Mrs. Ray and their daughter, Ove. Mrs. Ray and Ove wore extremely long dresses. Their sleeves were long, even in hot summers.

When Mr. and Mrs. Ray's buckboard arrived at the Antioch Church schoolhouse, several buckboards and wagons were there. Single adults rode their horses and tied them to the fence posts that bordered the schoolyard. Others, such as Granny and Papa (Dad's parents), lived within one-quarter of a mile.

To save on gas, they always walked. Granny had worked hard all her life. She never missed an opportunity to improve the economy of her family! Granny often quoted the old adage, "A penny saved is a penny earned." Then, with her many years of economic scrimping, she would laugh and add, "Especially for paupers!"

Papa always visited the church early and warmed the building before the cold parishioners arrived. In summer, the school windows were opened wide. Everyone brought paper hand fans. Fans were free from the town merchants with an advertisement of their stores. A wooden "hold" stick was glued or stapled to the cardboard paper fan.

The Antioch Church schoolhouse had no bathrooms, only short, bushy trees, brush, and tall grass in two fields. A women's and girl's field (east side), and a men's and boy's field (north side). Only babies drank liquids in church. No nursery. Mothers who nursed their babies covered any exposure with handkerchiefs or headscarves. Otherwise, frowns or a cleared throat could get everyone's attention!

"Dinner On the Ground" occurred a few times annually at the Antioch Church schoolhouse. The ground table consisted of a long row of tablecloths stretched over the school ground and guarded by a few bold women. Granny was one of them! Rocks anchored the tablecloths. The school had an outside hand pump that could be used for water. Before the pump upgrade, water was carried in wagons. On Sunday morning, the Antioch schoolhouse that doubled as a church was filled—without advertisements. Everyone arrived ready to sing, whether you were in the volunteer choir on the stage or seated at the small desk chairs.

Reflecting on Mother's solo journey, she listened to the Holy Spirit's gentle, inaudible voice in her heart. Her January 1939 cold and courageous venture gave our family a landmark beginning spiritually. Proverbs 14:1 (NIV), "The wise woman builds her house, but with her own hands the foolish one tears hers down."

Mother, a twenty-year-old with two children and an unknown future, wanted her family preserved—not dismantled by economic and spiritual storms. She attended church penniless. Her gift to God was her hungry heart—all that He required!

In Matthew 11:30 (NIV), Jesus' words implied, "Veta, stay close to Me. If you stay close to Me, I will lighten your burdens; My strength will carry you!" Because Joseph, his earthly father, had a carpenter shop, Jesus knew all about yokes. A mature ox was placed in a yoke with a young, immature ox. The older ox carried the heavy load. As he matured, the younger ox carried more. He eventually became like the older ox. An important factor was to construct the yoke to keep the oxen close to each other. The closer they were together, the more the younger ox became like the older ox and the stronger he became. *Reader, Jesus is in the yoke with you and me! Be confident in His strength!*

Brave-hearted Mother, thank you for your barefoot wade across the icy-cold water of Indian Creek—alone—that January 1939 Sunday morning. You were broken, repentant, and teachable. Like ripples in a pond, your decision to follow Jesus became Heaven's legacy for your family! You did not permit life's challenges to define you! You chose God's immovable values that initiated a legacy of faith for generations—our forever heritage! Because of your courageous heart, God caused your

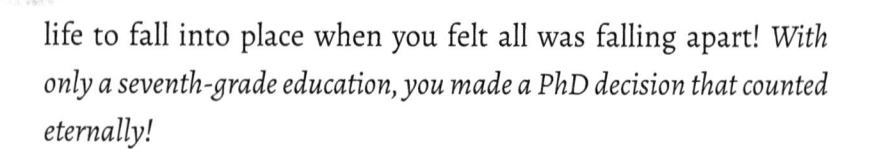
life to fall into place when you felt all was falling apart! *With only a seventh-grade education, you made a PhD decision that counted eternally!*

Mother Dumped
Her Backpack

The church service began promptly at 10 a.m. The stage was filled with a choir of volunteers. Singing traditional hymns from the heart was the agenda for the first thirty minutes. Neither the church nor the school could afford a piano. There was no guitar. When the congregation sang from their hearts, Heaven took notice!

A widowed lady speaker, Mrs. Hulsey, was the guest minister. When the altar invitation was given to accept Jesus Christ, Mother quickly went forward. Despite her fears, she was determined to follow her heart. Tears that streamed down her face were tears of desperation. Christians knelt beside her and prayed. Mother was willing to birth the necessary struggle for a breakthrough. *The Holy Spirit transformed the dry desert of her life into an oasis of joy!*

Immediately, her heart weights—hidden hurts, untreated bruises, and camouflaged scars—released their grip. Formidable scars of pain were gone! The Holy Spirit lifted a huge emotional backpack from her shoulders. Poisoned roots were dug up. Bitterness no longer controlled her emotions. She was infused with a stable anchor of hope. As a new believer, the apostle

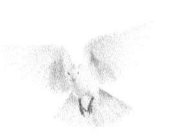

John's words of encouragement written hundreds of years ago to Mother and every desperate heart said, "All who have this hope in him purify themselves, just as he is pure" (1 John 3:3, NIV).

Mother's life was unstrapped! From personal experience, David proclaimed the inspiring words, "Cast your cares on the Lord and he will sustain you; he will never let the righteous be shaken" (Psalm 55:22, NIV). Emotionally and spiritually, Mother's season of struggle became manageable. Life was lived with the hope and the inner strength that all Heaven provided her. No more unhealed wounds to trigger revenge. The Holy Spirit used her insecurities to bring her heart to its needed inner peace.

It was not an introduction to God that she could have earned. Her experience with God is perfectly described in Ephesians 2:8–9 (NIV), "For it is by grace you have been saved, through faith—and this is not from yourselves, it is the gift of God—not by works, so that no one can boast." With His gentle dignity, the Holy Spirit had tenderly escorted Mother as she pushed through her challenges to discover her only anchor of hope, Jesus Christ. Mother was anxious to get home to share with Dad.

Mr. and Mrs. Ray were ecstatic about her spiritual decision! In their buckboard ride back to Indian Creek—where the Rays continued eastward—they encouraged her to attend church. They said, "Goodbye, Veta. We will look for you each Sunday morning. You are always welcome to ride up the hills with us to church."

Again, Mother waded back across Indian Creek. On her return trip, there was a spring in her step. She felt the sun— now at high noon—was shining just for her! Gone was the

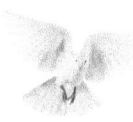

wall of doubts and fears she had wrestled with on her early morning venture. As she relayed this story to me, Mother said, "Barbara, I had never felt so clean inside my heart! I turned my face toward the sky, lifted my arms toward Heaven, and sang through the woods and up the long hill home. When I arrived home, Chester was not so happy from his morning with you!"

Dad had an excellent tenor voice but was not singing as he babysat in the shack! His first words were, "Veta, that baby cried from the time you left this house! Don't ever leave her with me again!" After she quieted me, she told him she had prayed at the altar. He seemed unimpressed. Dad was aware of church rules. After a decision for Christ, Mother was not aware of the church's expectations. She only knew that her heart felt emptied of its heavy weight. Her inner burdens had been exchanged for peace. However, Dad understood that the church's rules often differed from one's relationship with God.

The following Saturday night, Dad played the guitar and called the moves for the occasional community square dance. Mother's sister, Susie, stayed home with Kenneth and me. Mother went with Dad and danced—something she loved to do. She did not know the church considered dancing a sinful exercise. Dad later relayed to Mother the criticism certain church members had leveled against her dancing. Mother never went to another dance.

Sadly, neither did she immediately return to church. She felt very embarrassed. Again, the inspired words of David, the psalmist, still rang through the centuries, "The unfolding of your words gives light; it gives understanding to the simple" (Psalm 119:130, NIV). Thankfully, God's Word also "judges the thoughts and attitudes of the heart" (Hebrews 4:12, NIV). With inner strength and confidence, Mother ignored the harsh criticisms. The Holy Spirit had choreographed her breakthrough to inner peace. She no longer felt executed by her inner hurt. She wanted to stay free inside. No longer was she fighting battles in her mind and heart. Jesus bridged the gap between God's holiness and her sin and confusion. She was freed from her past insecurities and fears. Her spirit soared to achieve her fullest potential as a wife and mother.

Jesus spoke beautiful words in Scripture to grieving disciples worried about Jesus leaving them. In John 16:13 (NIV), Jesus promised His worried disciples that He would send them a teacher. The Holy Spirit. Silently, in daily moments of prayer, the comforter's invisible arms sustained her. The Holy Spirit did not permit someone's avoidable and regrettable remark to smother her newfound peace. *Because Mother leaned into the Holy Spirit to define her, the faith legacy of the McDonald family was preserved.*

Dare Hijack the Holy Spirit's Role?

Small hillbilly country churches in the Ozark Mountains of Arkansas have suffered from judgmentalism. Large affluent church leaders and constituents have also maimed, injured, wounded, and battered their own. The world has suffered religious wars.

Sadly, church administration or members may not give the Holy Spirit (the helper) time to nourish and mature new believers in their relationship with Jesus Christ. Church boards and constituents sometimes forget that the Holy Spirit has dignity, grace, forgiveness, and love. He doesn't injure or destroy us in the process! *When we embrace the wind of the Holy Spirit, He doesn't break our wings! He never grants permission to destroy a brother or sister in Christ—especially a new believer! Redemptively, the Holy Spirit knows the recesses of every heart that needs repair. He is the ultimate heart surgeon!*

Solomon's Holy Spirit-inspired words have rung through the ages, "A word fitly spoken is like apples of gold in a setting of silver" (Proverbs 25:11, ESV). A verse to be memorized. How different life becomes when we put our minds in gear before speaking! Personally, I have often needed to recall this verse.

And I have experienced what it is like to talk before I think. Sadly, Christians can become victims or victimize others. It happened in the Scriptures. Healing and forgiveness were also experienced in the Scriptures and are still available today for all who seek restoration. The Holy Spirit never destroys hungry hearts. He heals.

Is not judgmentalism the highest form of "self" idolatry? When we judge or champion the judgment of others, do we not elevate ourselves to God's throne—push Him off—to finalize a job He is not doing fast enough? Or, perhaps God has not done the job according to our wishes?

Regretfully, there is someone before God continually who accuses all of us! First Peter 5:8 and Revelation 12:10 (KJV) describe Satan as the accuser—the deceptive roaring lion—who seeks to devour the weak prey (*you and me!*). If we help Satan do his job, we work overtime for him without pay! Sadly, when we judge, we set the penalties for God's judgment of us. (See Matthew 7:1–2, NIV.) Satan, our accuser, will be destroyed. (See Revelation 12:10, KJV.)

My husband, Jack, now in Heaven, gave me the above analogy many years ago. A phrase he prayerfully inscribed into his sermons was, "Church should be a very *safe* place—the *safest* place in this world!" Jack felt that the church was responsible for creating a *safe* environment (*safety net*). It is paramount for each person to have a *safe* refuge—a fortress. (See Psalm 91:2, NIV.) *The Holy Spirit brings His correction at the right time, in the right way, in the right place, in the right order, and with love!*

Jack said, "If we put on God's glasses, we will see people as He sees them. Can we not love the ones for whom He died? That includes you and me! Jesus never asked us to love someone He

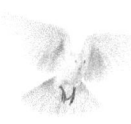

has not already loved! *He does say that if we love Him, we will love others!"*

Jesus and His disciples did net fishing. We do the same as we thread strands of love around the individuals with whom the Holy Spirit has us intersect (spiritual net fishing). We do not select the people; the Holy Spirit chooses them. Ananias would not have chosen Paul! (See Acts 9:1–19, NIV.) The net of love becomes so strong that the Holy Spirit draws the person to Christ in the perfectly woven net—made by strands of love from Christ's followers—you and me!

The Scripture gives clear instructions on what specific issues need to be addressed by the governing body of a church. Dare we ever go beyond what the Scriptures stipulate? Personal bias and a desire for control can forge non-biblical parameters that wound and possibly destroy the sheep. The great shepherd of the church exhausts all efforts to rescue, preserve, and shield His precious sheep. Ezekiel 34 (NIV) *describes God's defensive love for His sheep. If we don't love His sheep (believers in the church), will a spiritually wounded person believe God loves them? Enough to give His Son, Jesus, to die for them?*

Before his death, my husband, Jack, told our daughter, "I am not concerned about my final test with pain. The only question I ask God is, 'Have I loved every person in the churches I have pastored as You love them? I have tried. If I failed, please forgive me.'" Jack's goal as a chaplain and pastor was to love every person as God loved them, regardless of their response to him. Why? The people are God's sheep—not the pastor's property— nor the property of the church's governing body.

Jack continually reminded me that Jesus gave the key definition of a follower of Christ in John 13:35 (NIV), "By this

everyone will know that you are my disciples, if you have love one to another." What a remarkable statement by Jesus to His disciples, whom He taught for three years! Love is the true Christ followers' fundamental stamp of authenticity! Will others know we are disciples of Jesus if we do not have love? Jesus answers, "No." Ouch! Jesus never asks us to love anyone He has not already loved enough—without exception—to die for their sins! Without love—the key ingredient to Christianity—don't we diminish the Spirit's repair of our hearts and hinder His work in the lives of others?

As a new believer in Christ, Mother was judged shoddily. Perhaps they had also been victims and lacked biblical insight. The Holy Spirit illuminates our hearts to Heaven's perspective as we read God's Word. He restores love and unity. Hurt and division only come from an evil taskmaster. Deep-seated hurts and unkind words are regrettable. The Holy Spirit loves the offender and the offended.

The Holy Spirit healed Mother's heart and gave her an added blessing. In September 1940, Dad made his decision for Christ. Immediately, his voice and musical abilities were used for the choir and special music. Their life of faith and service together began. *The Holy Spirit has never failed to heal the heart that reaches out to Him!*

Joseph was renamed Barnabas (Son of Encouragement) by the disciples because of his spiritual influence in the early church (Acts 4:36, NIV). The church needs more "Barnabas-like" pastors (shepherds) and members—who are images of the great shepherd. Barnabas' name is undoubtedly written in God's remembrance scroll (Malachi 3:16, NIV).

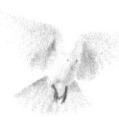

Saintly and "renamed" Barnabas sold his land for church needs (Acts 4:37, NIV) and was a bridgebuilder throughout the New Testament! The next verse (Acts 5:1, NIV) is the story of Ananias and Sapphira, who sold land. Both were land sellers in the same church but with different motivations! *The Holy Spirit was personally grieved!* Read Ephesians 4:30 (NIV); *the Holy Spirit can forgive us for wrong choices in life, but not for wrong choices about Him!*

God has blessed me with Barnabas-like friends in thirteen states and Bermuda. Though there are more, I name four treasured friends God gifted me.

Nancy (Cook) Gianopulos, my maid of honor and the wife of Reverend George Gianopulos, has been a close friend since 1957. Our golden years of friendship included college, dating chats, marriage, children, churches, and life. A great pianist, piano teacher, pastor's wife, and mother of four. *My North Carolina long-term friend is a rare treasure!*

Lillian Ferris, wife of Captain (Ret.) William A. Ferris (deceased), a friend since 1969. She taught me the protocol for officer wives. She cried with us when we lost our baby, Janae. She lovingly kept Gregory for the three weeks I was hospitalized. She listened to my hurts, functioned as a spiritual advisor, and loved my family. She fought a long and noble battle against COVID! Lillian is a "Barnabas" to me—and many others worldwide—*my San Diego encourager in her ninetieth year!*

Cassandra Marchese, wife of Michael Marchese, who lives in the State of Washington and whom I have not seen since 1987, has always been spot on when she texts, "Are you okay? You are on my heart today." A mother of five and a grandmother, she

has other ministries—like creating jewelry masterpieces and giving them to individuals in rest homes. *Her servant-heart is tuned to the inaudible voice of the Holy Spirit!*

Rhonda VanZandt—mother of five children, and an avowed atheist. In mid-life, she and Saber met and fell in love. Saber introduced Jack to Rhonda. Jack visited them often, and Saber taught him how to make his unique fly rods. Jack made one for our daughter, Jana, and our granddaughter, Alexandra. Rhonda loved Jack's visits *and felt accepted by him.* As he watched her carvings, she asked him all the questions she had battled with life, churches, Christians, and the Trinity in whom Jack believed. He respectfully answered her questions. Saber, also a fantastic cook—prepared tasty meals. (Saber was taught to cook by nine aunts who had raised him in upstate New York.)

The rest of the story? Jack married Saber and Rhonda and blessed their Alaska cabin and their talents. Rhonda's heart is forever sold out to Jesus Christ. Since Jack's death, she and Saber have called Jana and me monthly to check on us.

In December 2019, with severe COVID, she stared death in the face! Rhonda's heart had stopped for ten minutes in a helicopter between Fairbanks and Anchorage! Many people prayed for her. Our daughter, Jana, was outside on a Virginia night observing the Star of Bethlehem, which was visible for the first time in 800 years!

She came inside and said, "Mom, I prayed for Rhonda as I stared at the Star of Bethlehem in awesome wonder. I prayed God would give her a miracle just as He did for others when the Star of Bethlehem appeared on that first Christmas! I felt a holy presence as I prayed."

Rhonda survived COVID!

Her exquisite carvings continue to grace many homes! She lovingly paints the faces of individuals—incredible replicas—as gifts to them! A carved shepherd's staff is created for ministers, and unique and welcoming signs are made for churches. *Rhonda—a former atheist—expresses God's love!*

Nancy, Lillian, Cassandra, and Rhonda have been "encouragers" to me. They embraced the "wind" of the Holy Spirit's nudges *and lifted my limp wings to fly above life's storms!*

Dad and Mother's Courtship and Marriage

Dad and Mother met at a country square dance when he was eighteen. She was sixteen. He completed elementary school. She finished the seventh grade before she was needed at home. She loved school and was a good student. If a country student attended high school, they would have to find someone in the small town of Berryville or Eureka Springs with an extra room. Room and food were exchanged for the student's work—cooking, cleaning, laundry, ironing, and babysitting. Few farm girls or boys could move ten miles away from their parents. They were sorely needed at home, especially when the family had several children. Transportation and visits were difficult.

Dad arrived to pick up Mother on "Old Babe," his mare, for each date. Mother's parents lived on a small acreage in Grandview, Arkansas. She was the third child of eight. Her father, Ed Warren, worked on the railroad tracks across the county. Her mother, Martha (Summers) Warren, was a housewife who continually prepped to meet the family's food

needs—a great gardener and canner. The family's root cellar was filled with her beautiful vegetables, fruits, and sausages.

Dad lived in the Antioch community across King's River, approximately ten miles east. He was the youngest of three. When living in Arkansas, Dad's parents had always worked on their farm—selling milk and eggs. When times were tough, they sold pigs and calves. His mother, Mary McDonald, was an excellent prepper. She maintained a large garden, fruit trees, and fruit bushes.

Dad was a guitarist for the dances within the surrounding communities. He could play seven instruments—harmonica, fiddle, mandolin, steel guitar, banjo, piano, and regular guitar. His forte was the guitar. He called all the community dances. He was never privileged to take music lessons—a naturally gifted individual. He studied on his own.

As a seven-year-old, the Hollywood talent scouts visited Dad's school in California. Talented and fearless children voluntarily went on stage and performed. Dad simultaneously danced and played the harmonica.

A knock was heard on the door while the family ate supper that evening. The Hollywood talent scouts offered to "buy" Dad from Granny and Papa to make him a movie star. They loved his talent and charisma—a fearless natural performer.

They said, "We will make a big star out of him! You will be delighted to see your son in the movies!"

Fortunately, my grandparents said, "No, thanks. We're going to keep our son."

Though in the lower class economically, they loved their children.

For my family, the Holy Spirit choreographed that moment in our history. The Holy Spirit is gentle and inviting. His purpose is to bond families, not to separate them. Dad was grateful that his parents refused the Hollywood offer.

On January 8, 1936, a cold afternoon, Dad unexpectedly stopped by Mother's home and discovered her using a washboard and two tubs at a nearby spring. She washed the family laundry two days a week. Only one of the eight children was married. She and her husband lived with the family. Mother's hands were cold and raw from scrubbing the soiled clothes. He planned to tell her he was leaving for California to find work.

Dad was saddened when he saw how hard the beautiful girl he loved worked for the family. She was five-foot-three and weighed 117 pounds. They had dated for one year. She was now seventeen; he was nineteen. He knew he did not want to leave her behind, especially with another interested rival.

Courageously, Dad popped the question of marriage. He suggested they would leave for California within a few weeks. He woke up Cinderella inside her heart! She answered, "Yes, but I don't have a new dress for the ceremony."

Excitedly, he left with a promise, "I'll return in three days and have your dress with me."

Three days later, Dad returned with the new three-dollar light blue dress he had personally chosen. She loved the dress! Her few clothes were packed in a small bag. She put on her new dress. They climbed on Old Babe and rode eastward to his parents' home across King's River in the Antioch community.

Mother was not sure her parents would approve of their marriage. The family would keenly feel her absence, especially

her sisters, Susie and Mary, and her brothers, Jimmy and Johnny. Dean, the youngest, was too young to remember. The family did not realize this date was out of the ordinary! A date that would change Mother and Dad's lives forever! At my young age, it did not occur to me to ask Mother what they said about her not returning home that night! Her dates had curfews.

Before arriving at his parents' home, they stopped by the home of a justice of peace. Dad had the necessary papers. For the sum of one dollar, their wedding vows were performed. The justice of peace gave his daughter the dollar. With the dollar, the young girl purchased her first Bible. The date was January 11, 1936.

Veta Marie Warren, Seventeen Years

California (1936-1937)

Two weeks later, goodbyes were said. Dad, Mother, her oldest brother, and a friend left for California in an old Model T Ford. Dad's parents dipped into their home-building savings and gave him some money to buy a car and gas for the trip. The car had no heater. Granny and Mother packed food for the journey.

After three weeks of non-stop travel, the party of four reached Sanger, California. Mother recalled, "The weather was so cold we continually covered up with blankets." January 1936 was one of the coldest in US history. There was no money for hotel or motel stops. Fortunately, Dad immediately found work on the large farms and grape vineyards. At the age of nineteen, he drove large equipment and maintained and repaired engines. He had enormous potential to become a mechanical engineer. In his early years, he maintained or overhauled his own vehicles. His brother, Roy, was exceptionally talented in mechanics.

Seventeen months after their marriage, Kenneth, their twelve-pound son, arrived. He was born at the home of my paternal grandmother's sister in Sanger, California. After four days of labor, the doctor came to the home on June 3, 1937, and

delivered the baby. Mother said, "Barbara, for those four days, the pain was so severe that I prayed to die. I didn't know what I was asking because I wouldn't have been prepared to meet God."

When their baby was six months of age, Mother and Kenneth returned to Arkansas with friends. Dad followed three weeks later. The Ford car was unable to make the return trip. They had enough money saved to buy a few cows. Dad was able to graze them on Papa's pasture. Due to the 1930s depressed economy, there were no jobs available. Nobody had expected the depression to last so devastatingly long. They survived on small semimonthly milk checks for almost five years. Those checks purchased the main staples of cornmeal, flour, sugar, salt, and pinto beans. Matches and coal oil were needed for the lamp and lantern.

Granny supplied our eggs with her chickens. Her large garden gave us healthy vegetables, which she and Mother managed. The cows gave us the milk we needed. One pig each year was our supply of meat—Mother canned delicious sausages. Our pork meat lasted a few months. Once or twice each month, we ate fried chicken at Granny and Papa's house. Papa had several bee gums (homes for bees). He supplied honey and honeycombs to our family table. Dad fished Indian Creek for freshwater catfish—a tasty meal. He also caught squirrels, which tasted wonderful to hungry children. He could always get one or two Canadian geese flying south yearly. Granny and Mother made lye soap for cleaning hair, dishes, and laundry.

Kenneth, Barbara, and DeWayne

June 3, 1940: Kenneth (three years); Barbara (twenty months)

Our little family grew to five members. My brother, DeWayne, was born in July 1940. The above picture was taken shortly before DeWayne's birth. Unfortunately, there was no baby picture of him. Our great-grandfather, Matthew Summers, sponsored this picture. When his great-grandchildren were in town, he personally took them into the photography shop and paid for their pictures—most often with him.

After we lived in the rent-free backwoods shack for several years, my parents were ready for a change in early spring 1942. Mother was expecting her fourth child. They packed three children across Indian Creek to ride to the grocery store and church. Once or twice monthly, our grandparents drove us to the Boyd Church schoolhouse.

Dad brought Old Babe, his beloved mare, from his parents' farm home on Saturdays. Old Babe took us one by one across Indian Creek on Sunday mornings. For five years, including winters, Dad and Mother walked through the woods and crossed Indian Creek. When they visited the Boyd Church schoolhouse in the spring of 1942, they were offered a rent-free shack on a wagon trail road in the Boyd community. They would no longer have to forge Indian Creek. Economically, life could improve. The 1930s Depression lingered into the 1940s. Survival for farm families was the most difficult. Empty boarded-up farmhouses were scattered across rural communities. High school graduates taught school in many farm communities.

If Only the Shack
Could Tell Its Story

Granny's 1930s Dodge left a dusty clay-orange trail as we winded slowly down the extra-narrow country road. Toward the end of our March 1942 ten-mile trip, the bottom of her car was scraped by the tall, stiff weeds between the bumpy wagon road tracks. Nobody but Granny drove the Dodge.

She and Papa purchased their car in California. Granny loved to drive! It gave her the status she needed—the only senior lady in our hillbilly community who drove. There were few cars in the community. Most were the early Ford models. A relatively new Dodge—with a lady driving—was eye-catching in hillbilly country!

Suddenly, a weather-beaten shack appeared on our left in the middle of a field. I remember the first sight of my new home at three years of age! The abandoned shack was not unlike one seen in a Gunsmoke movie. Early settlers survived tough, rugged years as they carved out an existence on the old homestead. *If only the shack could tell its story!*

The shack was similar to the one we moved from in the Antioch community. The former shack was located deep in the woods. It had doors between the two rooms. The new shack had

only two outside doors. One went into the kitchen; one went into the bedroom. The new shack had easy access to the narrow wagon-trail road—a crucial factor to Mother and Dad. Work would, hopefully, become available for Dad on the larger and more populated farms. Dad and Mother had not inspected the house in advance. They were ecstatic to move out of the woods. No more winter wading of Indian Creek!

Our closest neighbor owned the rent-free shack. Aged, loose boards nailed to this unpainted and tin-roofed shack were a very dark gray. Arkansas common rocks were slowly sinking into the ground as they assisted in the stabilization of the fragile porch frame. The old porch floor had wide cracks and broken boards. The rocks underneath the house appeared stable and robust.

Our family was thankful for a free shack—we called home—on a wagon road. Mother and Dad never complained about our accommodations. There was a kitchen and a bedroom. The rickety porch door entrances to each room were without screen doors. As in our previous shack, we lived very simply. Day by day, we survived. The family kitchen was the room on the left. The kitchen had a handmade wooden table and a working wood cookstove.

The room on the right had two regular-sized aging iron rail beds. Mattresses were used and thin. Both mattresses had imprints of the noisy, broken, rusty springs upon which they slipped and slid—no mattress covers. Mother placed "feed-sack" sheets (four farm animal feed sacks sewn together to make one sheet) on her and Dad's bed. She spread a string-knotted quilt over the second bed. This quilt was stuffed with outgrown and worn-out clothes covered by four animal feed sacks sewn together. Arkansas life exhibited all the effects of the Great Depression. If neighbors had any extra furniture, they would gladly loan it to a needy family. The furniture they owned had been passed to them. Grocery orange crates were used for bedside table clocks and radios. The orange crates would be turned backward to keep important papers in the divided section away from children.

Nancy Sue arrived on May 2, 1942. Mother, Dad, and our new baby slept in the bed on the left. Three feet from their bed was the bed for my two brothers and me. We three were still short enough to sleep crosswise to have more individual space in Arkansas's sizzling summer climate. Kenneth, DeWayne, and I had never heard of air conditioning. No electricity. No refrigerator. No ice chest.

Mother's few dresses and Dad's two shirts and overalls hung on a wire nailed across a corner of the bedroom. Kenneth, DeWayne, and I stored our clothes in a cardboard box.

Nancy Sue's clothes were in a single box. Our family was worried about our new baby. She cried almost continually while she was awake. The doctor seemed baffled about her health.

Kenneth, DeWayne, and I were not aware that, culturally, we were known as extremely poor "hillbillies." Except for winter, we were barefoot most of the time. Mother and Granny patched our clothes. Granny darned the socks for all of us. We were delighted to wear "hand-me-downs." Dad's sister, Aunt Marie, occasionally sent a box of clothes she obtained from different thrift stores. We waited expectantly as Granny emptied the box. Hopefully, something our size was in the box. Mother

never asked Granny for a dress as most of the dresses would fit either of them. Granny often shared. Everything was new and beautiful to us! The clothing was used by someone or braided into a throw rug and placed at a door entrance, next to a bed, in front of the wash pan and water drinking bucket, to cover a hard chair or bench, or in front of a cookstove for Mother or Granny's tired feet. Granny also used them for her quilt patterns. Nothing was wasted.

The shack was within walking distance of the Boyd Church schoolhouse. That was the fun time of our week. The children loved the nuts from the Ozark Chinquapin tree that grew on the school property. Many of the farm families sang in the volunteer choir, and many regularly stood and gave personal testimonies of how good the Lord had been to them that week. Neighbors checked on the welfare of their neighbors, and those who needed help on their farms scheduled their volunteer labor. All the adults made sure they greeted the children. That made us feel important.

Daily Shack Activities

Without screen doors, we battled battalions of flies and gnats daily in southern summers. Flies eventually parked on the ceilings at night—making it much easier for us to sleep.

Spit baths were common except for Saturday evenings. Mother ensured we received a cold bath in the washtub on the porch. In the same water, DeWayne was bathed first; I was second, and Kenneth was last. She washed our clothes in the tub with a washboard. Nancy Sue was bathed inside the house in a basin of warm water.

Sunday was our "look your best" day. Everyone's ears had to be clean! "Rusty" ears were a big issue with Mother. Hopefully, our ears were thoroughly cleaned when our hair was washed with Saturday's weekly tub bath. If we had no shoes for church, our feet had to be clean. The toenails had to be trimmed. One comb accommodated the family hair grooming. Toenails and fingernails were trimmed with large scissors.

Mother abhorred bad-looking teeth. If we didn't have a toothbrush, we cleaned our teeth with toothpicks and a "wash rag" (washcloth). Along with our one lamp, salt, and pepper, toothpicks were always placed in the center of the kitchen table.

The drinking water bucket sat on a simple wooden bench in the kitchen. It contained our cistern water. The family's common long-handled dipper served as the common drinking cup. Without needed summer rain, cistern water was used sparingly. Next to the water bucket sat the family's wash pan. It was used to wash our hands before meals. The family's one drying towel hung on a nail by the wash pan.

The one treasured jersey cow we brought from the farm was a gentle friend. Trooper, our dog, kept her near the shack. Dad milked her in the mornings for our breakfast of milk, biscuits, and gravy. Mother milked her near the porch before dark when Dad arrived home late. Mother had me sit on the bed by Nancy Sue as she milked.

We had no chickens because our yard was not fenced. A neighbor gave us extra eggs. Granny also brought us eggs, jelly, and salted pork from their smokehouse. Papa and Granny graciously milked the cows we left on their farm. She and Papa visited a couple of times each month and brought my parents their small milk check from the milk plant. There were no food banks or free meals.

Suppertime

It was a hot and humid evening in late July of 1942. Our one dimly lit lamp was centered on the table where Kenneth, DeWayne, and I waited for our supper of cornbread and milk. Kenneth had turned five years old in June. October would be my fourth birthday. DeWayne became two on July 13. DeWayne was tired and hungry. His high energy was a joy to me. Dad was not home. He was working on a neighbor's farm.

Mother could not come to the kitchen and bake our cornbread until Nancy Sue was asleep. At three months, she slept little. Her cries seemed continual until her exhausted tiny body could fall asleep. Otherwise, she was always in Mother's arms. Mother had me assist with DeWayne and help her with small chores.

Matches for lighting the cook stove fire were in a jar high on a wall shelf. We were not allowed to touch the matches. It was the most cherished part of our day when we ate together as a family. Cornbread and milk nourished us and made our tummies feel full and secure.

Because Mother was always busy with Nancy Sue, DeWayne became my little sidekick. Kenneth, DeWayne, and I were never sick. As DeWayne grew, he became a loyal and fun playmate. He

was still young and unaware of the dangerous snakes and other insects. We played "house" together close to the porch. The field had no fenced yard. We used sticks and rocks for room dividers. We wrapped rags around our stick dolls. We used sticks to construct our rooms and furniture. Even at two years of age, DeWayne had learned to open our playhouse stick door and say, "I'm home!" Just like our Dad!

During the day, he and I also chased butterflies and caught grasshoppers. Kenneth preserved the grasshoppers for his fishing trips with Dad. We couldn't catch fireflies after dark unless Dad was home. Mother was concerned about the stealthy snakes and their nightly search for food.

Kenneth seldom played with us. He was our "big" brother and enjoyed slingshot skills with his friend. They made slingshots from the perfect "Y" limb that grew on the small branches of trees. An old inner tube preserved from a tossed, worn-out tire provided the rubber band for the slingshot. Small pieces were often used as fire starters for our stove. He and his friend became very skilled shooters. They found warped boards to make rabbit gums that enhanced our family cash. They dug ground worms and found special insects under rocks for their fishing trips. DeWayne and I were afraid of their fishing lures!

It was dark; Dad was not yet home. Hopefully, he made a few quarters as he worked for a farmer. They often took longer than expected to cut and store a field of hay. When he worked late, they usually invited him for supper. If they couldn't afford to pay, Dad worked for free. They sometimes sent food home with him. That's Dad—a neighbor who cared! Neighbors helped one another survive!

We enjoyed a neighbor's extra tomatoes and corn-on-the-cob for summer suppers with our nightly diet of cornbread and milk. With no garden area fenced and plowed, Mother could not plant her own garden. For a few weeks, neighbors blessed us with seasonal scallions and radishes. Kenneth, DeWayne, and I used the scallions as straws with our milk. What fun we had! Dad was the only one who loved the white radishes better than the red ones. Pinto beans were cheap and were bought in large bags. Mother gave me the responsibility of searching for tiny pebbles commonly left in the beans. She warned me of the danger to our teeth and stomachs. Afterward, I washed the beans until the water was clear. We loved the smell of the beans as they simmered on the wood stove.

Quarters were needed to buy more cornmeal for our nightly cornbread; flour was needed for our morning biscuits. Everyone's tummy had to be refilled each day. Dad never stopped searching for work to meet his family's needs and our sick baby's necessities. Dad and Mother prayed for a real job for Dad. If he earned one dollar per day, they felt blessed. He was fortunate if he obtained two or three days of pay each week.

Dad made contacts for one-day jobs or more when we were at church. Our family attended the Wednesday evening prayer service. We were always present on Sunday mornings and Sunday evenings. People encouraged one another and prioritized neighborly relationships.

Occasionally, we were invited home with the Charlie Minnick family on a Sunday afternoon. That was my first introduction to homemade Angel Food Cake. Charlie's wife, Ollie, was a super cook. She was a prepper and always had a huge garden. She made hominy in huge black cooking kettles in her yard. We enjoyed her fantastic meals. We had the choice of many vegetables along with her fried chicken. She also made her family's bread. Charlie did not have a full-time job either, but he always helped Dad find work somewhere. Mother had no sewing machine. When I admired the dresses Miss Ollie had made for her daughters, she surprised me with the same dress! The adults communicated with the children and lifted unknown burdens off growing little backs!

We all felt safe each night when we returned to the same crowded room. Except for Nancy Sue's crying, we slept peacefully, knowing Dad was home. Over the summer, Kenneth, DeWayne, and I learned to sleep with our baby sister crying. Mother endlessly bounced her on their squeaky mattress with its noisy springs to quiet her. Mother sometimes fell asleep in the straight-backed chair with the baby asleep in her arms. Mother and Dad whispered when they talked about our baby sister's health.

Trooper

Our hound dog, Trooper, always sat on the porch before our screenless kitchen door. We were safe when he was near. He waited—just outside the door—for any leftover cornbread. After our biscuit and gravy breakfast, Trooper received a little of the same! He guarded our home and unfenced yard against harmful varmints. Mother didn't worry when we played near the porch as long as Trooper was near.

Because of our baby's health, our supper wait was often extended. We, children, became famished. No leftovers. Trooper's eyes expressed such disappointment when no food remained for him. He scouted off for his middle-of-the-night exercise as he chased for food in the nearby woods.

Trooper alerted us when strangers approached our shack. He lay by our open bedroom door on hot summer nights and ensured no varmints entered our bedroom. Foxes, groundhogs, possums, skunks, squirrels, rabbits, snakes, mice, and deer were common to the Ozarks.

Trooper escorted us to the crumbling outhouse behind the shack, protecting us from snakes and varmints. Missing boards made it wise to ensure one's "peer through" visits were timely. Outdated Sears catalogs were out-house treasures.

Trooper helped Dad catch squirrels for a meal with meat. He assisted in finding geese that were flying south for winter for a special family meal. We loved Trooper.

"You, Lord, preserve both people and animals" (Psalm 36:6, NIV).

Depression Aftermath

Our small community suffered from the 1930s Depression aftermath. There were no jobs. There were no food giveaways. The Berryville Bank was thirteen miles from us. Distance did not matter because nobody needed bank services.

People who became terminally ill died at home, but never alone. Over the generations, many home deathbed testimonies deepened faith and spiritually encouraged the family. No person died alone. Farmers could not afford hospital charges. They lived too far from town for a doctor to drive to their homes without pay. If a family member went to the hospital, it was incredibly difficult to visit them. In order not to die away from one's family, individuals preferred to stay at home. Who wanted to die alone? Farmers had deep faith, honesty, pride, and loyalty. Integrity was a treasured virtue. They did not beg for medical services; they placed their lives in God's divine hands.

Neighbors went to California to work in grape vineyards and other seasonal fruits and vegetables. A coveted job there took at least two or three weeks of travel. Food was packed for the long trip. They rotated drivers and slept in their crowded Model-T Fords. They cooked one campfire meal daily on Route 66 and also made coffee.

If they were fortunate enough to own a home or small farm in Arkansas, the windows and doors were boarded until they returned. Neighbors guarded their house. Family survival was at the top of everyone's agenda. Once the family arrived in California, a friend or relative loaned them a tent. Sometimes, they found a cheap shack on a big farm. The orchard irrigation ditches provided water for bathing and washing clothes. Mosquitoes' nets were needed against those "ever-present" guests in California.

Again, Dad and Mother conversed about work in California. Dad needed to go alone as they had no car. Mother was afraid for him to leave us. They had not anticipated a problem with their baby's health. Problems do not make reservations. Most farm babies were healthy. Dad's search for work never ended. Mother prayed he would earn enough money each week for cornmeal and flour—our daily diet of cornbread and biscuits. Pinto beans were our protein staple.

Our two-room shack provided a place to sleep and protected us from the elements. Because of the stress of Nancy Sue's unknown illness, Mother and Dad retired each night, exhausted. Mother often cried as she prayed with her baby in her arms. We had never seen Mother so unhappy. If Kenneth were home, he motioned us to go outside with him. When DeWayne and I were in the room, I took him outside, and we played games with our rocks and sticks. My brothers and I didn't understand the sorrow that had settled over our once-happy family. Our family life had become profoundly serious—little laughter. Scary dreams and nightmares began to disturb my sleep each night.

World War II

One main topic of discussion in our home was the war. Quietly, Kenneth and I listened to the adult conversations. War was continually a subject of prayer at church. New words were continually aired on the radio and in our home: Germany and Hitler, England and Churchill, France and de Gaulle, Italy and Mussolini, Russia and Stalin, Japan and Tojo, and the Philippine Islands. Kenneth and I did not understand how large the world was, but everything we heard was frightening.

We heard our country's underwater ships, called submarines, were fighting with enemy submarines. Submarines and big ships were sunk; airplanes were shot down. We had never seen a picture of an ocean. No newspapers. The garbled radio enabled a vivid imagination as we sat and listened. We heard about concentration camps. Dad explained that innocent people were imprisoned.

Nightly family time was when we listened to the news on our static radio. Mother and Dad sat on their bed. Mother held Nancy Sue. Sometimes, two-year-old DeWayne fell asleep in Dad's arms. That was a special time for him. Kenneth and I instinctively understood our role as the older two children. He was five; I would soon be four.

Single men and fathers went to the war from our community. Kenneth and I watched a military vehicle on our narrow country road pick up a young man who had been called to the war. We asked Mother about the strange, noisy truck with open back doors. We thought he was taken to jail! She said the Army picked up men who had no transportation. A few men returned to our community in caskets draped with our American flag.

Kenneth and I became frightened when Mom and Dad whispered about what would happen to our family if Dad had to go to that scary war. Mother cried. Military classification letters were worrisome to our parents. They obviously felt they could not carry another burden. Mother had me watch for the mailman and rush the mail to her. The mailman's car and the large milk truck were the vehicles we saw daily. In our quiet country environment, we heard them coming on the road. During those frightening times, my dreams and nightmares worsened. Mother found our soiled clothes outside by the rain barrel one morning. Asleep, I often stood by their bed and stared at them. Children express their fears and burdens in unusual ways.

At my young age, I never imagined that a few men who fought in those fierce battles—even prisoners of war—would eventually become my dearest friends. My young mind could never have fathomed that my future husband would conduct funerals of World War I and World War II servicemen and women. *A treasured and patriotic generation of young single men, husbands, and fathers* who risked their futures for America and the world. Thousands returned in caskets; others were buried in the oceans, seas, or on foreign soil. *We must never forget!*

Our Little Baby Sister— My First Prayer

When our tummies were hungry, time passed slowly. We waited for Mother to get Nancy Sue to sleep in the other room. Mother told us to remain at the table for supper until she came to the kitchen. It was almost dark; DeWayne was extra hungry. My job was to keep him entertained until Mother arrived. We played finger games, made funny faces, sang songs, and learned new words. Kenneth told stories of his adventures. He and his friend constructed rabbit gums, made slingshots, and dug worms for potential fishing trips with their fathers. They kept the worms in fresh dirt. Dirt crawlers did not interest me! DeWayne was intrigued by them.

Nancy Sue was a gorgeous baby with naturally black curly hair. It was thick and shoulder-length at birth. Kenneth, DeWayne, and I had very straight hair. Mother said my hair was stringy. That did not sound attractive.

Though only twenty-four years of age, Mother continuously held Nancy Sue, her fourth child, close to her chest. She smothered her with kisses and sang to her as she gently bounced her on the old, thin mattress that covered the rusty bedsprings. At night, she bounced her in the straight chair. Sometimes,

Mother permitted me to sit beside her and cup Nancy Sue's feet in my hands.

As children, we did not understand the gravity of our little sister's health. Since her birth, a strange hush had settled over our family's little shack. Dad and Mother whispered when they discussed our baby. The doctor had told Mother that our baby had to be taken to St. Louis for stomach surgery. Sadly, Dad and Mother accepted the impossible. Poverty was *deathly* real. We did not understand their deep pain, but Kenneth and I felt their brokenness.

St. Louis was a long way from where we lived. We had no health insurance, no money, and no car. The few people with a car needed it for transportation, home, and farm supplies. It was late July, and everyone was busy with their crops and harvest. When crops were ready, they had to be harvested. It was a hard and slow job. Horses and wagons were used to gather the crops. Poor farmers had no tractors. Seasons did not wait. The farm family's survival depended upon the timely harvesting of their crops. Granny and Papa had a car; they had no money. There were no supportive health agencies.

After Nancy Sue was asleep, Mother would walk from the other room across the noisy loose porch boards into the kitchen. After starting the cookstove fire, it took an hour to finally bake a big iron skillet full of tasty golden cornbread. DeWayne was sleepy and anxious.

Suddenly, Mother entered the kitchen, where we hungrily waited. Her first words were, "Barbara, while I'm baking the cornbread, go into the bedroom. Nancy Sue is finally asleep. Lie down on the bed beside her. Put your finger on her upper lip so you can feel her breath. Be careful! Don't wake her up! Make sure she keeps breathing. If she stops breathing, come back and get me right away! I'll start the fire in the cook stove and bake our cornbread."

Quickly, I climbed off the chair. Mother spoke with urgency! Is something wrong? It scared me to know Nancy Sue was alone, but darkness terrified me! Quickly, my dusty bare feet raced across the broken and creaky boards of the porch. To enter a room without a light was eerie. Nancy Sue had to keep breathing! Mother's words struck panic inside me! It was a hot summer night, and there was no screen door. Trooper did not follow me. He wanted cornbread! Hopefully, he will be rewarded. When Trooper was with me, I always felt safe. A pitch-black room without a screen door was creepy. My baby sister needed me to protect her; I had to be brave-hearted.

Outside the shack, the tree frogs and crickets noisily screeched. Scattered among the oak and elm trees along the road, the night owls had undoubtedly watched me enter the bedroom door. My overactive imagination and fear of the dark convinced me I was helplessly alone. Dark nights intensely overpowered me, and I saw scary images.

Quietly, I lay down by Nancy Sue and placed my small right index finger across her tiny upper lip. She continued sleeping. In the lonely desperation of that moment, my young heart ached for answers to questions I could not understand or express. Inside me was a deep fear of the unknown—fearful thoughts I could not intelligently express—even to my parents. Life was so simple, yet so complicated. A secret sorrow had thrown a canopy of grief over our family. What had happened to us?

At the age of three years and nine months, while I monitored my sick baby sister's breathing, I thought about the God who lived high above us—higher than the airplanes that sometimes flew above our shack. How high was God? My first thoughts of God. My first prayer! Before that night, God was only someone to whom the adults talked. Did God see me lying there by Nancy Sue? Did He know Mother was afraid Nancy Sue might stop breathing? What happens when she doesn't breathe anymore? Will she be taken to Heaven before us? How does she get there? How long before we see her again? Will she remember me? Will she be lonely in Heaven without Mother? Will she miss Dad, Kenneth, DeWayne, and me? My heart desperately communicated with the unseen God I did not know.

Mother and Dad said that the Lord gave gifts to us (like Nancy Sue), and sometimes He takes back the gifts (Job 1:21, KJV). How does God take Nancy Sue from our house to His? Does God have a table in Heaven with enough food for everybody? Do we all have to die to get to Heaven? Why can't we all go together? Nancy Sue would be terrified to go alone. She doesn't know anyone in Heaven. Will Trooper be in Heaven, too?

God seemed so powerful, frightening, and far away. Why would He give Nancy Sue to us and then take her away? Would He take Kenneth, DeWayne, and me from our parents, too? How can we really know someone who lives so far from us? Why does God hide from us? I want to see Him! Does God hear the prayers of a little girl like me? My heart broke for answers.

While Mother built the fire in the kitchen cookstove and gave Kenneth and DeWayne some attention while the cornbread baked, I struggled for answers to my deepest concerns.

Awkwardly, I whispered my thoughts and fears to God. I never removed my pointer finger from my baby sister's upper lip. Helping Nancy Sue live was more important to me than a growling tummy. She breathed continually, but her breath was exceptionally faint on my finger—tiny puffs of thin air. I still remember it well.

How I wanted Nancy Sue to quit hurting! Except when sleeping, her stomach pain always caused her to cry. "Please, God, stop her hurting and crying," was my whispered simple prayer. My dreams of playing with Nancy Sue had faded. She was too ill for me to hold. I guarded her breathing while she slept and cuddled her tiny feet while Mother bounced her.

Mother's footsteps quickly came across the rickety porch back into the room. She hadn't thought of supper for herself!

Excitedly, I whispered, "Mother, Nancy Sue kept breathing! My finger has felt her breathe all the time I've been in the room."

Mother urged me forward, "Go back into the kitchen and help DeWayne eat his supper. When you are finished, put the dishes in the dishpan. Kenneth can carry the lamp back to this room. You bring DeWayne back." She didn't ask for cornbread; she must really be worried about our baby.

Silently, I scampered out of the dark bedroom. My feet hastily sped past the wide cracks of the old porch and joined my brothers at the table. I felt comforted to be back in a lit room. It was dark outside, so we knew Dad had eaten with the farmer and his family.

My thirty-pound body was hungry. Quickly, I crumbled the warm cornbread into DeWayne and my glasses of warm milk. He was hungry, and so was I! There was leftover cornbread for

Trooper, our loyal dog! We fed him his cornbread as we ate. It tasted delicious as we solemnly finished. DeWayne was almost asleep in his chair. Trooper waited and followed us from the kitchen to the bedroom porch door. He faithfully slept on the porch before the bedroom's open door.

In that previous lonely hour, I was unaware that God had always known me! Psalm 139:13–16 (NIV) says that God knitted us together in our mother's womb. The Holy Spirit, my heavenly choreographer—whom I did not know—lit a lamp of faith in my heart. Maybe the God who lived so high above us listened when little girls like me talked to Him. My tiny seed of faith was amazingly small and simple. Though I knew little about Him, my talk with God helped! My heart told me that God was real—just like the adults at church believed. I wanted to know more about Him. *Strangely, I felt more secure and nearer to Him than my simple, childlike thoughts could have dreamed.*

The Loneliness
of Suffering

Nancy Sue's health was fast declining. The paramount concern of my parents was not for our family's needs but for a miracle recovery for their baby. Since her birth, Mother and Dad struggled for basic needs. Public jobs were non-existent in our county unless one was a schoolteacher or owned a grocery store, feed store, or gas station.

Only one teacher taught grades one through eight. The teacher may have had a semester of college or may have only finished high school. Children walked to school. One truck picked up the milk from the farms and transported it to the milk facility in Berryville. Life was amazingly simple and uncomplicated.

Summer ushered in tomato picking season. My parents hoped that tomato season would meet Nancy Sue's medical needs. To get to the tomato fields, parents and children all climbed into the wooden bed of a big truck. We were picked up near our shack because we lived on a drivable road. Every able-bodied person walked from valleys and backwoods to board the truck. People were desperate for work to merely exist.

Women and children sat on wooden benches constructed to fit the sides of the wooden truck bed. Mother held Nancy Sue

close to her chest the entire trip. They felt it was a *matter of life and death* to earn money for their baby's medical needs. Dad instructed me to sit by Mother. Kenneth and DeWayne were kept with him. Men either sat on the floor or stood and braced themselves by holding against the boards on the wobbly sides of the uncovered truck. The journey was quite noisy as we traveled along the bumpy country roads to big fields of tomatoes— over the Missouri state line.

Mother and Dad were fast pickers. Kenneth, their helper, enjoyed "alone" time with his parents. Mother spread our feedsack blanket as a pallet for Nancy Sue and DeWayne. I watched the two children and kept all insects off the blanket. As our shade disappeared, Mother advanced our blanket nearer to them. She also nursed Nancy Sue at scheduled intervals. In a different environment, Nancy Sue was quiet that day. Her big blue eyes followed my every bounce to entertain her. DeWayne and I had a beautiful day with her—our imaginary doll!

Mother and Dad steadily worked many rows of tomatoes for an exceedingly long day. They would be paid by the bushels picked. No checks would be given until all the fields were harvested. They were grateful for the few earned dollars.

Dad and Kenneth worked alone for the remainder of the week. Dad's fingers were extremely agile. Mother kept Nancy Sue, DeWayne, and me home due to the summer heat. Kenneth enjoyed his "big boy" feeling with Dad.

My parents were forced to depend upon God for Nancy Sue's health. There were no phones, internet, car, or money. Each day became a bit more difficult. The gift of life is subject to

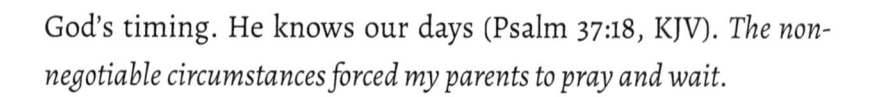

God's timing. He knows our days (Psalm 37:18, KJV). *The non-negotiable circumstances forced my parents to pray and wait.*

An Incredible
Scene Unfolded

It was Labor Day, September 7, 1942. Our family attended a special evening service at the Boyd Church. The Sunday minister remained for a Monday evening service. We walked from our shack to the church. Mother carried Nancy Sue. DeWayne sat on Dad's shoulders. Kenneth and I skipped along beside them.

To bounce Nancy Sue should she cry, Mother chose to sit at the front left large school desk of the Boyd Church schoolhouse. It had no desk in front of it. Mother laid Nancy Sue on her lap. I sat beside Mother, cupping Nancy Sue's tiny feet. Dad, Kenneth, and DeWayne sat with the men on the other side of the church. The usual custom.

Guest ministers received an evening meal and breakfast for time donated to a small audience. After the service, congregants with little money would slip them a dollar or less. Depending on the minister's residential distance, others donated produce to the minister. Farm families, not wealthy in material possessions, were affluent in faith.

In the last moments of the special service, time was reserved for prayer. Before the service, Dad requested the minister pray

for Nancy Sue's health. The minister and Dad came and stood directly in front of Mother, Nancy Sue, and me.

As the minister prayed, Nancy Sue raised her tiny arms—stretching her hands and fingers—toward Heaven. She was four months and five days old. Her blue eyes were wide open. She had been silent throughout the service. Her face glowed. She saw someone we did not see. Guardian angel? Was he holding her hand and fingers so straight? She was oblivious to the minister, Mother, Dad, and me. Her gaze was solely upward. She lowered her arms and lay peacefully quiet when the prayer was finished. The minister, Mother, and Dad all broke into sobs. My heart was crushed as I watched my parents weep quietly but brokenly—a hallowed five minutes. Silently, I watched that mysterious, incredible scene unfold. Nancy Sue had never raised her hands like that before.

That sacred prayer time was unforgettable to Mother, Dad, and me. Our heavenly choreographer, the Holy Spirit, orchestrated that experience—a never-to-be-forgotten holy encounter. One month short of being four years old, I remember it as though it occurred yesterday. Nancy Sue was definitely in the "embrace" of the Holy Spirit (the "comforter"). *What a visible demonstration of Heaven's love for our precious four-month angel!*

Who had Nancy Sue seen with her upstretched arms? What did she see that we did not see? Mother and Dad felt that what they saw was a sign, but they did not know its meaning. By the next morning, they felt that they understood the reason for their baby's upstretched arms. *Mother said she believed Nancy Sue had seen Jesus' beckoning arms reaching for her.*

Our Little Angel Says Goodbye

The following morning, I awakened to a heavy silence in the room. Nancy Sue was asleep. Mother and Dad whispered. They tried not to wake my brothers and me. They seemed alone in their own world as both gave their full attention to our baby. As young parents, what heavy burdens they had carried since her birth. Mother was crying; they both appeared to be incredibly sad. What were their mumbled words about Nancy Sue's raised hands at church last night? Again, Mother and Dad quietly talked about the "sign" of her upraised arms.

Silently, I sat in bed—with my back against the wall—and watched my parents cry softly. Mother tenderly embraced Nancy Sue tightly to her chest. She was brokenhearted. Though still a young father of four children and in need of his own solace, Dad did his best to comfort Mother. Our little shack bedroom was cradled in a holy moment that would forever be memorialized in my heart. The Holy Spirit, our heavenly choreographer, was present in the room. His presence was felt...even by me. What had happened?

Nancy Sue was incredibly still. Mother's crying did not awaken her. They were unaware I was monitoring the anguish

of their private and sacred scene. It was not the time for me to ask questions. Then, I heard Dad quietly say, "I'll go get her to come and help us." With stooped shoulders and tear-filled eyes, Dad slowly left the room. He did not glance in our direction.

After Dad left the shack, I asked softly, "Mother, is Nancy Sue going to wake up?"

Sobbingly, she said, "No." Shocked, I said nothing more. A lump formed in my throat. Tears fell freely. When Kenneth and DeWayne awakened, I whispered to them that Dad had gone to bring our neighbor here. Nancy Sue was not going to wake up today.

As we watched Mother softly crying, Kenneth, DeWayne, and I—like three toy soldiers—quietly sat with our backs to the wall. Mother was grief-stricken and sobbing helplessly. She kept looking at our baby sister. Heavy sorrow overwhelmed the room. We had never witnessed death before. Our young and tender hearts felt a profound and intense loss. Nancy Sue would now be taken from us.

We wanted to stop Mother's tears—see her smile, laugh, and play with us again. Our inquiring eyes asked questions we could not express. *We all grieved through our valley of why.* We would never hold our baby, watch her grow, or play with her. Nancy Sue's long summer with pain had ended. Our loss was deep. Her visit with us was too short. She never knew how much we wanted to keep her. What happens next? The three of us sat in suffering silence. *That unexpected morning of September 8, 1942, revealed a hushed scene of shock and grief. Nancy Sue had quietly passed away in her sleep in the early morning.*

To bravely face the day was too much for Mother. She continued to sit in their bed with Nancy Sue in her arms. *She could not*

bear to release her. Her tears would not stop. How could she cry so long? Kenneth, DeWayne, and I weren't thinking of breakfast with biscuits and gravy. Our sorrow for Mother was inexpressible. DeWayne was only two years old; he, too, was silent.

Trooper lay on the porch in front of our bedroom door. He, undoubtedly, felt our deep pain. He, an intelligent friend, understood the hushed environment.

Dad had walked one-half mile from our shack to the neighbor's home. It had a pretty sofa and several nice chairs. Their kitchen had a table with a beautiful tablecloth. Kenneth, DeWayne, and I played with them in their grassy yard. Her daughters attached empty sewing thread spools to my heels, and we pretended to walk in high heels.

Our neighbor's car promptly arrived outside! Our small neighbor lady promptly entered our bedroom. She placed both her arms around Mother and our baby. She shed tears of genuine compassion. Lovingly, she lifted Nancy Sue out of Mother's arms and wrapped her in a blanket. With her arms empty, Mother covered her face with her hands and continued crying. Dad sat by Mother and tenderly embraced her.

Our neighbor then picked up DeWayne, sitting on my right, and put him into Mother's lap. She knew the importance of filling Mother's empty arms. Once again, he was in his role as the youngest child. Just two years old, it had been an extra-long summer for him. Since Nancy Sue's birth, she suffered continually. DeWayne had abruptly been cut off from quality time with Mother. Farmer wives, like our neighbor, bravely faced emergencies head-on—without a doctor or nurse's help—for their entire lives.

Within minutes, we were crowded into a 1930s Model-A Ford Coupe and driven to the home of our paternal grandparents, Freeman and Mary McDonald (Papa and Granny). Mother held Nancy Sue. DeWayne cradled on Dad's lap. Kenneth and I crunched into empty spaces.

Trooper stayed home and guarded our shack. Our neighbors gave him food and water. Loving farm neighbors were priceless treasures.

When we arrived at our grandparents' home, Granny lovingly carried our baby to her and Papa's bedroom. She immediately fed all our empty tummies. After bathing Nancy Sue, Granny placed her into the beautiful baby basket, which was filled with soft cushioning. The basket was placed upon her large California antique trunk by the south window in their bedroom—my birth room. Nancy Sue had been named after Granny's mother, Nancy (Stanley) Hayhurst. Our baby remained in the basket until Dad and Granny brought her tiny coffin home. *Crushed dreams—Dad's tomato work check purchased Nancy Sue's tiny coffin.*

Nancy Sue's Funeral and Burial

We stayed with Granny and Papa until after Nancy Sue's funeral. Each day, Granny took me around the farm hillsides and gathered herbs. She used the herbs as preservatives for Nancy Sue's body. The climate was hot; there was no air conditioning. Granny permitted me to observe how she kept our baby's body preserved.

Nancy Sue looked like a sleeping doll in the white wicker basket. Several times each day, I walked into the quiet room to check on my baby sister. Precious memories were engraved upon my wounded spirit as I touched her face, smothered her with kisses, held her tiny hands, and wrapped my fingers around hers. Her soft, naturally curly hair shaped beautifully around my fingers. Since the day she came to our home, my pretend baby doll—Nancy Sue—had not been touched so much by me. The time I spent with her was a healing balm to my broken heart.

Daily, Granny patiently answered all my questions about Heaven, God, and Jesus. As Granny and I stood by her little casket, Granny gave me the Bible's promise that we would see Nancy Sue again. She would never be sick anymore. God would

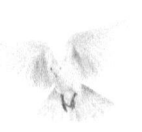

give her a new body in Heaven, but she would look the same. Nancy Sue wouldn't forget me. Granny said that someday she and I would live in Heaven, too. Granny said, "God has plans for us that are as beautiful as the mansion He has built for us." Uncluttered faith from Granny with six months of formal education! Her understanding words healed my wounded heart.

Nancy Sue's little coffin was placed into Granny's Dodge and carried to the little stone church at the High Cemetery near my grandparents' home. Neighbors dug her grave.

Granny's foreknowledge of my grief-stricken heart helped to eliminate all my questions before the funeral. After my sister's illness and death, I did not experience nightmares or negative dreams. Thank God for grandmothers with caring hearts who have experienced God's love. God has His own special purposes for grandmothers and grandfathers. Granny and Papa were close to me for their entire lives and continually gave me words of wisdom.

A powerful memory of the funeral was the tiny coffin sitting in the right exit corner of the little stone church. My toughest memory was the day of the funeral. When she was placed in her coffin, the lid was closed. Granny said, "Now, Barbara, Nancy Sue can't be touched again. You will see her one more time. They will open the coffin lid again at the close of the service but don't touch her anymore. You can touch her now before we close the lid." One more time, I combed her hair, stroked her tiny hands and fingers again, and kissed my beautiful baby sister, Nancy Sue, goodbye.

Through the funeral service, Granny and Papa were comfort pillars of strength for Kenneth and me. Kenneth and I sat between them. Lovingly, Granny kept her arm around me

throughout the service. She pulled me close to her and patted my shoulder. Clinging to Granny was the most natural thing for me to do. Emotionally, she kept me together and gave me hope for our future. Kenneth had shied away from looking at Nancy Sue before the funeral. It was too painful for him. DeWayne was spending all his time with Mother. We needed Granny and Papa's arms around us through that final hour with our baby sister. Since Nancy Sue was born, Kenneth and I had unconsciously acted much older than our physical and emotional ages. More maturity had been expected during our baby's illness—a tough summer for all of us.

Papa kept his arm around Kenneth—never leaving him untouched. Dad kept DeWayne on his lap as he sat with one arm around Mother. Mother never stopped crying. Our baby's short visit with our family had taken its toll on Mother and Dad. Economically, life looked extremely bleak for them. Their expectations and prayers for her health had not happened. Dad said, "Someday, we will all understand why God took her from us."

At the close of the funeral service, we all stood by her coffin and looked at her one more time. Her little coffin lid would soon be closed forever. Her long, dark curls were so beautiful. Everyone talked of her beauty and her hair. Our family remained by her coffin until Mother had the courage to walk away. Dad stayed close to Mother and kept one arm around her. He held DeWayne on his other arm. Granny held my hand tightly and let me peer at our little doll until the lid was closed. She continually wiped the tears from my face. The coffin lid was closed ever so quietly over our little angel, our beautiful baby, Nancy Sue.

Granny was a fantastic gardener. Her fresh red and pink roses covered our baby's tiny grave. Mother had also made a beautiful sweet pea arrangement out of crepe paper that was stunningly beautiful. Creating the wreath provided comfort to her broken heart.

Though the Boyd, Antioch, and High community farm families were extremely busy, they sacrificed their time to honor, grieve, and encourage Mother and Dad. The little stone church was filled with our neighbors and friends. Most farmwives who attended the funeral took one of Granny's roses home to memorialize Nancy Sue. Granny said I took one too. A flower was kept in a kitchen sink window or in the center of the dining table.

In the fall of 1942, Mother cried often. Kenneth, DeWayne, and I did not disturb her until she talked again. As she fought her lengthy battle with grief, we often saw Mother on her knees praying. We quietly listened to her prayers. Her grief overwhelmed us with forever memories. Severe headaches paralyzed her. We missed our baby sister, too. Mother took us to visit the grave often. We walked through the woods and waded Indian Creek. If it were too cold to go outside, we quietly sat on the floor with our backs to the wall until she finished her prayer. If the outside weather permitted, Kenneth would lead us outside. We played until she called for us.

One month before Nancy Sue's death, Dad became twenty-six; Mother became twenty-four. To them, the economic depression of the 1930s had become a fierce, relentless adversary. Would it never end?

Six and one-half years of marriage were history. Kenneth was born in June 1937. Mother turned twenty in August before

I was born in October of 1938. DeWayne was born in July 1940. Nancy Sue entered our family in May of 1942.

Those lean and lonely years strengthened Mother and Dad's faith. The most difficult test of their faith was not poverty but the unwritten chapters of Nancy Sue's life. It seemed our little angel only stayed a few weeks with our family. Her short visit of one hundred thirty days left a forever imprint upon our lives.

Our baby's uplifted arms to an invisible Heaven—on the eve of her death—was an unforgettable sacred holy epiphany. Tough times forge steel faith. Like church bells, treasured family sounds would one day toll again with life's simple, rich music—a family that laughed, played, sang, and prayed together.

Nancy Sue McDonald (May 2 to September 8, 1942)

Mother at Nancy Sue's Grave—Fall 1942

Nancy Sue, your one-hundred-thirty days
In our rent-free shack were far too few.
You are engraved in our hearts.
We will hold you in Heaven.
...Dad, Mother, Kenneth, Barbara, and DeWayne.

As shown above, the little stone chapel is still standing.
The High Church and Cemetery.
Located ten miles north of Berryville, Arkansas.
An extension has been added to the front.

Mother purchased Nancy Sue's small tombstone many years later with an angel engraved at the top of the stone. Engraved on the stone are the words:

Nancy Sue
Inf Dau of Chester & Veta
McDONALD
May 2, 1942
September 8, 1942

Psalm 139:16 (NLT), "You saw me before I was born. Every day of my life was recorded in your book. Every moment was laid out before a single day had passed."

The Original
Mcdonald Homestead

James and Elizabeth Mcdonald's Original Indian Creek Homestead
(Indian Creek flowed west on the north or back side of the home.)

In January 1939, when Mother waded Indian Creek and boarded Mr. and Mrs. Ray's buckboard on the day of her spiritual conversion, she saw the remains of the above-fallen homestead. James and Elizabeth McDonald never graduated

from their wagon to a buckboard. Their homestead was on the hill above the wagon trail road next to Indian Creek. A hill that would later have great significance in Mother's life. *She could never have imagined the future impact of that original homestead on her family.*

In the picture, Great-grandmother Sophia Elizabeth (Wooley) McDonald stood at the shack's front door. Great-grandfather James Odis McDonald was seated in a rocking chair on the "leaning" back porch. A visitor, probably Grandpa McDonald ("Papa"), is seated across from him on the right. Granny was usually the family photographer. Great-grandpa's long johns are blowing in the wind! Dad told me Great-grandma's hollyhocks were planted in the foreground. Dad returned to the homestead in the 1980s, gathered the hollyhock seeds, and planted them on his final lawn. They grew beautifully.

In the community, Great-grandpa was also known as Uncle Jim; Great-grandma was known as Aunt Elizabeth. They homesteaded in Carroll County; Indian Creek flowed through their property. Jim and Elizabeth's children were raised in the tiny shack. Freeman, my grandpa, was one of them. There were at least nine children in the family.

Great-grandfather was a powerfully strong man. He cut the trees that built their cabin. He made the shingles for the roof. A freshwater branch flowed from south to north through his property and emptied into Indian Creek. Indian Creek flowed east to west across his property. He settled in a location where they would not fear water shortages.

The mountain on the west side of the branch suffered erosion. Great-grandpa terraced the exceptionally long and tall hillside for a great distance—lengthwise and widthwise.

Arkansas rock—large and small—was abundant on his property. The forceful water branch was deep and a short distance west of their house. His shack was placed on the opposite hill with a scenic view of where the branch and the creek intersected. There was a small flat section of grazing land. A large black walnut tree was near the intersection of the branch and Indian Creek. That is where my Mother had paused in 1939 to put her shoes and socks back on after crossing the creek to go to church alone for the first time. At specific depths, the branch walls were six to eight feet in depth. In addition to his farm work with only the crudest implements, it must have taken Great-grandpa years to terrace the mountainside (1870–1880s). The terracing was still solid when I took my children there in 1973.

When he arrived in early 1870, Great-grandfather discovered a cave-like spring underneath the root of the enormous oak tree immediately north of the shack. Amazingly, he dug out the spring without doing any damage to the life of the tree. They couldn't afford a drilled well but could get enough water for drinking from that pure spring—delicious water! Perishable foods and farm milk were kept chilled in the spring.

Their children bathed in the creek from spring to late fall. Their fireplace heated the creek water for basic needs in winter. Indian *Creek never stopped flowing.*

Sunset Years of Paternal Great-Grandparents

James Odis Mcdonald and his wife,
Sophia Elizabeth (Wooley) Mcdonald.
Their last picture together before health and poverty
caused their permanent separation.

As a young girl, Mother was taken by her maternal grandmother, Susan (Stanley) Summers, to the home of Great-grandpa and Great-grandma McDonald. They walked three miles just to help them—clean the house, bake food, wash and iron clothes. Mother recalled she was afraid of Great-grandpa's long beard!

Due to poor health, in the 1930s, Great-grandpa and Great-grandma were separated to live with different children in their sunset years. Granny and Papa were in the grape vineyards of California to earn money to build their home on the nearby acreage. *The 1930s Depression and aftermath deeply affected the elderly poor.*

It is easy to observe why Great-grandpa and Great-grandma "held loosely" to meager earthly possessions but kept an iron-clad grip of faith in the dreams of their future home—Heaven. *My great-grandparents' faith was their most cherished treasure.* Their faith became their legacy. They were charter attendees of the first services in the Antioch Church schoolhouse. *My parents both became Christians there.* Their children, grandchildren, and great-grandchildren have all attended the Antioch Church. Most of them, including myself, became Christians there. DeWayne, my brother, and Myrna, his wife, still attend.

Isaiah's ancient words to patriarchs of faith, such as my great-grandparents, echo through the centuries,

> "As for me, this is my covenant with them," says the Lord. "My Spirit, who is in you, will not depart from you, and my words that I have put in your mouth will always be on your lips, on the lips of your children and on the lips of

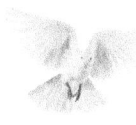

their descendants—from this time on and forever," says the Lord.

Isaiah 59:21 (NIV)

Great-grandmother Sophia Elizabeth (Wooley) McDonald
"Eyes that Portray a Beautiful Soul."

Great-grandmother, your life exemplified the true meaning of the Cross (not my will, but Thine be done). Selfishness died within the soil of your heart. It was rich in Heaven's dividends—beyond earthly comparison! You and Great-grandpa gifted the McDonald family with a legacy of faith! The inheritance that matters!

My Paternal Grandparents

My paternal grandfather, Tim Freeman McDonald, loved his family of origin on Indian Creek. When he turned eighteen, there were no jobs. For the economic welfare of his family, he ventured to Oklahoma Territory with a friend. The Indian Nation tribal chief loved Grandfather and taught him many survival skills. He wanted Grandpa to remain with them. He stayed for one year. He had great respect for the Indian Nation.

Papa's parents loved their children. Children understood their parents' hardships. Papa never criticized his parents. Tears filled his eyes when he spoke of them to me, especially his mother. He loved her dearly. He had little education—he could read, write, and add. God schooled him with wisdom and integrity.

When Papa returned to Arkansas, he met Grandmother, Mary Isabel Hayhurst. Granny told me that when she first saw Papa, she told her mother, "Mother, he is the man I am going to marry!"

Tim Freeman McDonald & Mary Isabel (Hayhurst) McDonald
Grandparent's Wedding Picture: December 10, 1906

Indian Territory Marriage License
December 8, 1906

To find work, he chose the City of Grove in Oklahoma Territory. Their marriage ceremony performed in Oklahoma Territory is shown above.

The landlord supplied them with a small shack on the property. Oklahoma became a new state in 1907. Roy, their first son, was born in 2008. Granny told me they were extremely lonely. "Freeman worked long hours on the owner's farm. On Saturdays, I would push Roy in the buggy into town (six miles) to see people. I carried our food and water with me as I had no money. By the time we arrived, we would be covered with dust from the unpaved road! It was a lonely life!"

In Arkansas, Granny's mother worried, "I know the reason Mary hasn't written is because they have no money for stamps." She sent them stamps; Granny immediately responded.

The owner of the large farm had no children. He knew how poverty-stricken Papa and Granny were. He and his wife begged to adopt Roy. They offered them any price they wanted for their son. My grandparents said, "No." Sadly, childless couples did not have the adoption possibilities that we have today.

After a couple of years, they returned to Arkansas. They tried to eke out an existence working for other farmers for several years. Aunt Marie was born in 2010. My dad, Chester, was born in 1916. Granny and Papa have two deceased children, King Tim Freeman McDonald and Betty Jean McDonald.

Papa and Granny's Children: Roy, Chester (Dad), and Marie

Our Move to Indian Creek—Mcdonald Homestead

After Nancy Sue's death, Dad built a small house on the original Mcdonald homestead. Nancy Sue's grave was less than one mile from our house.

Dad built our kitchen where the leaning porch of the homestead picture was located. A cement screened-in porch was adjacent to the kitchen. Our front entrance into the living room was on the north side. The back door entrance was the screened-in porch.

Our family used Great-grandpa's original spring for drinking water. Our house was built in the same location. Eventually, a well was drilled. We kept the perishables (milk, butter, cream) cold in the spring. We had no refrigerator. Compared to the cistern water in the Boyd community, Great-grandpa's spring water tasted heavenly.

Kenneth, DeWayne, and I swam in Indian Creek in the 1940s, just as Great-grandpa's children had done in the 1870s. Our winter bath water was heated on a pot-bellied wood stove in winter. Our clothes were carried to Granny's house and washed

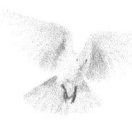

in her Maytag washing machine. A real treat! Granny always cooked the family a delicious lunch loaded with vegetables.

Dad recycled any possible boards from Great-grandpa's collapsed shack to build our house. A sawmill was less than a mile away. He and Papa drove the wagon through the backwoods trail to get the two-by-fours from the farm trees cut for the house. Papa and Dad always worked together. Neighbors helped build our home before winter. Their volunteer work was in addition to their farm activities. They cared. Except for Sundays, Dad stayed with Granny and Papa while he built the house. Our new house was visible from Granny and Papa's home above us. Granny said, "We love to look out our window and see the light in your house."

By Thanksgiving, the house was livable. It still had the rough flatboards showing on the outside. We could see the two-by-fours and the black tar paper insulation inside. There was no money for sheetrock, paint, finalized wood flooring, or linoleum. It was better than the shack. Kenneth, DeWayne, and I were happy to have our house, yard, creek area, branch, spring, and black walnut trees. We loved to be near Papa and Granny!

Our family gathered near the living room woodstove each night and listened to our static battery-powered radio. The World War II news continued to be scary. The war began thirty-two days before I was one year old. My parents had grave concerns about the war. Basic items of food were not available. We substituted granulated sugar with Karo syrup and brown sugar. Mayonnaise was a rare treasure!

Neighbors donated chickens to Mother. After a year, she had several. She sold a few dozen eggs each month to stores for grocery cash. Boards from Great-grandpa's shack, unusable on the house, were used to build the chicken house. They needed safety from hawks, crows, foxes, snakes, and weasels.

Snakes love eggs. On one occasion, an exceptionally long black snake swallowed ten of Mother's sorely needed eggs. At a distance, I counted the huge round bumps on the snake's back and said, "Mother, I've never seen a snake with bumps!"

Mother said, "Barbara, those bumps are my eggs!" Mother retrieved her eggs!

In the spring of 1943, Granny and Mother enlarged Granny's vegetable garden. Kenneth, DeWayne, and I were trained to help. There was an abundance of canned vegetables—cabbage, sauerkraut, beans, corn, beets, peas, and various pickles.

Years before, Granny had started peach trees that yielded canned peaches, jelly, and jam. She never tossed the seed away from a tasty piece of fruit. She planted it! Granny had also planted gooseberry bushes. We canned gooseberries for pies and jam. All the vegetables were kept in Granny's outside storm cellar.

Granny always picked blackberries from a neighbor's farm. She then gave the owner as many blackberries as they desired for payment. After the owner's wife separated her portion of the berries, Granny filled the container more than requested. All I visualized was the hard work of picking berries! When we were away from the owner, I said, "Granny, why did you give her more berries than she already took?"

Granny said, "Barbara, learn to give more than you are requested, whether on a public job or when you round off the berries!"

One morning early, Mother, Kenneth, DeWayne, and I went with Granny to pick blackberries. We were unaware that the

owner had forgotten to lock away his dangerous bull. Suddenly, the bull charged toward the berry patch. He bellowed loudly. Mother said, "Barbara, you and DeWayne run to the car and lay on the floor and the back seat!" Granny, Mother, and Kenneth climbed trees.

The bull came to the car and tried to push it over. Granny was terribly upset that the bull rocked her hard-earned car! DeWayne found it difficult not to look at the bull who had smeared saliva over Granny's car windows. DeWayne kept crying, "Barbara, he is going to get us!" It seemed forever, but the owner heard Granny and Mother's screams! When he arrived, Granny was out of the tree and trying to scare the bull away from her car! She gathered large sticks and several of Arkansas's plentiful rocks! Granny—usually one hundred pounds—facing an adult bull whose average weight was between 1,100 and 2,200 pounds! A courageous grandma! DeWayne and I had a super story to tell Dad and Papa!

At young ages, Kenneth, DeWayne, and I rode in the wagon with Papa and Dad to gather hay. We also planted and gathered corn from the cornfield. DeWayne and I were chosen to carry cold afternoon drinking water to Papa and Dad in the fields. Granny's small Hotpoint refrigerator accommodated four small ice cube trays. She bought it after a summer of work—the year I was born—in the California cannery with her sister. The refrigerator was a cherished treasure on Arkansas's sizzling summer days!

Granny and Papa would do without needed groceries to have the extra fifteen cents for three sodas from the Coca-Cola water cooler for three grandchildren. They bought twenty-four large sodas for one dollar when they could afford them. On a

scorching summer day, Kenneth, DeWayne, and I walked all the way to their house for such a treat! They always gave us food and one soda. We always had permission to lift her tablecloth and spoon a dip of Papa's honeycomb to keep our energy high! She faithfully centered it on their table in a tall, crystal-lidded dish.

One summer morning in 1943, Great-grandfather's large, steep ravine water branch became a target of paralyzing fear. Mother decided to sell her eggs to the grocer for basic items. Going to the country store was one of the biggest events of our week! If Mother had money remaining, she purchased us a large bottle of soda for five cents each.

Kenneth was in the passenger seat of our old Ford car. DeWayne and I were in the back. The car started immediately, but when Mother drove forward, she realized the steering was disabled. The downhill grade gave the old Ford speed. No brakes! Mother kept a death grip on the steering wheel. We were headed straight toward the deepest gully of the branch!

Mother prayed, "God, please help us! Don't let this car go into the branch. Help us now!" Kenneth, DeWayne, and I were in silent shock! Only a few trees along the field side of the deep branch were large enough to stop the car! Immediately, I visualized us falling into the deepest section of the branch. We would never see Dad, Granny, and Papa again! As the car approached the branch, it miraculously turned toward one of the trees. We hit the tree so hard that the car lurched backward and stopped. A God ovation! *Yes, the Holy Spirit was there when we needed help!* The heavenly choreographer of our lives! The outcome could have been different! Joshua 1:9 (NIV) says, "Have

I not commanded you? Be strong and courageous. Do not be afraid; do not be discouraged, for the Lord your God will be with you wherever you go."

Dad was shocked when he arrived home to see his car had collided with a tree along the bank of the water branch! The radiator and front bumper were severely damaged. After a quick discussion, Mother was promised he would notify her when our car was not operational! He repaired our car and gave me a penny to find the bolts and screws.

Before we acquired our used Ford, transportation to church was different. Kenneth and I walked along with Mother and Dad. DeWayne was carried. Dad sometimes permitted me on his shoulders on Sunday and Wednesday evenings. He carried DeWayne in his arms. Kenneth guided us with the lantern or flashlight.

We had moved back to the Antioch community during Thanksgiving week in 1942. Kenneth was five; I was four. When he turned six in June 1943, he began first grade. When Kenneth arrived home from school, he would teach me the words in his lesson. He taught me how to count. My mother taught me to add small numbers. Mother read the remainder of Kenneth's schoolbooks to me. He only read the stories he enjoyed. Starting school was my greatest wish!

Monthly, the Berryville School superintendent would visit the Antioch School and fill up the stage's cedar closet with books. Kenneth checked out books and brought them home daily for us to read. After I began school, I read all the history and biography books each month. Sadly, I didn't place more emphasis on math!

Mother worked on puzzles for hours with us. Later, I positioned the puzzles on the top of its box to give us pictures to display. Sometimes, Mother let me place them on her vanity dresser! Mother taught us marble games. If we lost, she explained why.

Dad purchased her vanity dresser at a farm sale. It was fun to comb DeWayne's hair, my hair, and Mother's hair. Dad let me comb his hair, but not for long. Dad was not blessed with a barrel of patience! Kenneth would never permit a girl to comb his hair! Primping in the mirror was fun!

Mother was delighted with the simple buffet Dad bought her at a farm sale. She acquired depression glass in oatmeal and other boxes of food. The depression glass was proudly displayed in her buffet. The person who loved it more than she was me. It was fun to rearrange the pretty dishes. The most beautiful area of our home.

Slowly, for Mother and for us, life returned to normal after our baby sister's death. Often, Mother drew pictures while Kenneth, DeWayne, and I played. She loved to draw flowers and faces. She worked diligently to teach us to write flowing cursive (script). With only her seventh grade education, she wrote beautiful cursive.

When Kenneth was in second grade, nothing made me happier than being in first grade. The school gave me new friends. Quickly, I became envious of the beautiful clothes others wore! Their lunch buckets were always filled with good sandwiches, fruit, and dessert. Jealousy filled me! Even at an early age, comparing our family to other families became a formidable problem. Sometimes, I ate my lunch away from others.

My heart cried once when my brother ran to me for his lunch. I handed him one slice of white bread that I had butter-fried on the cookstove. He was so disappointed. He looked at me and said, "Barbara, I don't want that!" He had hours to wait before supper. That was all we had for lunch.

Financially, life improved when Dad managed the milk route for farming communities. His paycheck came from the milk plant. He financed a truck and was strong enough to lift large milk cans. Mother and Dad were happy about the financial turnaround. Mother obtained war ration stamp books for Kenneth, DeWayne, and me. Pictures of my World War II stamp books are shown below with my parents' signatures.

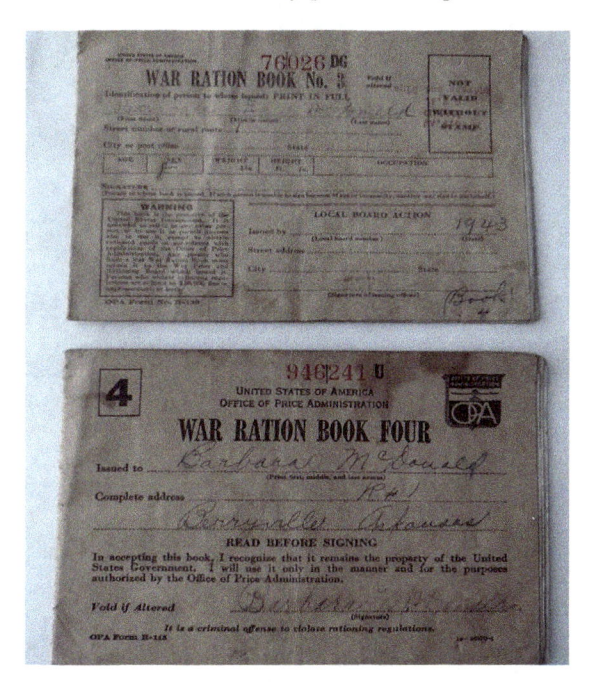

My World War II Food Ration Books
Dad signed my name on the 76026;
Mother signed my name on 946241.

Papa and Granny's Home

Papa and Granny McDonald—What a difference you made in my life!

My Fun Times with Papa and Granny

When I stayed overnight at Granny and Papa's house, I thought of myself as a princess! After Granny removed the combs and hairpins from her hair, she enjoyed me combing it before bedtime. I combed Papa's hair in various styles. Once, I braided the top of his hair with the braid pointing upward! He never complained. We laughed when he saw himself in the mirror!

At our home, we had no partitions between the rooms. Papa and Granny's house had partitioned rooms. It frightened me to sleep alone in a separate room! On my first night alone with them, Granny placed me between her and Papa. At four years of age, I remember Granny slept in a long gown, and Papa slept in his "next-day" long johns. She put one of her long gowns on me. As it graced the floor, I was sure I was the most important granddaughter in the world!

Granny positioned me in the bed between her and Papa. Granny said, "Now, if you hear us snoring, just wake us up, and we will stop." Papa was quiet about me waking them all night long! He must have said something to Granny! On my

remaining visits, Papa slept alone. He worked hard on the farm and did not need his granddaughter's disruptions!

Mother and Dad only permitted one child to stay overnight with the grandparents. One afternoon, DeWayne and I both wanted to stay. Mother said I could visit for a while, but then I would have to come home. When it came time to go, I refused to leave. My disobedience made me feel guilty. However, I loved to eat at Granny's table and stay overnight. The guilt was quickly forgotten.

Granny, DeWayne, and I slept in her extra bedroom that night. He was three; I was five. DeWayne slept between Granny and me. She placed her arm around DeWayne as he went to sleep. That was something she usually did for me! That night, I silently cried myself to sleep because I thought Granny loved DeWayne more than me. I felt Granny punished me because I disobeyed Mother. The next morning, I asked why she loved DeWayne more than me. She said, "Barbara, my arm is not long enough to reach over both of you! I don't love DeWayne more than you! I love you both the same!" She was only four-foot-ten and never weighed more than 95–105 pounds.

As DeWayne and I walked home, it was a bit scary to approach Mother. She told me I would be spanked with a buckberry switch the next time I disobeyed. Those switches would bend but never break, and they really stung my legs!

Kenneth and I helped carry our soiled clothes to Granny and Papa's house each Monday. Granny's wringer-style washing machine was a rare farm treasure. She drew well water and filled huge black iron kettles on an open firepit. The water was always hot when we arrived. Mother and Granny washed the

whites in hot water and rinsed the clothes twice. With each rinse, Mother threaded the clothes through the wringer of the machine. The colored clothes were next to be washed until all the clothes were finished. The washing machine was then thoroughly cleaned inside and out. Granny repositioned it on her screened-in porch and protected it with a special cover she had sewn. It lasted for her lifetime.

Those wringers did a fabulous job pulling hair! The top of my head was wringer-level. Twice, my hair was caught for a few moments before Mother reached me. That side of my hair was thinner for months. Mother warned me of carelessness!

When Monday morning's wash was finished, Granny always served a lovely meal. Papa and Dad came in from the field to join us. Everything was scheduled. When safely away from Mother, I whispered to Granny each week and said, "Granny, are you making a blackberry cobbler today?" She never disappointed me.

She served iced tea with our lunch. Dad would drink three to four large glasses. Hot biscuits were added with the fried chicken or bacon from her winter slab. Papa's honeycomb and Granny's homemade jam were on the table. She taught me to peel and fry potatoes (white or sweet). When a farmer told me I had fried the sweet potatoes just as he liked them, I thanked him and said, "Granny taught me!" It was then I saw him give Granny a big wink!

Each Monday, I dusted all of Granny's furniture. Her hand lotion, hair oil, Pond's Cold Cream, face powder, hairnet dish, special hair combs, pictures of her children, parents, Papa's sisters, and her and Papa's wedding picture were all positioned on her long library table. After all items were dusted, a beautiful ironed embroidered dresser scarf would be placed on it. One afternoon, Granny said, "Well, Barbara, I really don't like my stuff sitting in a slanted manner. You have always done better than that!" Quickly, I changed everything facing forward!

Granny always listened to "Judy and Jane," "Stella Dallas," and "Mary Noble" on KWTO radio as she quilted. Mother quilted with her until the clothes were dry.

The happiest year of Kenneth's childhood was when our cousin, Roy Leo Noel, came from California and lived with Papa and Granny. Papa improved all of Kenneth's and Leo's hunting and trap-setting skills. He had many rabbit gums and two or three hound dogs. He, Kenneth, and Leo fed the three horses— Queen, Ribbon, and Dixie—balanced and trimmed the horse hooves for the horseshoes and often fed the cows together. Kenneth and Leo regarded Papa as their hero.

Papa and Granny never experienced an extra pound on their bodies. Granny broke her leg in the Huckleberry Patch in her early seventies. After recuperation, she soon walked again. Papa once broke a rib but was soon back to his chores. What role models they were to me!

Grandparents: God's Assignments of Love

Granny and Papa never represented money to grandchildren. They were cisterns of love. They invested time to teach us thankfulness, responsibility, and accountability. When there was a lull, I asked, "Granny, can we go 'junkin' in your trunk?" We unpacked her large antique "Californie" (her pronunciation) trunk in her bedroom. She told me where her Sunday hats were purchased and other simple treasures. When all the items were unpacked, and all the stories retold, she and I carefully repacked each item. It was a fun time together. She laughed with her friends about our "junkin" time!

The one small light bulb at the top of each ceiling was turned on by pulling the long string hanging from it. Standing in a chair, Kenneth could reach the string. Papa would hold me so that I could get my turn. Because Kenneth always insisted it was his turn, Papa kept track of whose turn it was next! Simple pleasures! They used lamps to have light closer to reading and needlework. We had no electricity in our house.

As Granny and I fed her chickens, gathered eggs, and worked in her garden, she and I talked about the imaginary trip we would take on Route 66 to California—just the two of us. She

described Oklahoma, Texas, New Mexico, and Arizona to me. She described the sheepherders living in the colorful caves and mountains of the Southwest. We enjoyed hours together on our imaginary trip! Granny was the only adult who did imaginary things with me.

Granny was known as the best quilter in the community. She usually cut and pieced one quilt each month. The next month, it would be on her quilt rack to be completed. She said, "Before I die, I want to make sure that each of my children and grandchildren have one of the quilts I made to remember me." She did this year-long for years. Her beautiful quilts—with only the highest-grade cotton—became a beautiful part of her legacy. Every child and grandchild received at least one of her quilts.

On one occasion, a minister asked Granny to create two quilts. That was four months of work. She quilted for hours throughout the day and night. With pride in her work, Granny presented her quilts. The minister loved them! She handed Granny ten dollars for the two quilts! Granny painfully laughed as the minister walked away and quietly said, "Well, that surprised me, Barbara! Maybe the ten dollars will help me pay for the cotton!" Granny had hopefully expected twenty-five dollars for each quilt. The buyer had just sold their farm to the government. The farm was replaced by Table Rock Lake and Dam. Granny never mentioned the transaction again. Her remaining quilts were made for the family.

When neighbors helped bring hay from fields to their barns, the neighbor who owned the barn served hot meals. More than three times, I remember one neighbor who approached Granny mid-morning and said, "My wife doesn't feel up to doing the

meal today, Mary. Would you cook the meal for the workers?" She was not given food or money to fulfill their obligation. Granny's neighborly heart said yes. She served her food joyfully and without complaints. Proverbs 11:25 (NIV), "A generous person will prosper; whoever refreshes others will be refreshed."

Granny was a generous and genuine neighbor. As a midwife, she delivered most of the babies in the community. When the mother was frail or weak, she remained in their home for as long as needed. She told me, "Once with a severe breach birth, I stayed three weeks." Granny cooked, cleaned, washed, gardened, and cared for the family. Never was anyone charged for her work. Will there be rewards in Heaven for those who express the love of Christ—*loving their neighbor as themselves?* Granny served "needy" neighbors whether or not they attended church.

Heaven's reward awaits Papa and Granny for helping the poorest of the poor. They always checked on the sick. Their comment, "What are we in this world for if it is not to help our neighbors?"

Papa's hound dogs supplied the extra money in animal furs for their simple Christmas gifts each year. Granny always made sure his dogs were well-fed. He and his dogs were extremely loyal to one another. Papa's words still echo, "Mary, do you have the food ready for my dogs?" Their health and hunting ability represented food and gifts.

Papa, Granny, and our family shelled walnuts from the walnut trees on the property. A very messy job. Walnuts were shelled by all families who had the trees. Several ladies would keep some walnuts to bake delicious black walnut cakes and

candy for Christmas. Kenneth, DeWayne, and I always wished
Christmas came more often!

Even when our Christmases were meager, Mother purchased
four pounds each of Papa's favorite milk chocolate-covered vanilla cream drops and orange slices. Granny loved peppermint
candy and candy canes. Granny and Papa were delighted to be
with our family on Christmas. Presents to them were small.
They appreciated a family supper and pork chops.

As children, Granny and Papa's Christmas gift was an orange. Occasionally, a peppermint stick. After years of hard
work in California, they had their house, car, washing machine,
refrigerator, and Martha Washington cookstove. Their yard
flowers began as cuts in their living room. *Uncomplicated lives
of gratitude.*

Memorial Day—Dinner on the Ground

A Long-Standing Community Tradition
Waiting for "Prayer of Thanks" and Pictures

On Memorial Day, a church service was conducted in the High Church and Cemetery. People who attended other churches filled the chapel. Ancestors were always remembered in songs, testimonies, and sermons. "Dinner on the Ground"

was the custom. The church service was followed by a beautiful "Ground Buffet," as shown in the above picture. Families usually brought at least two prepared dishes. The afternoon was enjoyable visiting with friends. The children played on the road and hillside.

The deceased were not forgotten. They were remembered with reverence and respect. Families brought their fresh and homemade flowers to the cemetery and distributed them to the graves before 10 a.m. Recent deaths were also given extra flowers. A healing balm gesture to grieving families. It was their way of saying, "We haven't forgotten your loss."

Granny always invited me to assist her in distributing flowers on the graves of her ancestors and the unknown soldiers from the Revolutionary War. She was the lady with the most roses in her yard. The soldiers' headstones—Arkansas thin, tall rocks—did not always have a name. Granny made sure they had fresh roses. She said, "Barbie, I don't know if these graves were soldiers of the North or of the South, but they deserve my roses. These young men have mothers who have never known where their sons were buried. I'm doing this for their mothers, too. Their sons died far too young. I still have my two sons." Since burial, their graves have been cleaned yearly, along with the other graves.

Granny told me of the sufferings of the Civil War, "My paternal grandmother, Lucy Hayhurst (in the picture below), was on the farm alone with her children. Her husband was away. The soldiers took her food from her house and smokehouse. She and the children had a tough survival. She sifted the dirt in her smokehouse where their salted meat had been stored over the

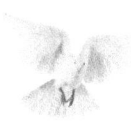

years to recoup needed salt for fish, squirrels, or rabbits they caught for food."

Great-grandmother Lucy Hayhurst—Civil War Survivor
Great-grandmother Lucy Hayhurst (seated in the chair on the right).
Papa (Freeman McDonald) holds my dad, Chester, and stands behind.
Great-grandmother Lucy. Granny (Mary McDonald) is to
the right of Papa.

Sitting by Granny in Church

My most affectionate memory of Granny was sitting with her on the single seat of the front school desk in the Antioch Church schoolhouse. She kept her arm around me during the service. That was something I loved! When the sermon was dull, I laid my head on her lap. I loved listening to my favorite preachers. We had a different preacher each Sunday. If Granny had any gum, she sneaked me a stick. Granny chewed tobacco twists, and she dipped snuff. My cupboard still has one of her snuff glasses. She lost one or two of her permanent back teeth throughout her lifetime. Her only dental visits were with the two problem teeth. On her last visit to the dentist, he said, "Mary, if you just massage your gums five minutes each day, you will never lose another tooth." She never lost another tooth! She brushed her teeth faithfully, occasionally with soda, but rinsed with salt water.

Except for singing in the choir, Granny was silent in church. Only a couple of times did I hear her give a testimony. Her tone expressed the brokenness of one who felt unworthy of God's love. In the Ozark culture, nobody felt God needed them for His success. They sensed extreme unworthiness because Jesus

Christ had died for their sins. How could they repay Him? They sought to live a life that portrayed their appreciation for His death. *Quite the opposite of what we now hear—does God exist—if so, is He relevant? Farm families did not doubt that God was real and relevant!*

For the last twenty years of her life, she never failed to read multiple chapters of her Bible weekly (often fifty). She always told me she felt unworthy of the Lord and had no unique talents. She felt under-educated and had always wished she could have been a nurse. She deserved the title of a Licensed Practical Nurse for the many babies she delivered and her home care, not only for the mother and baby but for the families! For as long as she lived, she was the one person who stayed up all night with anyone who was dying at home. Granny and Ollie Minick visited, cleaned, disinfected, cooked, bathed the patient, changed the beds, washed clothes, and ironed. Granny worked at home during the day and would stay with the dying person at night. Granny was requested by the dying because they knew she served them in the most loving ways. Granny and Ollie exemplify how the Holy Spirit defines His net fishing—"strand-by-strand of love." Granny's many years of being available to the Holy Spirit to serve the poorest of the poor filled her heavenly treasure chests. She gave her hands and feet as Jesus' hands and feet to the poor and dying. Her only reward would be the future—Heaven. She never thought of an earthly monetary return. Long-term care was unknown; *Granny was the Antioch, High, and Hoodie communities' long-term care. She most often walked or rode a horse.*

Seated by Granny in the Antioch Church schoolhouse, the Holy Spirit tugged at my heart. The usual order of the service

was for everyone who enjoyed singing to come upon the stage and sing in the choir. Twenty singers were the usual volunteers. They ranged in age from twelve to seventy years—as long as one could stand and sing! After his conversion, Dad played the guitar. There was no piano. *Granny always sang, and I sang by her.*

The attendees were poor farmers. Granny dressed her Sunday best. When overnight at their home, she permitted me to choose her costume jewelry. Church had no membership roll, church board, or formal choir. The volunteer choir sang from their hearts. From then until now, I have never heard more beautiful singing. They sang of a life to come—an authentic heavenly mansion far from where they now lived. *When they sang about Heaven, they felt rich in what truly mattered most—enduring eternal riches. No earthy possessions would go to Heaven with them!* The following songs were the usual favorites:

"Amazing Grace."
"Everybody Will Be Happy Over There."
"In the Sweet By and By."
"Just Over in the Glory Land."
"Just a Little Talk with Jesus."
"Heaven's Jubilee."
"I'll Meet You by the River."
"In the Sweet Forever."
"Glad Reunion Day."
"When the Roll Is Called Up Yonder."
"What a Friend We Have in Jesus."
"Where Could I Go but to the Lord?"
"Won't It Be Wonderful There."
"You Can't Do Wrong and Get By."

One of the grandmothers could not read. However, she had memorized every song. She had a beautiful soprano voice. Her son led the choir. Their voices were always on pitch. Her children and grandchildren were singers. The choir usually sang for thirty minutes—many times longer. The choir did not clap their hands while singing, but the song leader devastated the shaped notes hymnals. He kept time as he beat the hymnal against his hands! They sang about a coming time when poverty, sickness, separation, and death would be no more. The Antioch Church schoolhouse was the community's *lighthouse of hope* for their earthly and eternal future.

Though the people in the pews were not in the choir, they always sang, too. A spirit of thankfulness, love, and genuine unity was dominant. Any individual was free to start a song during the testimony service. Dad immediately found the chord in which they were singing on his guitar, and everyone joined the singing. New songs were introduced in such a manner.

The Antioch Church attendees had never heard of a programmed worship. They worshiped God—whether or not the minister was present. Their iron-clad faith and steadfast hope were in God alone. Their faith—*deeply believing God was who the Bible said He was and would do what He promised He would*—was *their greatest hope and legacy.*

Seated next to Granny on the small school desk seat at the Antioch Church schoolhouse, the inaudible voice of the Holy Spirit spoke to my heart with every altar invitation. No child my age went to the altar! And I told nobody how my heart beat extra fast during the song of invitation. The Holy Spirit tugs occurred as I understood the sermons. God was real; I felt His

Holy Spirit speak to me—like my first prayer for Nancy Sue. Never did I doubt those feelings of conviction!

When I asked how old a child should be before they became a Christian, Dad said, "Jesus went to the temple in Jerusalem at the age of twelve. When children go younger than that, they probably don't understand the commitment they are making."

Incredibly, one can lack knowledge of the Bible (as I did) and feel the King of Heaven's presence at a young age. In today's world, one can easily find the most accurate translations of Scripture but never bother to respond to the Holy Spirit. The Holy Spirit finds hungry hearts regardless of their age. "God, don't let me die before I become a Christian" was my secret prayer each night.

Service began with an opening prayer followed by the song service. Before the next congregational prayer, verbal prayer requests were given. They were requests for families in need, "Remember the Smith family; his father has passed. The grave will be dug early Wednesday. The funeral is at 1 p.m." The *only* announcement to the community. If in winter, the congregation ensured the grieving family had wood for warmth. Food donations were arranged. The Antioch Church schoolhouse church services were about gratitude to God and community outreach. Capable men worked. *Common sense and integrity were strengths, not weaknesses.*

Women unexpectedly died in childbirth. Mother's cousin died birthing her first child. Papa's sister died while birthing twins. Her arms were raised to Heaven, thanking God her twins were born healthy. Neighbors helped children who lost their mothers.

Elderly community members died of simple pneumonia. Cancer patients died at home. *Nobody died alone.* Neighbors did their chores, cooked food for them, and babysat the children. *Suicide was unknown; love overcame the fear of the future.* That's the spirit of the community in which Papa and Granny were raised. They lived what they had been taught. *As they grew older, it must have been difficult for them to comprehend how the community became more self-centered and unaware of their neighbor's needs.*

Papa and Granny's Spiritual Role in Grandchildren

Papa was relatively quiet about his faith. Twice, he gave a testimony at church that I remember. Each time, he spoke with tears and a trembling voice. He mentioned the many times he talked to the Lord near the water branch below his barn— kneeling down on the grassy knoll. He said that knowing Jesus meant everything to him. Once, I heard him say, "My time with God down on the hillside makes all my troubles disappear."

The faith his parents passed on to him was deep and solid. In every way, he was one of the most loyal men I have ever known—to God, family, neighbors, and country. He never passed judgment—even when others did. How does the Holy Spirit enable a believer with three months of education to encourage and refresh the lives of others—only plant seeds of peace? That was Papa! He did not have a religion that enslaved and entrapped him! Papa had a relationship with Jesus! He knew what it meant to deny himself. His self-love had died; Jesus' love was all-important to him. That did not make him a non-person but a new person. Papa had learned what Jesus meant

when He said to pick up our cross. The Cross is recognized as a metaphor for death. Someone has also said the Cross is where "God's will" and "our will" cross! At such an intersection, Papa had learned to say, "Not my will, but Thine be done." And I witnessed what it was like for him to follow Jesus. A follower is a disciple or a student who applies what Jesus teaches. (See Matthew 16:24–25, NIV.)

In later years, a very tender moment in my life was when Papa received a Sunday school award. He had attended one year without an absence. After the church service, I was seated in the car, holding one of my siblings. He came and handed me his award. I said, "Papa, you earned that award! It's yours to keep!"

With tears, he said, "I want you to have it, Barbara." So, without saying more, we both cried. He had invested fifty-two Sundays for that award. Papa and Granny loved and trusted me; I never wanted to disappoint them—my dearest friends. His closest relatives had made heartbreaking decisions. He wanted his grandchildren to make intelligent life decisions. *With spiritual insight, he saw beyond this life where true and eternal rewards are given for the right decisions.*

The Holy Spirit, my life choreographer, gifted me with the legacy of Granny and Papa—who lived lives of tenacity and faith. Were they perfect? *No.* They were just like you and me. As for education, Granny had only been able to attend school for six months. She lived close to the school. It hurt her deeply when she could not attend. A knowledgeable and brilliant lady. Papa received three months of education. Would today's society mock their lack of education? With limited education, they

could both read, write, add, and live honorable lives. They were never arrested or jailed for any reason. God gifted them with wisdom, integrity, and common sense. They were never too busy or elderly to help, share, and encourage. They didn't blame God, nor anyone else, for life's problems, material shortages, or physical incapabilities. *What a rich heritage! Accountability exemplified!*

Earth is sometimes referred to as the "womb of heaven." By the time we are ready to enter Heaven, this world has changed so much that it is no longer home to us! Granny and Papa would no longer enjoy living on their farm. They matured beyond this life—their nine months of earthly living were finished. They were ready for Heaven's environment! The message I learned from my grandparents is that we need less of life's stuff. *We must live a life of love with a servant's heart—Christ-centered versus self-centered! Heaven-centered versus Earth-centered!*

Recurring Memories and Dreams

After I skipped on the beaten path to Papa and Granny's house, I knocked on the front door to surprise them. Granny's clicking footsteps were easily heard outside the door. Due to her poor insteps, she always wore just under a two-inch heel, size four shoe. Their hearts always welcomed me with love. There was always too much work to be done for naps. In her spare time, Granny crocheted and quilted; Papa often sneaked a nap in his rocking chair between projects and chores.

Since her death in 1966, I dreamed I returned to her door. After the knock, I heard her heels popping across her linoleum—totally worn out until she painted its designs with sponges. She opened the door, and I awoke! Someday—soon, I hope—the door of Heaven will open, and Granny and Papa will greet me! *It is difficult to imagine their awe as they entered Heaven's love and majesty!*

The Holy Spirit (the remembrancer) brings back memories. Jesus said, "But the Helper, the Holy Spirit, whom the Father will send in my name, he will teach you all things and bring to your remembrance all that I have said to you" (John 14:26, ESV). The remembrancer has brought to my memory inspirational

life events that have spurred me on in my faith journey. Memories have included Granny and Papa. The Holy Spirit knows that memories of my grandparents have kept me focused on Heaven. Thank You, Holy Spirit, for the precious memories You preserved for me. As I author this book, Granny has been in Heaven for fifty-eight years. Papa has been in Heaven for fifty-seven years.

When I reflect upon the Ozark Mountain people—hillbillies—where I was born and raised, only one thought stands tall in my mind. *They had few material possessions but were generous with their most precious gifts—love and time.* Today, there are material possessions but so little of the neighborliness that the community once knew.

When I visited the Antioch Church, I reflectively saw Granny and Papa seated in the first and second rows of the church. In real life, as they became older, they were noticed less and less at church. They never enjoyed an "Elderly Appreciation Sunday." Families are busy. No Sunday lunch invitations or a drive-by to check on them. One by one, all their friends passed away. The elderly were given little honor in the community where they had given so much. Heaven is different! *They will forever be rewarded for their humble deeds!*

As I authored this book, a friend in India mentioned that the youth in his area bow to the elderly when they meet them—often touching their feet! They bow and touch to show appreciation for the life, wisdom, tenacity, integrity, guidance, and presence of the elderly. It would be rewarding if every church in America created an adoption agency—within their church—for the elderly. No, not to have them live in their homes—only

to be loved! One call each week to them would be a beginning. Thanksgiving meal? Christmas presents? Time out for an ice cream cone? A phone call and prayer once a week? There are thousands of ways to say, "We love you! We will miss you when you are in Heaven!"

In 1967, Grandpa was near death. Dad said, "Papa, do you want to go home with us?" Papa shook his head "no" and pointed toward Heaven. His spirit undoubtedly experienced close communion with the Holy Spirit before Dad asked that pivotal question. He envisioned something much more precious than going back to see the farm he loved—the one on which he was born and raised. He was prepared to leave it all and move to the eternal home his parents had first told him about. *His spirit could hear his angel chariot coming!*

When I reflect on Papa, two Bible verses always come to mind. "You keep him in perfect peace whose mind is stayed on you, because he trusts in you" (Isaiah 26:3, ESV). The second verse is, "Great peace have those who love your law; nothing can make them stumble" (Psalm 119:165, ESV). I have visualized Papa escorted by angels as—alone in his hospital room—he stepped out of time into eternity. A holy moment with heavenly escorts! My first notification that Papa was in Heaven was a letter returned to me in Massachusetts that was marked "Deceased."

The Antioch community lost a great man of love and peace. Simple faith in his heavenly Father. Integrity was not his weakness! A sense of responsibility for right and wrong. His friends were gone when he stepped out of time into a beautiful eternity. *His funeral was small in number but rich in presence.* My imagination explodes when I visualize his welcome into Heaven's majesty—*God's land of equal justice!*

In 1966, Granny was dying. I sent a goodbye letter from Massachusetts. Kudos were given to her for the times she fed my hungry stomach and the many times she drove me to church—like the night I became a Christian. In my letter, I asked her to tell me her feelings about her homegoing. She said, "Tell Barbara that with all the sense that God has given me, I am ready to go."

Mother told me that Granny sobbed so loudly as she read my letter to her that she could be heard crying throughout the facility. *Granny needed to hear how much she was loved and that she would be missed by those she loved so much—her family.* She had told me more than once that she felt unworthy of Jesus' death for her sins. *Isn't that how we all should feel?* The first Bible verse we memorized as a child speaks hope and life to the dying because it promises eternal life. (See John 3:16, KJV.)

The Unexpected—
March 1945

Hesitatingly, I said, "Mother, can I please sleep at the foot of your bed tonight?" Mother was shocked! Never had I asked to sleep with my parents! Independence was my forte—*as long as I could see them!*

She responded, "Why do you need to sleep with us? You can see us from where you sleep!" My uneasiness was mysteriously real.

As she walked away, I persisted, "Mother, please. Just one time. I can see you from my bed, but I don't want to sleep alone tonight."

Slightly agitated, she said, "Okay. You can sleep at the foot of our bed. Only this one time!" Mother had her reasons. Nightmares were common occurrences to me. Mother needed a good night's sleep. Nobody needed my restlessness!

"Mother, just for tonight—I promise," I said. Picking up my little pillow, I hastily climbed under the covers at the foot of their bed before Mother changed her mind! She occasionally did just that! My nightmares were common family knowledge. Kenneth and DeWayne slept peacefully. Nobody understood

why I had them, especially me! *Mother would never have forgiven herself had she not allowed me to sleep with them that particular night.*

The Holy Spirit nudges individuals in mysterious ways— never intrusively—even through the worried voice of a little child. As a six-and-one-half-year-old, the Holy Spirit choreo- graphed my emotions and words. My parents later echoed that the Holy Spirit gave me the urge to sleep with them. *He kept us all near one another that fateful night.*

Dad, Mother, Kenneth, and DeWayne slept in the two beds at the south end of the non-partitioned side of the house. The house was built in a square form. From the north end of the liv- ing room, we could go into the small kitchen. Also, at the north end of the living room—next to my bed—was the exit door from the living room. The kitchen had a south exit door onto the screened-in porch. There was no door at the south end of the long room where my parents and brothers slept.

Reflecting on that day, Granny had said, "It's late. Why don't you have supper with us tonight?" Granny always made sure we had a nourishing meal. She and I always anticipated the free dish she would find in specific food items, especially oatmeal, flour, and cornmeal. Granny's favorite color was the green depression dishes. With her green eyes and brown hair, she naturally loved green. She loved to feed guests at her table, especially her family. She never failed to permit me to choose the table dishes for the meal. I stood in one of her kitchen chairs to reach for the dishes. The silent praise she received as she watched her grandchildren devour their meal was the only "thank you" she needed. *She had a servant's heart.*

Granny mixed her cornbread in her mother's bowl. She baked the cornbread and fried the potatoes in big iron skillets.

There were onions, assorted pickles, canned beets, sauerkraut, pinto beans, and Papa's delicious honeycomb smothered in honey. Granny kept the honeycomb in her antique crystal pedestal-lidded dish.

When anyone in the community discovered a hive of bees on their property, they contacted Papa. He took his smoker and safely transported the bees to his property. Many times, I watched him put his hands into the hive. The bees nested all over his hands and arms. They never stung him.

Granny and Papa's common staples for lunch and supper were cornbread and pinto beans. In summer, her meals included fresh garden vegetables. Her garden lettuce was tasty! *Most notably, on that March evening of 1945, our supper meal at Granny and Papa's home had a historical and safety significance.*

That night was the only time I remember Granny not going to the barn to help with the milking. She was convinced she was the only one who could get the most milk from her cow, Mandy. She measured the output! Mother had the same opinion about her cow, Jersey! On one occasion, Granny mentioned her cows had reduced their milk supply because Papa milked them while she was in California! Mother made the same remarks about Dad when he milked her cows! Two economically minded women! Their words did not disturb Dad and Papa!

Granny and Mother prepared the meal while Papa and Dad milked the dairy cows. We had no barn. Our few cows were milked in our grandparents' barn stalls. DeWayne and I stayed in the barnyard long enough to give the barn cats milk. Kenneth was enamored with the ever-popular Lone Ranger and Roy Rogers programs on the radio.

We delightfully gathered around Papa and Granny's supper table and filled our hungry stomachs. Granny's eyes danced as we devoured her food. Papa generously passed the food to anyone who could eat more. What beautiful memories! After the dishes were cleaned, we said goodbye and walked down to our home by Indian Creek. Everyone was exhausted.

We were unaware of how the Holy Spirit had choreographed our schedule to share supper together in my grandparents' home. We arrived from Berryville later than intended. Granny insisted on supper with them. She and Mother hastily prepared the meal. Dad and Papa immediately went to the barn and milked the cows. *On that fateful night, the Holy Spirit knew our family of five needed protection from a hot stove with burning coals in our small, unfinished home. He used Granny to make that happen!*

Dad continually improved our house to get it finished. He bought needed supplies when money was available. The house had no partitions or inside doors. Black tar paper covered all the walls until money was available. Patience and money would get everything finished—even our cellar. Dad manually dug the outside cellar but waited for the money to cement its floor, walls, and overhead.

The house porch had a cement floor. Mother kept the huge lard can on the porch from the winter's pork butchering. Dad's few tools, chicken feed, canned fruits, and vegetables were there. Muddy shoes were cleaned there before entering the kitchen.

The milk route Dad managed provided the money for basic staples. The remainder went to the bank for the truck payment. Because the wagon trail road from Granny and Papa's house to

ours was extra rocky and bumpy, Dad always parked his truck next to Granny and Papa's garage.

The Holy Spirit, our heavenly choreographer, had orchestrated our supper, the parked truck, and my request to sleep with my parents. By the next morning, we would call those incidents miracles.

Exhausted, we were anxious for bed! A night we thought would be just another night—changed our lives forever! *Never— in a million years—could we have imagined how different tomorrow would be.*

Unstoppable Winds

When Dad blew out our lamp that night, there was no indication of rain or strong winds. It was an ordinary evening except for supper at Granny and Papa's home and my request to sleep with Mother and Dad. Soon, we were soundly asleep.

Suddenly, fierce winds pounded debris against our unfinished house! We were unaware that a tornado with a 300-foot-wide ground path had barreled through the woods above our home. It narrowly missed the Antioch Church schoolhouse. The winds were so noisy that Granny and Papa had not heard their porch roof blow off! The tornado set down on the two hills above our home and uprooted giant oak trees. When Dad awakened, he said it sounded like a freight train approaching. He jumped to his feet and slipped on his overalls. Mother was up immediately but terrified! They felt helplessly afraid for our family! When we knew a storm was imminent, we walked to Granny and Papa's cellar and slept there all night. March 1945 caught us unaware.

Dad and Mother sensed the house was buckling from the horrific winds. Dad said, "Veta, grab Barbara; I'll grab the boys!" With no more than a distance of three feet, Dad reached to enfold his two sons in his arms. Sadly, before Dad reached

Kenneth and DeWayne—like a sandwich—the winds doubled the mattress over their bodies as he watched. Mother said she just fell over my body as a protective shield. My parents' last memories were that we were drawn upwards.

Mother told me, "We were drawn upward with all the debris of the winds as the house, and everything in it, broke apart. It was like we were in a whirlwind. While going up, everything went black for Chester and me." While asleep, Kenneth, DeWayne, and I became unconscious.

Dad regained consciousness first. Rain torrentially poured down as if in buckets. Without pause, lightning danced angrily over the sky above us—no glowing starry night. From the lightning, Dad saw where Mother and I were sprawled out on the ground. He wondered if we were alive. Dad painfully tried twice to stand but was unable to move his legs again.

Thankfully, Mother and I were still by one another when we landed on the ground. Perhaps Mother hung on to me tightly through the entire destructive forces. We will never know. She had me wrapped in her arms when she went unconscious. Mother's fall over my body undoubtedly protected me and kept me with the family. Thankfully, we were not dumped unconsciously into the rushing mad waters of Indian Creek.

Dad kept calling Mother. She finally became conscious and stood. He realized she was in shock when he said, "Veta, pick up Barbara!"

Her bizarre response was, "Where is she?"

Dad said, "She is lying on the ground beside you. Pick her up! Sit her down beside me." With only her right arm, Mother swooped me off the ground, carried me over to Dad, and

dropped me. I became conscious! Dad was relieved that two more family members were alive! We later discovered why she only used the right arm.

The night was forever imprinted on my memory. The entire hillside was visible from the constant lightning. The rain was relentless, and the thunder was explosively loud. The quiet night had become a dramatic devastation.

Mother stood silently by me—still in shock. She uttered nothing to us—just stared at the wreckage. The rain poured over my face, but I also sensed another taste that was not rain on my face.

Dad said, "Veta, you must get Mother and Dad. Tell Mother to bring her car to take us to the hospital. We need to find Kenneth and DeWayne. They may be under this rubble."

"Which way do I go?" she said. At that point, Dad felt the lowest depth of despair. He knew she was hurt more than he realized, but she was his only hope of getting help. The lightning continuously illuminated our hillside with pain and destruction—displaying our devastation as bright as day. How many tornadoes might still be coming?

Dad pointed south to her and said, "Veta, go in that direction to Mother and Dad's house. Stay on the road!" Mother put her head high in the air and started walking toward the wagon trail road that led to my grandparents' home. Dad sobbed even louder as she left.

He somehow felt he had to keep me by him. He could have sent me to Granny and Papa's house. Perhaps he was worried about his demise before anyone arrived. Maybe it was because he knew the water branch was running swiftly and was afraid

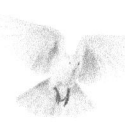

I might not make it through the rough waters. When the lightning flashed, he could undoubtedly see my bloody face and didn't know how seriously my head was injured.

After whirling us within the debris, the winds had dropped us, along with broken boards, windows, and piled-high wreckage. We were dropped on the north side of the house, which was a hillside. At the bottom of the small hillside was one row of trees, a narrow wagon trail bluff road, a deep bank, and Indian Creek. The tornado rainfall had overflowed the banks of Indian Creek and flooded the adjacent cornfield.

As the lightning flashed, Dad was looking for Kenneth and DeWayne. The mattress had folded over them as he tried to reach them. *He kept calling, but they did not answer. Were they on the hillside? Dropped into the raging waters of Indian Creek?* His heart was sick with concern. He hoped his parents' home was still standing when, and if, Mother arrived there.

Our "911" Farm Neighbors

As the lightning flashed, I saw the pain on my almost twenty-eight-year-old Dad's face. Between his painful groans, loud sobs, and desperate prayers, he called across the hills to our neighbors for help. After tornados, neighbors waited outside their homes and called the names of other neighbors until they answered. Their voices rang through the Ozark hills until they knew families were safe. There were no phones. Neighbors deeply cared. What a beautiful community we had. Neighbors who loved one another! Handshakes were pledges of loyalty. Their loyalty manifested with intensity during tornadoes!

Between sobs, I said, "Dad, what happened to us while we were asleep?"

He said, "Barbara, a tornado destroyed our house! I've got to get help to find Kenneth and DeWayne. I can't walk anymore."

Stunned, I cried silently, "Why did God do this to us?" My thoughts went wild! Nobody taught me to blame God; it came naturally to me.

Dad's worry over Kenneth and DeWayne's whereabouts made me feel helpless. My young mind vividly remembered

losing my baby sister. God took her. Had God taken my brothers in this tornado?

Dad was relieved when Kenneth and DeWayne both cried for help. They were doubled up inside the mattress. We couldn't see the mattress. They had destroyed sections of the house on top of them. Debris was spread everywhere. Dad asked if they were hurt. Kenneth said, "Dad, we're not hurt; we can't breathe! Get us out of here, please!" Their fearful, heartbreaking cries broke Dad's heart. Mine too. He felt so utterly helpless.

Dad said, "Son, I am hurt. I can't walk, but I am getting help. Stop crying. Try and lie still. You'll be free soon!" Dad was so relieved! His entire family was alive!

The hidden hand of God doubled the mattress over Kenneth and DeWayne, protecting them from the boards, nails, and glass blown in the tornado-force winds. Thankfully, in our unconscious state, none of us were dumped by the tornado's powerful winds into the overflowing rushing waters of Indian Creek! Dad's greatest fear! As I sat on the ground by Dad, I heard its raging waters. We could see it flooding the field.

In his pain, Dad was ecstatic that Kenneth and DeWayne were near us and alive. Thankfully, nobody had to search for them. Bodies can travel miles in a tornado. Clothing and other household items were found miles north in Missouri. Who knows how many items drifted down the surging creek waters? They were deep and forceful. Most loose items were never found. Our family's legacy could have been changed forever had it not been for the invisible arms of God holding us. When Dad spoke of tough trials or life's stressful situations—whether when he had failed or others had felt they failed—he always said, "Except for the tender mercies of the Lord, none of us would be here."

Jesus said in Luke 12:6–7 (NIV),

> Are not five sparrows sold for two pennies? Yet not one of them is forgotten by God. Indeed, the very hairs on your head are all numbered. Don't be afraid; you are worth more than many sparrows.

The McDonald family—and the entire community—knew that God watched over the McDonald sparrows (our family) that memorable night.

As I sat by Dad, I not only listened to his passionate prayers, but we both heard the fearful cries of my brothers. Kenneth kept saying, "Dad, we're going to smother to death if you don't get this stuff off us. We can't move." DeWayne, who was not yet five years old, was terrified. He called both Mother and Dad to help him.

With their cries and fear, Dad was worried they would exhaust the oxygen they needed. Smashed in the mattress, the darkness and weight of the debris were scary. Dad told them to lie still so the debris would not shift. He was relieved they were alive and comforted them by telling them Austin and Emerson were coming. Only strong arms could remove that heap of wreckage. We did not know if they were on the very bottom or somewhere in the middle of the mountain of rubble. Dad was unaware whether his parents were okay and if their home was destroyed. With Mother in shock, he wondered if she had lost her way, stumbled and fallen, or wandered into the woods between the homes.

To our left, across Indian Creek, a lantern appeared. It was our neighbor to the west. We could see him and his lantern at the edge of the water. Dad was so relieved. He started calling, "Come help us. Hurry! Our house has blown away!" To our dismay, our neighbor walked back toward his home. With all the thunder and rain, he did not distinguish Dad's words. Later, we discovered that because Dad was loudly sobbing and praying, he thought it was an all-night prayer service! He would never have left had he known about our desperate situation. Dad cried as he saw his lantern going back toward his home, "Oh, no, he's going back home! I've got to get Austin ('Aus') and Emerson ('Punch') to answer me!"

Despite his pain, Dad kept calling, "Aus, Punch, can you hear me? We need help! Can you hear me? We are hurt! Help!" Perhaps they had assumed the neighborhood was okay and had not listened outside their homes.

At first, Emerson and his wife, Laura, thought a rooster was crowing, a usual occurrence when chickens are frightened. Possibly, one of our roosters had been blown near their home. Any rooster who lived through the tornado would have crowed to regather the flock. They soon realized that Dad was also calling for help.

Dad and the Ray brothers were friends as teenagers. They attended dances and double-dated together on their horses. They stole watermelons from farmers' fields and enjoyed teenage watermelon feasts. Granny had often complained about how the Ray brothers would go to their house while she and Papa were in the Sunday morning service and eat one of her Sunday dinner pies. She never added that perhaps her own son, Dad, had secretly invited them down and enjoyed the pie with them!

When Dad became a Christian, he went to farmers, apologized, and paid for the watermelons he had stolen. Their lives had now changed. They were each happily married, each family had two children, and attended church together. No longer did Granny's pies disappear on Sundays! Dad had taught Emerson to play the guitar.

It was music to Dad's ears when Austin and Emerson began to answer him. "Chester, we hear you! We'll be right over just as soon as we can get across Indian Creek!" It had been a heavy downpour for most of the night. Austin and Gladys had two young boys, Billy and Bobby. Emerson and Laura had a young son and daughter, Odell and Myra Lou. They could not leave their children home alone. Another tornado could be forming. They placed their children on their shoulders. They found the safest location to cross Indian Creek and came to our rescue.

Reflect with me on the definition of true neighbors. Austin and his family—with their lantern—walked a good distance to Emerson's family residence. Then, they walked down a hill and waded across an overflowing creek. They trudged along a muddy trail alongside Indian Creek to reach our wreckage. The rain had not stopped its deluge of the countryside. Genuine neighbors are gifts from God. Because they hurriedly came to our rescue, there was no time to find their horses bedded down somewhere in a grove of trees. It was late into the night as they walked across the overflowing creek during the storm's aftermath. Their time helping us was spent in their wet clothes with no complaints. Could one find better neighbors? They

fulfilled the adage, "Love isn't really love until you give it away." Love is more than just words. Love is not only a noun; it is a verb—action! To love is to give. Love transforms our behavior. Love changes the hearts of individuals and nations. Love cannot be passive; it is graced with action. The McDonald family was touched forever by the love of neighbors that March night in 1945.

During the interlude, the lightning exposed our chickens, running back up the hill from the creek area to find their chicken house. Not understanding the situation, I said, "Why are our chickens running up the hill? They're clucking loudly! Some of them look crippled. Where have they been? Their guts are hanging all the way to the ground! Why did they leave the chicken house?"

Dad said, "Barbara, they're looking for their house. It was blown away, too. Now, they are trying to find their way back. Many of them are hurt." My childish heart felt so broken for them. My sobbing voice joined with Dad's. We loved our chickens and enjoyed gathering eggs. Mother sold the eggs for a few dollars each month. We had ample eggs for breakfast and baking. We each had a special chicken that we called our pet. Only a few of the more than fifty chickens survived the storm. How many injured floated down the creek, we never knew. Our pet chickens did not survive.

Trooper, our loving and protective dog, did not survive. We never saw him again. We really missed Trooper, a long-time friend.

Meanwhile, Mother managed to get to Granny and Papa's home. She was in her very ragged gown and barefoot. They

asked her what was wrong. Her response was, "I don't know." She walked in circles and stared at the ceiling. (Mother only remembered consciousness when her feet stepped into the raging waters of the branch. She also recalled when she opened the unlocked door to their home. Those two incidents were all she could remember about her walk to their home.) Few people locked their homes at night. *Imagine!*

Papa and Granny were shocked by the entire situation. They "walked" back down to our home with flashlights. Sometimes, fallen trees and tree limbs would obstruct the wagon trail roads in tornados. By the time Papa, Granny, and Mother arrived on the scene, Laura and Gladys had made Kenneth and DeWayne presentable enough to leave for the hospital. They shared their clothing with Mother.

Dad's pains and sobs grew more intense. Even today, I remember how sad and helpless I felt for him. In a broken voice, Dad said to Granny, "Mother, why didn't you bring your car? We need your car! I can't move, and I'm in terrible pain." With his horrific pain, I'm sure he wondered how things could worsen! More than an hour had now passed. To him, it must have felt like an eternity. Granny hurried back home to get her car. As time passed, he continually cried and often screamed in painful prayer.

Immediately, Grandpa wedged a two-by-four under the wreckage while Austin and Emerson began taking a side of the house off my brothers. What a relief to Dad! Their mattress still had them safely sandwiched inside. However, oxygen was diminished. A vast section of the house was on top of the mattress. Kenneth and DeWayne couldn't see or move at all. As they

lifted the house off of my brothers—lifting as carefully as they could—a sharp object ripped a long, deep gash from the ankle to the knee in the muscles of DeWayne's leg. As a five-year-old, he was terrified and in horrific pain. Thankfully, his ankle, knee, and bones were not damaged. The neighbors hugged my brothers—something Dad could not do. They stopped crying. Gladys and Laura bandaged DeWayne's leg to slow the blood loss. Fortunately, Kenneth only received a scratch on his knee. The rain kept pouring over all of us. There was no place to shelter for protection.

When Granny returned, our neighbors loaded us into Granny's Dodge. Dad had to be lifted—as gently as possible—by the men. He was "seated" in the back seat for the first ten miles of his one-hundred-eighty-mile journey. He didn't ask us to double up in the car. That would have been much less painful for him. He was not self-centered but family-centered. Dad was so glad that his wife and three children were alive. *He had to wonder if he would be with them much longer.*

Granny drove the car; Papa held Kenneth in the passenger seat. Mother held DeWayne and sat on my left in the back seat. In her shocked state, her maternal instincts responded. She wrapped DeWayne closely in her arms. He quit crying. She never spoke to any of us—she wasn't aware of her injuries. I knew not to ask her any questions. She was not well. Her shock must have made her immune to the large nail the doctor discovered driven into her back.

Dad was to my right. He was almost twenty-eight years old and weighed less than one-hundred-fifty pounds. It is impossible to describe his incredible moans or comprehend the pain he suffered. For as long as I live, I can still hear his screams as we drove over that wagon trail road, crossed the rocky flooded branch, and drove over the ruts and rocks. Papa opened and closed the fenced gate by their house so the cows would not get out of the pasture. We did not know if our cows and horses had been injured. Dad continually moaned with every stop or bump in the road. Tears streamed down his face. Those wagon roads and hills were solid with bountiful Arkansas rock—large and small. That was the first and last time Granny's car was ever driven over that road! Much like the trails in a Western movie—not filmed on the plains of Kansas but in the high country of Colorado.

It seemed like a forever ride into town. Nobody was talking. Dad's prayers and cries filled the car. Silently crying with Dad, I reflected on the God who had taken Nancy Sue from us. Is Dad going to be taken from us, too? Was this the last time I would ever sit by Dad? Was he going to be alive in the morning? He was hurt so badly that nobody could talk to him, and he seemed to be dying with his pain. It seemed like Granny and Papa were worried. My heart was filled with more fear than I had the ability to express.

Grandma Etta Ray was our neighbor. Her farm bordered the opposite side of the creek. She was the widow of Buck and the mother of Austin and Emerson. Her trees swayed against the roof of her home the night our home was destroyed. Austin, his wife, Gladys, and their two sons, Bill and Bob, spent the night with her because she had a cellar. Bill told me, "Grandma had a giant cedar tree near her house. The tornado twisted and broke it to only a few feet in height."

Odell, Emerson's son, remembers Grandma telling the story of the tornado that blew the McDonald's home away and how the family had been hurt, especially Chester. Her home was a short distance across the creek from the McDonald home—the tornado's direct path. Her husband, Buck, was deceased. She clasped her hands above her head and said, "Except for the mercies of the Lord, my house could have been destroyed."

Grandma Ray was the lady in the buckboard in the first story of this book. She and her husband, Buck, had picked up Mother after she waded the January 1939 icy-cold waters of Indian Creek. Mother rode in the buckboard with them to the Antioch Church schoolhouse the Sunday she experienced a spiritual transformation.

Dad Leaves Us

At the hospital, Dad was immediately placed on a stretcher and transferred to an ambulance. My eyes followed his ambulance until it drove out of sight. His exhausted body welcomed sleep from such horrific pain. His injuries were unknown but serious. He had no feeling below his waist. His shoulder and several ribs were broken. Sadly, with Mother still in shock, she was unaware of the circumstances. His parents, Kenneth, DeWayne, and I, were unable to say goodbye. They rushed to get him to a more capable medical facility.

With brave-hearted courage and acting alone after the tornado, Dad discovered his family alive. He persisted until each person was rescued and taken to the hospital. The US Marine Corps would have given him a medal of honor.

The next stop on his ambulance journey was thirty miles south. They did not remove him from the ambulance at the Harrison Hospital—just gave him more morphine. The next stop was Little Rock, Arkansas, another one hundred and forty miles south of Harrison. The current Arkansas highways were not on the drawing boards. It was a two-lane road with dozens of hills and curves. He finally arrived at a reputable bone specialist. We had to wait for the diagnosis.

After the ambulance escorted Dad away, we were taken inside the hospital to get our wounds treated. With love and courage, though they were worried about my father—their youngest son—Granny and Papa assisted the one doctor with their two grandchildren.

DeWayne and Mother were treated first. Mother suffered a concussion, a damaged shoulder and chest, a broken collarbone, and a nail driven in her back. She was in shock for most of the night. Mother was brokenhearted when she learned the enormity of the tornado fallout and Dad's condition.

Crushed glass was embedded in her scalp. It took several days before all the glass was removed. She showed Kenneth and me where her scalp was hurting. After we found the glass, Granny would pull the shards out with tweezers. Mother had chest pains and difficulty breathing for months. In certain positions, her left arm shook uncontrollably.

DeWayne's leg was immediately sewn up. It took a long time for a gash that had cut through his leg muscles to heal. Thankfully, his bones were uninjured. After he and Mother were cared for, they were placed in a room together in one of the few beds of the small hospital. By morning, Mother was out of shock but very weak.

Papa kept Kenneth on his lap in the waiting room. The nurse placed a bandage over his scratched knee. The doctor said I was too frightened to be given any painkiller to sew up the gash on my right forehead. The gash was almost three inches long and was to the depth of the frontal bone. Two people came to hold me still. My hidden anger toward God exploded. I said, "Why didn't God just kill us and be done with it?"

The doctor said, "Now, now, little girl. God didn't do this to you! It was that nasty tornado!"

I said, "It was God that sent that tornado! Wasn't it Granny?"

Granny was embarrassed, "Now, Barbara, you'll be okay. This will only hurt for a little while. I'll stay right here with you. Don't talk now; keep quiet, and it won't hurt much!"

More than anyone else in the world, Granny knew how hard it was for me to see my baby sister, Nancy Sue, leave our family. She comforted me as the doctor sewed up my forehead. She kept her face near the left side of my head. She made sure I could see her and hear her whispers. She was deeply aware of what the possible loss of our father could mean to us. Granny and Papa were suffering silently because of their son's—our dad's—serious condition. They never focused on themselves— only their son's family.

The Holy Spirit always had Granny there for me when my needs were the greatest. That night was no exception. Psalm 91:11 (KJV), "For he shall give his angels charge over thee, to keep thee in all thy ways." *For reasons known only to the Holy Spirit, the "angel" God often sent me as a child was a one-hundred-pound lady I called Granny.*

Dad's Courage

Dad's iron-clad bravery can only be compared to that of a front-line United States Marine fighting for his country— fighting as the last one standing. Like our brave marines, he would have been called the Eleazer of the Old Testament.

Eleazer was one of King David's three bravest warriors. In one fierce battle, the Scripture relates the story of how Eleazar stood his ground and struck down the enemies when all the other soldiers fled in fear. *His hand grew so tired that it froze to his sword.* The Lord gave a great victory that day! When the "runaway" soldiers returned to Eleazar, the battle was over! (See 2 Samuel 23:9–10, NIV.)

Dad never gave up hope for his family. He trusted God and persisted until everyone was rescued. His lowest point emotionally was when he regained consciousness, only to discover he was alone. Seeing his family restored—one by one—was beyond his wildest dreams! God's mercy immeasurably touched Dad's heart as he observed the scorched-earth devastation! Because I sat by his side from the time I regained consciousness until he left us at the hospital, I have never forgotten his pain, tears, screams, and prayers.

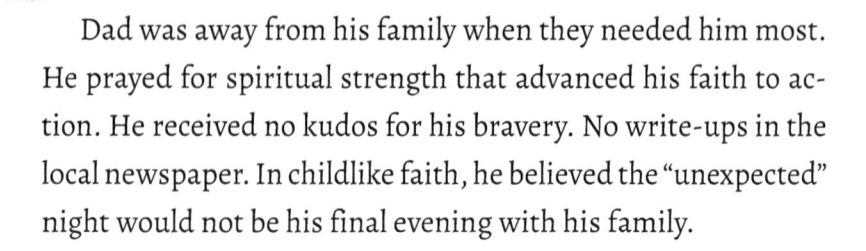

Dad was away from his family when they needed him most. He prayed for spiritual strength that advanced his faith to action. He received no kudos for his bravery. No write-ups in the local newspaper. In childlike faith, he believed the "unexpected" night would not be his final evening with his family.

Papa and Granny—Our Immediate Refuge

Upon our return to their farm, Granny and Papa realized their front porch roof had been blown away. No windows were broken; the outhouse was destroyed. The boards were scattered over their hillside. Granny and Papa laughed about that loss! Dad's milk truck had suffered no damage in their driveway. No doubt, my grandparents had much bigger issues to occupy their thoughts. Would their son be paralyzed for life? What would Veta and our grandchildren do to survive?

Their son was seriously injured. Would the next information be a death message? There were no phones in the countryside. If he lived, would he ever walk again? No life, health, or property insurance. The Red Cross sent a message to Berryville Hospital within two days. We received the news from the church attendee who managed Dad's milk route.

Dad endured an exceptionally long trip for someone extensively damaged by the storm. His back was broken in two separate places. *The doctor said Dad's spinal cord was severed to less than a thread!* Several ribs, his shoulder, and his collarbone were also broken. Undoubtedly, he had really suffered the brute force of the wind and debris. No feeling in his body from his

waist down. He was in traction; he would never walk again. At almost twenty-eight years of age, Dad heard that news alone— no family members were present. *No different than a serviceperson in a war zone isolated from his unit, he suffered alone.*

The medical report saddened the family. The community empathized. At this low point, the apostle Paul's words echoed hope. Paul assured us that God could do more than we could ask or think with His power inside us. (See Ephesians 3:20, KJV.) Mother, Granny, and Papa never lost hope. Any worries they had, they kept them from Kenneth, DeWayne, and me. *They realized our burdens were heavy enough for children to carry.*

After the storm, as Dad's friend, Cecil Smith, was managing the milk route, he knocked on each customer's door and asked if they could donate anything to the McDonald family. He said he would pick up the donations for the next few days as he picked up their milk. From three communities, kindhearted farmers donated dishes, clothes, and any item they felt we might need to begin a new start in life. The farmers were not rich. Every farmer had their own economic struggles. Their hearts were filled with love, sympathy, and generosity. They gave out of their needs—*followed the words of Jesus*—"to love one's neighbor as they loved themselves." (See Matthew 19:19, KJV.)

When the clothing donations were delivered, one neighbor gave me my first silk dress. The blouse of the dress was white with a green collar. The skirt and sash were a beautiful silk green print. *That dress immediately transformed me into Princess Cinderella!*

Jesus remarked about the true test to determine if one is truly His disciple (John 13:34–35, NIV). If we genuinely love one another, *others will know* we are Jesus' disciples. To be loved

by our grandparents, church family, and neighbors was much more important to us than money. *Money could never have met our deepest need—only love!*

Scripture has emphasized encouragement to the grieved and brokenhearted. The McDonald family felt encouragement from friends and neighbors (Isaiah 61:1–3, NIV). The Scriptures above best describe the healing balm that saturated Mother, Kenneth, DeWayne, and my hearts from the love and donations of start-over items we received. Nothing was new. We didn't need new. Neighbors did not have an extra dollar in cash, but they still gave out of their possessions. Their neighborly love was more precious than gold. Love heals heart wounds—hurts that money cannot heal. We had the emotional support we desperately needed from a great community of neighbors as we hoped, prayed, and waited for Dad's unknown return.

Dad sent a letter detailing his severe diagnosis. He was stressed about the mortgage on the truck. The volunteer purchased the milk truck! Dad's major gnawing concern was off his worry list.

The day after the storm, several neighbors searched the scattered hillside wreckage and salvaged what few things could be saved. Two interesting discoveries were made. Mother's glass Daisy Churn was found unscathed—not even a chip! I was ecstatic! She always designated me to churn the family butter in that particular churn! Another interesting fact was that our five-gallon lard can was still on our screened-in porch. After the house was destroyed and sections of the cement porch ripped from the ground, the can of lard was still sitting in the same spot with only the lid lifted off by the tornado! And Dad's old Ford was still sitting in front of the house—it hadn't even

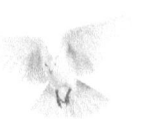

been knocked off the blocks! Our house—only a few feet from the car—was totally demolished!

For the next month, we lived with Papa and Granny. Mother, DeWayne, and I needed Granny's nursing skills. After my first night's sleep, I awoke extremely frightened. My eyelids would not open—totally glued! Mother soaked them with warm water for a long time and washed the inflammation away. It happened again the next night. That was when Granny scraped a potato, placed it on a white cloth, and laid it over my eyes. Until the inflammation from the gash on my forehead had dissipated, I slept on my back with Granny's scraped potatoes over my eyes. Thanks to Granny's special nursing abilities, neither DeWayne nor I suffered from an infection. Mother, DeWayne, and I slept in Granny's second bedroom. Kenneth slept on a cot in the living room. We were all served three meals daily. Granny and Papa did their best to make our transition into a new beginning as comfortable and loving as possible.

As I relay this story, I reflect on Granny and Papa's arrival in Heaven. I can see Jesus place their hands in His—servant hands that sacrificed—without considering remuneration from their many neighbors or us. They had never been told by anyone that their hands had been the hands of Jesus to so many different neighbors and friends. Hands that were responsible—in many different ways—for the sprinkling of healing balm to so many hearts. Yes, I think the Holy Spirit, our comforter, did permit Granny to live her dream of becoming a nurse—in the way He had predestined.

Papa always desired to be the best servant of God and the best husband, father, grandfather, and neighbor that he could possibly be. He accomplished his goal. He greatly influenced

my life. *He was one of three people I have known who rose above the community—and the church congregation—with his non-judgmentalism.* I have imagined Heaven filled with people like Granny and Papa! *They were surprised—I'm sure—when they realized that their treasure boxes in Heaven were filled!*

DeWayne's femur, knee, tibia, fibula, ankle, and foot bones could have been damaged for life. Instead, as an adult, he enjoyed many seasons of summer fun as he played baseball. At eighty-three years of age, DeWayne's scar is a permanent reminder of his March 1945 miracle escape from death. My frontal bone could also have been crushed, but it was not damaged. Kenneth, who was the oldest, had only a scratched knee. My parents mentioned many times what could have happened to their children in the tornado—but it did not happen. Each of us has lived the predetermined chapters of our lives.

In one testimony, Dad fought back the tears, saying, "Except for the tender mercies of the Lord, we all could have been killed. However, we are all present in church this morning."

Dear Reader, as I author this story for you, I am thankful for God's protection on that stormy night. What if any of our five family members had regained consciousness to find the remainder of the family gone forever? Heaven did not permit that to happen! What if I had not slept at the foot of Mother and Dad's bed? If Dad could not reach Kenneth and DeWayne only three feet away from him, Mother would never have made it across the length of the house to my single bed. She and I would have been separated from the family. God kept us all in one area—even after we were dumped on the ground—a miracle!

Temporary Home "On the Road"

A brother to Austin and Emerson had bought the farm on the main road above Papa and Granny's home. He gave us his home rent-free until they returned to Arkansas. The house had a cellar! After the tornado, Kenneth, DeWayne, and I were afraid to sleep in the house. We told Mother that a tornado could blow us away again! We slept through the first storm! We didn't feel safe without Dad, Granny, and Papa. We slept in the cellar for two months—even though it gave Mother headaches! It didn't help that we found a snake in the rafters of the unfinished upstairs of the house!

Mother needed spiritual strength to courageously monitor the fears of her children as she waited for her husband's return. She learned to maneuver challenges, overcome hardships, and conquer adversity.

The Antioch Church schoolhouse was only a five-minute walk. A county road was in front of the house, not a wagon trail road. We had a fenced yard and a well for drawing water. DeWayne and I had fun crawling through the small driveway culvert installed in the ditch to the driveway leading into the property.

There was a subtle shadow of grief over our family. Mother still suffered from chest pains. When her arm was in certain positions, it would shake uncontrollably. For furniture, we had a wood cookstove in the house and donated blankets for our cellar shelf beds. We each chose a room and placed our few clothes in a corner. Mother would leave the cellar each morning and walk down to Granny and Papa's barn to milk our cows. When she returned, she would wake us up and fix our breakfast.

We heard from Dad when the Red Cross volunteers came into his room and gave him a pen, paper, and a stamped envelope to write to us. We missed him! Mother seemed sad most of the time. Undoubtedly, she wondered how we would survive economically as we faced each day. We ate oatmeal for breakfast and cornbread and milk for supper.

Farmers could not afford insurance on their homes. We had none. As a family, most of our conversation was, "Mother, when is Dad coming home?" Kenneth, DeWayne, and I did not comprehend that Dad would never walk again. Perhaps God had instilled simple faith in our hearts that Dad would walk. We did hear the people at church request prayers for him. *Mother prayed each day for him.*

The church people asked God to turn our unfortunate circumstances into something good. Our community neighbors believed Dad would walk again if they prayed. No, it was not an easy journey for our family, but because of the tornado, our faith in God and His provision increased. Expectancy grew in the congregation as they prayed daily for a miracle for Dad.

Dad's Miracle

Prayer changes individuals, communities, events, and nations! The hidden hand of God restored our entire family! Our neighbors did much more than donate their used items to us—cooking utensils, a few dishes, and clothes. *Their greatest gifts were love and prayer.*

Tired farmers gathered in different homes each evening to pray for Dad's broken back. *They gave what they inwardly possessed—faith!* Farmers who lived uncomplicated lives and depended on God's rain for their crops developed an intensely personal relationship with Him. Their lives and their economy depended upon God! Most of them had generational testimonies of answered prayer.

"His delight is not in the strength of the horse, nor his pleasure in the legs of a man, but the Lord takes pleasure in those who fear him, in those who hope in his steadfast love" (Psalm 147:10–11, ESV). The two verses exemplify the child-like faith of those neighbors. Not one person in my home community had attended high school—let alone received an advanced degree. Nobody had the opportunity! They had, however, attended their "personal home school of faith and experience" with God. The most important school!

The doctor said Dad would never walk again. We never underestimate God's power and purposes! Consider Joseph's predicament thousands of years ago. The devastation he suffered caused what appeared to be irreparable harm to his family and his nation. He was wrongfully dumped in prison and forgotten by everyone in Egypt! His father, Jacob, had been told that he was dead! His brothers were aware of how they had wronged him. Dead or alive—they were not going to look for him! God made it happen quite unexpectedly for his brothers! *Wrong things were reversed.*

Yet, in Genesis 50:20 (NIV), Joseph was able to forgive his brothers. Repentance and forgiveness can fill one's life with its full meaning and purpose—totally changing our focus and behavior. Joseph expressed to his brothers that even though they had done him wrong, God had turned their wrong into the salvation of the Hebrew nation! *An entire nation successfully emerged from starvation due to Joseph's wrongful treatment! The Holy Spirit is an intelligent administrator. He arranges for everything to come out the right way, at the right time, and in the right order. No wonder we look at Joseph in the Old Testament as the person who most typifies Jesus Christ. Our lives may feel turned upside down. God can turn them right side up!*

The devastation the tornado had brought, especially to Dad—by earthly evaluation—looked irreparable. As faith multiplied in the hearts of the farm families, Dad woke up in the Little Rock Hospital one morning and moved his big toe! As the doctor made his morning rounds, Dad excitedly said, "Doctor, I moved my big toe this morning!" To Dad, this was big! He had felt nothing from his waist down since the tornado.

The doctor said, "No, Chester, that did not happen!"

Dad raised his flag of faith and asked, "Would you like to watch me?"

Surprised, the doctor said, "Yes, I would." Dad moved his big toe again. The next morning, Dad was able to do a little more movement. The doctor ordered another X-ray of Dad's back.

When the doctor saw that Dad's back was knitting back together beautifully—even the spinal cord severed to less than a thread—he said, "Chester, I'm writing in my medical notes that this was a miracle of God. I had nothing to do with your spinal cord and backbone knitting back together!"

Our God is a *creator*. Not only in the miracle of natural and spiritual birth but when there is a need for a physical rebirth! Dad needed God's hand to supernaturally repair his spinal cord. God did! Don't ask me how God did it! That is why it is called a miracle! It is beyond the doctor's understanding, but everyone knew a miracle happened to Dad!

According to 1 John 3:1 (NIV), *God enjoys lavishing us with His love!* Those words have depth! King David, a man after God's heart, had lived through many encounters with death. Yet, he always reminded God of His promises. In Psalm 139:16 (NIV), David informed us that all our days were ordained *before the first day was counted*.

Our life is over *only* when God says it is over! Yes! Our days are ordained (numbered) by God! Only when God says our life is finished—is it finished! God was not finished with Dad! God healed him completely! He retired as a cheesemaker from Kraft Foods Company!

Dad's Home!

Three months after Dad arrived at the Little Rock Hospital, he returned home. In a cast, he walked into the house on crutches! Kenneth, DeWayne, and I had never seen a cast. *We stared at him!* From his underarms to his hips, the cast surrounded him. We were afraid to touch it or him! He then had us print our names on the cast. We thought that was special! My parents did not know how they would make it economically or where we would eventually live. However, we were together again, and the Chester McDonald family had received a hefty dose of hope!

Each day, Dad got stronger. He was given an old guitar to replace the one he lost in the tornado. He spent most of his time in our rent-free house playing the guitar. His relationship with God soared to a higher level. His body responded to his faith. He continually spoke words of faith—not doubt—thanking God that he was growing stronger. During that time, he said, "Barbara, you are going to start singing alto, and we are going to sing duets." Alto had no meaning to me. For fun, I had always joined him as he was singing—even from another room.

Not yet seven years old, I responded, "Dad, I can't sing!"

He said, "Yes, you can! I will teach you!"

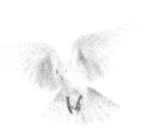

The remainder of the summer of 1945 was spent practicing with Dad. He set aside time each day to sing with me. We sang for as long as he desired! That was not my choice; I had no alternative!

Then, one evening, Granny and Papa drove us to Boyd Church. Dad was invited to sing. When he got on the stage with his guitar, he surprised everyone, especially me, "Barbara is singing a duet with me tonight. Come on, Barbara, we have a song to sing!"

My body stiffened with fear. Tears started down my face. He stood there looking at me, expecting me to approach the stage. People said, "Go on, Barbara, you can do it!" Mother—an intelligent lady—said, "Barbara, if you'll go up there and sing loud enough for the people to hear you, we'll buy you a doll." She knew my life-long desire for a doll.

I said, "You promise, Mother?" She knew what I wanted! The only little tattered doll I had finally been given was blown away in the tornado. Slowly, I walked up to the stage to stand by Dad. It was one of the longest walks of my life. At the age of almost eight, I was petrified!

Dad looked at me and said quietly, "Now, I want to hear you sing—loud." He meant every word he said! My tears had not impressed him! And the chorus had an alto lead. Mother said I had to sing loud enough to be heard if I wanted the doll! There were no microphones.

The doll was given a few weeks later. That was the first of many times Dad called me to sing with him. He also taught me to sing harmony to the songs with a high alto—a higher pitch I have never reached! *Precious memories*.

Dad's healing was not the only miracle that occurred. Everyone knew how great it was to own "road" property. In our rent-free house, the mailman picked up our mail, and the milkman picked up our milk. That saved our parents a lot of time each day. Mother did not want to rebuild where the tornado had destroyed our home nor walk one-half mile to pick up the mail. She prayed for her miracle—a home on the road!

To our surprise, a neighbor whose road property was adjacent to Papa's property gifted Dad and Mother five acres of land. That meant we did not have to move our few livestock. My parents were stunned but overwhelmed with joy. What generous hearts! *Neighbors who loved their neighbors! What a concept!*

1947—One Last Year in California

The Chester and Veta Mcdonald Family
L-R Front Row: Kenneth, DeWayne, and Barbara
(Two years after the 1945 tornado)
This picture was taken before we left for California—in May 1947

The tornado was in 1945. In May 1947, Dad and Mother returned to California to earn money to finish the house. We

arrived in California, borrowed a tent, and set it by an irrigation ditch next to a large tree near an orange grove.

DeWayne and I slept in Mother and Dad's old car to be protected from mosquitos. Kenneth slept in our uncle's car. Our cousin slept inside the tent. Our maternal uncle and aunt had driven to California with us and worked fruit vineyard jobs.

We lived by the irrigation ditch for several months. We took our irrigation dip baths in shifts. Men and boys bathed first— Mother, my aunt, and I bathed last. When winter arrived, we were given a rent-free tiny shack on the property of Dad's cousin. Both families shared the tiny kitchen—eating our meals separately. Our uncle's family was given the small living room as their living quarters. Dad, Mother, Kenneth, DeWayne, and I took the bedroom as our living quarters. Children slept on the floor. Dad and Mother had a rail bed we used as our only sitting area. Of course, there was an antiquated outhouse that graced the back area. My aunt gave me one dollar a week to wash the dishes for her family. My first paying job!

We lived in California for one year. Dad, Mother, my uncle, and aunt worked in the fruit vineyards and saved their money. Kenneth, DeWayne, and I walked to Centerville Elementary School. Before the school year began, we helped Mother and Dad in the grape vineyards.

The only place we shopped in California was the grocery store. Kenneth, DeWayne, and I were exhilarated as we packed our daily school lunches. Mother permitted us to choose our lunch items—a first-ever! That was the only shopping spree we needed! My dessert choice was the two-pack chocolate cupcakes. Mother permitted me to have one cupcake each day!

A vivid memory in my mind was the travel to and from California. In the late 1940s, children sold roadside items like beautiful rings, coin purses, and hair ornaments in Western states. On our return trip home, Dad gave each of us one dollar to buy a gift from them. It was the first dollar we had ever been given to buy whatever we desired!

Growing up, Dad lived many years in California. Unlike his brother and sister, Dad loved and called Arkansas his home. He said it would be his last time to go to California for work. It was. He anxiously returned to Arkansas, finished our new home, and never moved out of the state again.

Our parents paid the house loan and installed windows and doors in the boarded-up areas of the home. The top of the new basement became the front porch of the house. The floor of the basement was solid rock. At one point, the solid rock floor of the basement naturally divided to present a clear-flowing underground stream. Dad blasted through the rock, guiding the spring out of the basement and through our front yard. He built our smokehouse, small milk barn, and, of course, an out-house. Compared to our earlier existence, life was exceptional.

Maternal Grandparents— The Warren Family

Back Row, R-L (in order of birth): Grandpa (Ed Warren), Grandma (Martha Warren), Veva (Warren) McClelland, Cleve Warren, Veta (Warren) McDonald (Mother); Front Row, R-L (in order of birth): Jimmy Warren, Venita (Susie Warren) Brisco, Johnny Warren, Mary (Warren) Patterson, and Dean Warren.

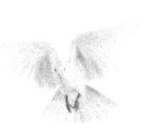

The above picture was Mother's family of origin the day before Johnny left for World War II. We saw Grandpa and Grandma Warren (called Mommie and Poppie by all family members) three or four times yearly. We loved to play with our cousins. Grandmother Warren fed us mashed potatoes and sauerkraut, along with other vegetables. Uncle Dean scraped juicy turnips from Grandma's root cellar when the grandchildren needed snacks. She grew all her vegetables and was an excellent canner. They lived in the Grandview community.

Dad drove our old Ford car across King's River to visit them in the summers. There was no bridge to cross, so he would get out of the car and evaluate the most shallow section of the river. Then he drove us across! Sometimes, the car motor flooded, but he never failed to get it across the river. It always started again. Crossing the river reduced our mileage to less than half the alternate route.

Mother's paternal grandfather, a champion swimmer, had accidentally drowned in King's River before Grandview Bridge was built. When his wagon began to sink, he rescued his son. He tried to free his team of horses from the wagon. He and the team were swept down the river. A horrific tragedy for the family. The tragedy was difficult for the son. He left the state and lived the remainder of his life in California.

In 1947, Mother's brother, Uncle Johnny Warren, lived with us for a few months. He returned home from the Navy. We excitedly listened to his Navy adventures. He gave Kenneth, DeWayne, and me one dollar or less each payday.

In early 1948, with a weak economy, Johnny returned to the Navy. The morning he left our home, I heard him say, "Tell

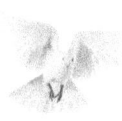

Kenneth, Barbara, and DeWayne goodbye for me." Mother cried as she said goodbye. I remember his footsteps on the gravel path as he walked around our home to the waiting car. His immediate goal was to earn enough money to marry his beloved fiancée. He had only been there for a few weeks when he was killed in a shipbuilding accident. That was difficult for us. The nightmares and dreams overwhelmed me. Fear terrorized me that I would lose my parents, too. Death seemed to threaten our family continually.

A few years later, their youngest son, Dean, injured his leg while wrestling with a friend. In subtle stages, the bruise became cancerous and took Dean's life. Sadly, Mother's parents buried two sons before their death.

Grandma and Grandpa Warren became Christians in their senior years. They were baptized together in King's River.

Grandma Warren honored my brother, DeWayne, by requesting him to come and pray with her before her death. Ministers had also visited her. Grandma lived to be ninety-eight years of age. With the rails up on the hospital bed, she climbed out of it on one occasion—successfully! She was blessed with great health throughout her lifetime.

One remaining member of Mother's family is Aunt Mary (Warren) Patterson. She was ninety-four last February. Until November 2023, she had lived in her home. December 1, 2023, she moved to Heaven. She was preceded in death by her husband, George, and two sons, Deanie and Donny. Aunt Mary said, "No mother should have to live longer than her children." Her remaining son, Danny, and his family live next door. Danny's daughter made her a proud great-grandmother.

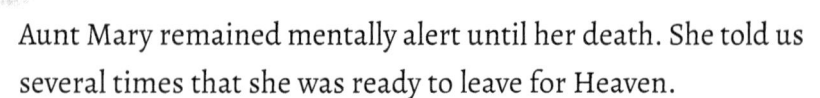

Aunt Mary remained mentally alert until her death. She told us several times that she was ready to leave for Heaven.

Grandfather Warren gave a profound testimony in a small country church not too long before he departed for Heaven. During the testimony service, he stood and said, "I asked God to permit me to attend church with all my family once before I go to Heaven. All my living children are here tonight, and I thank God He answered my prayer." Grandpa's secret prayer—publicly rewarded by God! He was a faithful husband and father who had worked hard labor his entire life to provide for his family.

New Family Members and New Church Building

A neighbor said to Mother, "Veta, everybody in the community has a refrigerator except your family. Don't you think it is about time you and Chester got one?" From inside the house, I heard her stinging words! At ten years of age, those words hurt! Deep pity for Mother rose up inside me! We didn't waste money! A refrigerator was not possible right now! On scorching hot days, I walked through the woods to Granny's home for ice. Granny's small Hotpoint refrigerator worked beautifully. For several summers, that had been my daily afternoon walk. Half the ice often melted before I arrived home through the woods. Granny loved to help us.

A refrigerator was welcomed shortly before my pleas for a sister were answered in 1948. Johnnie Kay was welcomed with immense joy. Her dark curly hair was like Nancy Sue's. Dad taught her to stand straight in one of his hands.

Two leather chairs, a steel spring cot, and a television were purchased. The Emerson Ray family brought popcorn and came

over to watch *The Andy Griffith Show*, *I Love Lucy*, and boxing matches.

From an early age, Johnnie Kay, like Kenneth, was a comedian. My youngest brother, Lonnie, was born two years later. He loved the outdoors, his pony, and his dog. The children played well together. On command, Lonnie trained his dog to chase me, especially when I had them dust the throw rugs! Their energy was unlimited! Kenneth, my older brother, drove the tractor in the hayfields. My responsibilities were household chores. DeWayne enjoyed the waters of Indian Creek and riding bicycles with his best friend. Later, he also drove the tractor for harvesters. He and Kenneth loved their first paychecks!

The Antioch Church schoolhouse was sold. A new Antioch Church was planned. One of the attendees donated the acreage—the same family who gave my parents their five acres on the road. Dad, Austin Ray, and the acreage donor each pledged fifty dollars to buy the lumber and cement needed to start the structure. All labor was volunteered. Dad left for Kansas, where he had wheat harvest contacts to earn money for his pledge.

On his first morning home from wheat harvest, the new pastor's wife stopped by selling dresses. When Mother told her she could not afford a dress, the minister's wife said, "Chester just returned from wheat harvest yesterday. You must have money."

Mother said, "Yes, Chester returned with fifty dollars. It is pledged for the church building." Mother never regretted giving the money. However, she did not appreciate the pastor's wife's pressuring remarks! She would have loved a dress! Country church members throughout the United States have *sacrificially* built churches scattered throughout their communities.

Dad eventually built a covered back porch on our two-bedroom home. He then made half the porch into a bedroom for Kenneth and DeWayne. Johnnie Kay and I slept in the second bedroom. It offered little privacy as our older brothers had to walk through our room to their room. It was great to only have one bed in one room for the first time!

In 1952, Dad was working on the roof of a Berryville building for thirty-eight cents per hour. Dad and my uncle had just received a one-cent per-hour raise! Uncle said, "You can keep your penny an hour raise!" He had one child to feed; Dad's seventh child was due in September. He kept his raise!

A few days later, the Kraft Foods Company manager in Berryville stopped and called to Dad upon the roof he was repairing. He knew Dad from the milk route he had with them before the tornado. He said, "Chester, how about starting to work as a cheesemaker tomorrow?"

Dad said, "I'll be there! What do I wear?"

The manager said, "White starched clothes—a clean uniform daily." The joy was unbelievable that Dad brought to our home that night! Dad purchased one pair of white clothes at Carr Dry Goods on credit. His word was as good as a contract. Mother washed, starched, and ironed them each day until the first check was received. Another set was purchased.

Mom was ecstatic! For the first time, they had health insurance. Her seventh child would be born at the hospital! Her other six children had been born at home. A doctor had been present with Kenneth's twelve-pound birth. The doctor arrived at Papa's farm—ten miles from town—after I was born.

Dad became an excellent cheesemaker. He obviously had a high IQ. Dad exceeded expectations in music, singing,

carpentry, mechanics, and as a cheesemaker. The manager later complimented, "I can tell by the taste of the cheese which vat of cheese Chester made."

Dad declined a job transfer offer by Kraft to move to their Springfield, Missouri, facility. He meant it when he said, "I will never leave this community again. This part of the Ozark Mountains is home to me!" Dad proudly called himself an Arkansas hillbilly. He would quietly isolate himself from anyone who felt they were "better" than others.

Before the seventh child was born, Dad's peers came to him for a donation for a needy girl in Berryville. He generously gave. They later brought the donations to him! The donation had been for our family's seventh child.

In 1952, Dad bought a 1948 Chevrolet for one thousand dollars—in perfect condition. It was the nicest car they ever owned. He made any needed repairs.

Dad worked twelve to fourteen hours six days each week. On many days, he worked sixteen hours. Mother worked eight hours Monday through Friday.

Due to the increase in our family, Dad built another room over the rectangular basement. There was a bed and a piano in this room. Dad found a Chickering piano for forty dollars. Granny took me to Berryville for a fifty-cent piano lesson twice each month. Our home was filled with noise and activity.

At thirteen years old, my heart was filled with emptiness and unhappiness. School was burdensome for me. My lack of clothes embarrassed me. Aunt Marie's thrift shop clothes from California didn't always fit. Bullying had occurred at school, which I never mentioned. My hurt was deep but

camouflaged. Teenagers who poked fun at poor people were highly unappreciated by me. Kenneth felt the pressures, too. When our last sibling was born, he refused to view the baby. Mother and Dad did not understand; I did.

One painful experience was seeing my favorite teacher on the street in our town. She was in conversation with another adult. I stood to the side and waited patiently for her to finish. It was summer, and I wanted to greet her. When she finished her conversation, she looked at me and turned her back. No other person was on the street. An experience I never relayed to anyone before this book.

Our community changed as we became teenagers. Farm families became more prosperous. In the 1950s, shiny cars, nice clothes, and having fun uptown were the rage. Hank Williams and Elvis Pressley were the idols of most country teenagers.

I did not attend school for the last three weeks of eighth grade. After a week's bout with sinus, alongside Granny, I picked strawberries for two weeks. When I was convinced my strawberry pints were ready to be counted by the checker, Granny's generous heart would always say, "Barbara, round off the top!" Reluctantly, I obeyed; I wanted new clothes!

Granny always told me how glad she was that I had the opportunity to attend school. Her parents needed her to work at home. She loved school and worked hard for the two three-month sessions she attended. She was an excellent reader and gladly read the Scriptures during her reading turn in Sunday school. She wanted to learn multiplication tables. At a young age, I found it difficult to teach her. Upon reflection, she would have been embarrassed to ask an adult. Granny took great pride

in how she looked and in everything she did. She had no idea how much I hated to face my peers each day. Had she known my reasons, it would have hurt her. Neither did my parents know. My heart desired significance—not to be shunned because my family was poor.

The promises of the Scriptures appeared to be for others, not me. The battle inside me was primarily a private one. In the lonely darkness of my struggles, the Holy Spirit kept whispering, "Barbara, I have a plan for your life." (See Jeremiah 29:11, NIV.) My heart longed to talk to someone confidentially for comfort and direction. Deep inside me, I longed for hope. *There was nobody I trusted to tell how I felt, and I did not feel anyone would understand.* Never did I want my parents to know how I hurt. They didn't need more pain. Their economic setbacks and reversals had been severe and extensive.

My Unsettled Heart

Due to pride and elevated expectations for life, anger slowly chiseled deep roots into my heart. The outhouse just outside of our fenced yard was an embarrassment to me! Continual financial needs stressed our family. Long hours, hot summers—forever combating flies—no air conditioning, a larger family, and unending financial burdens were heavy on my parents. Unfortunately, I internalized the family's struggles. Financial advancement was a slow process. Everyone in the community worked hard to meet their family's needs and gather the "stuff" of life that people felt would bring them respect and happiness.

Our once peaceful, friendly neighborhood was slowly disappearing. Everybody worked long hours to have a better home—if not the best—the newest car, the most fashionable clothes, and all of life's extras. Financially, pride told me our family was at the bottom of the economic totem pole. Television kept several families at home who had formerly attended every church service.

For miles around, everyone worked for the town's chicken plant. The competitive spirit of "keeping up with the Joneses" and "giving our children a better life than we had" silently dominated our community. On the other hand, there were severe

losses to the simple lifestyle of loving and sharing relationships the farm families once enjoyed. Traditional values no longer occupied the highest priority. Marital affairs, separations, and divorces became more common. Families in our community were torn apart.

One incident clearly revealed to me that our community had lost neighborly communication. The milkman returned to our home one morning after he had picked up our milk. In a tearful voice, he said he had passed the High Cemetery and discovered a father digging his baby's grave. That had never happened before! Men picked up their shovels and immediately went to the cemetery. After apologies to the father, he returned to his home. It was a dramatic realization that our community had lost its close bonds. Everyone had become too busy to be aware of one another's desperate needs—a neighbor's child had died! Eventually, paid grave diggers were hired. My grandparents would not have understood how that could have happened! Papa would have dug the grave alone for a neighbor!

Devastatingly, the Antioch Church suffered a couple of congregational divisions due to pastors who needed more experience to deal with conflicts. Many people felt shunned and set aside. My parents were two of those people. Feelings of isolation and lack of appreciation crushed them. Dad and Mother were always excited when the church hired a new pastor. The excitement was usually short-lived. In my heart, I felt the pastors always enjoyed visiting the more excellent homes where tables were more exquisitely set, a buffet variety was served, and the potential existed for social and financial advantages. Of course, there was a bathroom inside other homes! My critical mind never missed such interesting details.

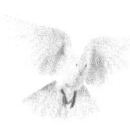

In that transition period, I began to feel that the community had nothing I desired. Inside my heart, I felt like two people. One person wanted to leave my family and go with my cousins to California. When they visited relatives in Arkansas, they begged Mother and Dad to permit me to go home with them. The other part of me felt absolute allegiance to my parents. They needed all the support I could give them. Thankfully, my parents never permitted me to leave. *Tenaciousness is not built inside us with a life of ease.*

Starting at a young age, my home responsibilities were huge. Though my parents never asked me to do the household chores, it was an unwritten rule. The daily ritual consisted of helping with the meals, doing dishes, battling summer flies, making beds, sweeping, dusting, and mopping daily, waxing, cleaning windows and walls, changing diapers, bathing children, combing and setting hair, yard work, and ironing.

On lunch hours at a laundry near her job—Monday through Friday—Mother washed clothes. The laundromat manager would have her machine and rinse tubs prepared for her lunch-hour wash. They were not automatic washing machines. We eventually had cold running water in the house. So, there had to be a lot of heating water for dishes and bathing. It was much easier when we finally purchased an electric range.

A few items had to be ironed daily, especially DeWayne's one pair of favorite jeans and other unexpected items. DeWayne and I each had enough personal pride to share with the community! Saturday was the day I ironed one huge washtub of clothes—clothes starched the "old-time" way. We had not heard of spray starch and fabric spray. Shirts, Dad's work clothes,

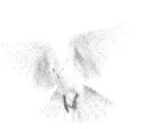

children's clothes, and dresser scarves were starched. Ironing began at 8 a.m. Everything was finished by 5 p.m. Ironing for the family began when I was in the fifth grade. I learned to be Mother's ironing helper in the third grade and loved it. In later years, the volume of ironing killed my enjoyment.

After the day's chores were finished, the children had to be bathed. The tub of water we kept on the porch throughout the day would be warm for their evening baths. We would refill the tub with water to keep the evening dairy milk cool until the following morning. An add-on bathroom was far into the future. One former community member from California drove by our home as I was bathing one of the children in the tub. They slowed down their car and laughed at our bathing scene. My face burned with embarrassment and anger. The person who drove the car and laughed the loudest was my age! After the three children's baths, I washed their hair inside the kitchen sink a couple of times each week. Hot water had to be heated.

Time was of the essence, and there was never a relaxed hour for piano practice. Once or twice each month, Granny begged me to go and take my fifty-cent piano lesson. Thankfully, she continually prodded me, though I had not practiced faithfully.

In the summer of 1952, life was miserable for me. Never did I doubt the existence of God. When Nancy Sue, my baby sister, raised her hands straight to Heaven at only one hundred and twenty-nine days old—the night before she died—I was extremely confident about the existence of God. The only time I thought of eternity was each night before I fell asleep. I prayed, "Jesus, please don't let me die without knowing You. I do want to be a good Christian someday. Please spare my life until I am older."

Deep inside me, I was angry with God. The feeling had been there since Nancy Sue's death. The tornado gave my anger another add-on. Financial family setbacks, resentment, and unforgiveness had deep clutches inside me. At that time, I did not understand that unforgiveness was a formidable weapon that enslaved me within my own prison walls. It was impossible to express my feelings, but I realized that unforgiveness was destroying *me*. "Forgiveness" is spiritual and physical healing we can give ourselves! If we seek forgiveness—whether or not another person forgives us—God does, and we are free! Jesus taught us to forgive as God has forgiven us (Luke 11:4, NIV). *The verse implies that He will not forgive me if I do not forgive!* Jesus makes His words simple and clear to us! He doesn't permit us to choose our personal alternatives!

My prison had me trapped; I saw no way to break free. My love for my family was unquestioned, but I was miserable. The only person that I felt understood me at all was Granny. She never criticized me. She always told me what I could become! She had no idea how empty and fragile I felt inside. Inwardly, I knew she could do nothing to change my situation, so I kept the hurts hidden. Undoubtedly, she was aware and prayed for me.

My heart understood that sin in our lives resulted in spiritual death. We are all born into this world as sinners. Heaven waits for those who are "spiritually" born again. A spiritual rebirth was a commitment I was *not ready to make*. I witnessed how difficult it was for Christian students to have the same loyalty to their faith during school hours as they had during church hours. When I became a Christian, I wanted to be committed totally to Jesus Christ. Stories my brother told our family convinced me the church youth had great difficulty with Christian commitment. Fortunately, a few young people had Christian friends their age they could chum with while in school.

Hope, to me, was too far in the future to contemplate. It was unclear what I wanted to do or be. However, I did not want the status quo. My life wanted a depth of meaning that I had not found. At night, the shooting stars, the Big Dipper, and the Milky Way caused me to concentrate on God. It was too difficult for me to fathom how someone as insignificant as me—an unhappy and unimportant individual—could be incorporated into God's divine plan. *How could God improve my insecure life?*

My Dream

One night, I fell asleep after my usual "God, don't let me die" prayer. In the night, I was awakened by a dream. After that traumatic experience, my life was forced to change direction. The frightening dream I kept secret from everyone—only between God and me.

In the dream, I stood in our backyard under the black walnut tree I claimed as my own. Suddenly, the heavens rolled back—just like a scroll. Immediately, the brightest image of Jesus in a glistening white robe appeared where the scroll had opened. Jesus had returned, and I was not ready! I said, "Jesus, please don't leave me here! Please take me to Heaven with You!"

Jesus looked tearfully at me, "No, Barbara, you have continually rejected Me!" His expressive eyes—so plainly visible to me—were filled with love, tenderness, and great sadness. It was too late to negotiate! The dream concluded; my body was cold; I trembled uncontrollably. The dream occurred around 3 a.m. I prayed until Mother called at 5:30 a.m. I said nothing about what had happened. She left for work at 6:15 a.m. The experience filled me with fear for my life. Jesus spoke truth to me in the dream. Since the night I prayed with my sick baby sister, I had known that Jesus was real. He had spoken to my heart

continually since that time, but I had never publicly responded to Jesus.

The dream occurred in early July of 1952. In August 1952, two young lady evangelists conducted unimpressive meetings at the Antioch Church. On August 21, 1952, an invitational hymn was sung for those desiring salvation. The Holy Spirit immediately nudged my heart! After such a dull service, I was shocked! I knew it was a decision call from God to me!

As a teenager, I was insecure, publicly shy, and angry with life's injustices. With my lips closed, I spoke the following words silently from my heart, "God, if You send someone to walk down the aisle of the church and kneel at the altar with me, I will keep my promise." Immediately, Charlie Minnick, seated in the front left corner of the church, stood up and climbed over the bench in front of him. No doubt! He was on his way to me!

Charlie was a tall farmer who usually wore denim blue bib overalls. In his bold fashion, he walked over halfway down the length of the church and turned into the wooden pew bench in front of me. The youth stepped forward so he could walk behind them. Nobody wanted him to stop and talk with them! He walked straight to me and said, "Barbara, don't you think tonight is your night?"

My heart pounded hard. God was serious! Never was a "now" decision more real to me! "What if I go down to the altar and nothing happens?" It was difficult for me to trust God!

Charlie gently said, "Barbara, we will stay with you until you know you are saved. I will walk with you to the altar. Are you ready to go?" With those words from Charlie—even though several young people were around me—I left the two rows of my

peers—the longest walk of my life—and walked with Charlie to the altar.

The greatest decision of my life—made in a hillbilly country church! *Where else would the people have loved me enough to pray with me for one and one-half hours?* Charlie knelt beside me and prayed. His wife, Ollie, immediately followed. Many others knelt with me. It touched my heart that many tired, hard-working people cared.

At thirteen years of age—less than two months from fourteen years—on my knees, I sobbed over my sinful, unforgiving, and unsettled heart. My soul needed forgiveness for the blame I had attributed to God. My life was lit with hope! My eyes and face were swollen from my sobbing. There was a real shift inside my heart. The world that had looked so bleak and dark to me for so long was the most beautiful, star-studded night! Hefty weights, insecurities, resentments, and unforgiveness were lifted from deep within my soul. Heaven cleansed me within and without.

The dead spirit inside me was brought to life by the Holy Spirit! Once the Holy Spirit indwells us at salvation, He begins daily communication and works in our spirit. He gives maturity and direction to our minds, emotions, choices, and decisions. As we communicate with the Father, the Son (Jesus), and the Holy Spirit, our life takes on purpose and meaning. The walls we have built inside ourselves, against others, and against God crumble.

Granny and Papa had brought Kenneth, DeWayne, and me to church. They were delighted to see their first grandchild respond to the salvation invitation.

As my brothers and I arrived home from church that night, from our parents' bedroom, came the usual question, "How was church tonight?"

"Okay," I said. My parents had not been at the service, and I was unsure how to explain the details of my conversion to them. The people who had prayed with me knew that I wanted to see if my heart would feel the same the following day before I declared myself a Christian. My brothers had not heard that conversation at the altar.

The second question from my parents was always, "What was the sermon about? Did the pastor say hello or that he missed us?"

That last question continuously stabbed my heart because I deeply cared for my parents. Before I had to answer their question, DeWayne blurted out, "Barbara got saved tonight!"

Mother said, "You did, Barbara?"

"Well, maybe. In the morning, I expect to know for sure." My answer shocked DeWayne and embarrassed me, but it stopped the questions.

Unfortunately, I had never understood the "exchange" at the Cross (Jesus death). Jesus took all my bad—my sins—temper, anger, envy, insecurities, and shame. In exchange, He gave me His righteousness, a new path, and a clean slate to start over again! When Jesus took my sins, they were no longer mine! *He paid the price of death for my sins so I could become His child—a new identity!*

One writer has said the Lord will subdue our iniquities (Micah 7:19). *Our sins are erased from God's memory!* Micah says that God has buried them in the depths of the sea.

Biblical scholars refer to the "depths of the sea" as the Sea of Forgetfulness! Jeremiah 31:34 (ESV) eloquently states, "I will forgive their iniquity, and I will remember their sin no more." *How great is our God!*

Life Is Worth Living

Morning came. Before Mother called, I was awake. It was the most peaceful sleep that I had enjoyed in months. No nightmares or scary dreams. There was no thought that I was waking up to another dull day of swatting flies and cleaning the house! Most nights, I watched shooting stars, wondered at the awesomeness of the universe, and listened to the tree frogs until my restless body fell asleep. That previous night, peace flooded me. My feelings on that first wake-up morning are best described in Isaiah 61:10 (NKJV), "He has clothed me with the garments of salvation, He has covered me with the robe of righteousness."

Immediately, the next morning, Mother wanted to hear about the service. They regretted their absence. As intelligently as possible, I told her about the service and that Charlie had walked me to the altar. Then I walked into the living room and picked up a handwritten book of songs Dad and I sang together. For the first time, I sang songs from my heart and felt their full meaning! The presence of the Holy Spirit was inside me. Our simple, small home took on a sacred beauty. The challenge of keeping it clean was still there, but the unresolved conflicts inside me were gone. My changed perspective on life was unbelievable—even to me!

While I was singing, Mother sat in the other living room chair. Her seventh child was due to be born in September. When I finished, she said, "Barbara, I am so glad you went to the altar last night. I didn't know how to deal with you as you were always so angry." She spoke words of truth from her heart. My heart was so regretful. She didn't understand my hurt and anger. To her, my life had been much easier than her life.

My parents had no problem with my morals or obedience, but inwardly, I was disappointed and disillusioned. For so long, I had carried anger and resentment. My personality was defensive. Justice versus injustice was important to me. Never did I challenge the senior members of my family. However, they knew my words were sharply executed when I felt my position was valid. Before my conversion, I preferred death if I had not feared God and believed there was a Heaven and a hell. *Sadly, at thirteen years of age, I had not felt that life was worth living.*

The morning singing occurred for several days. High school would start after Labor Day. The thought of going back to school was a daunting prospect. Day by day, financial challenges did not go away.

Due to pregnancy, Mother was unable to work. After her seventh child was born, Mother intended to start night shift work. She needed me to help with family obligations while she was at work. She and I both realized the enormity of the scheduling for the smaller children. Kenneth and DeWayne would be seventh and tenth graders. As she worried about what to do, I finally expressed my heart to her.

"Mother, I am now a Christian. My life has changed so much for the better. Never do I want to go back to the way I was. You

go ahead and go to work. Doing the work at home will be easier if I quit school and care for the little ones." That was September 1952; my fourteenth birthday was in October. Johnnie Kay was four; Lonnie, my youngest brother, was two; and Mother and Dad's seventh child was due by the end of the month. Mother returned to work when the baby was six weeks.

I devoted myself to the family, the Scriptures, and the church for three years. As I matured, I knew I needed to continue my education. Despair gripped me! My class was already three years ahead of me! My concern was daily told to God. A new minister came to the church. His wife had finished her high school by correspondence. Without telling me, she submitted my name for a representative to visit my home.

After a long journey and a three-hour conversation, he convinced Mother to invest six dollars each month for my high school education. She was a bit suspicious of the offer. One of his remarks sealed itself in my memory and convinced Mother she had made the right decision, "Mrs. McDonald, if you don't purchase this high school correspondence course for Barbara, you are going to limit her ability to succeed for the remainder of her life. She may never be able to get a good job." Mother accepted his offer.

Immediately, I threw myself into dedicated study. The Holy Spirit gave me the initiative and needed strength. After I finished supper dishes, I studied in the bedroom. Often, I fell asleep with the book in my hands. Any free hour was utilized for the studies.

Providentially, Mother brought home free religious magazines from the laundry each week for me to read. Those stories

made me realize I wanted to invest my life in eternal things. At church, I volunteered to teach a class of approximately twenty-five children each Sunday evening before the regular evening service began. The new pastor supported me completely. He sat as an observer each week, along with the parents of the children. That year, our church set a record for foreign mission giving. Most of that was due to the Sunday evening children's service. As the children grew, they all knew I loved them. From fifteen to seventeen years of age, I taught the class. It was the highlight of my week. Each Sunday afternoon was spent alone in the hay loft of our barn, where I studied and memorized my lesson for the children's evening service.

When I turned seventeen in October 1955, I submitted my application to Central Bible College (now Evangel University) in Springfield, Missouri. My application was accepted. My parents then firmly said, "No." There was no money for college. The subject was dropped.

My dedication to the family, especially to the younger children, continued. The children didn't need me. Love for them was my only qualification. As a young teenager, I had little knowledge or wisdom within me to be an adult in their lives from 6:30 a.m. until 5:30 p.m. However, they enjoyed one another as we were alone from daylight to dark, especially in winter. No phones. They expected little out of life but appreciated what they received.

Except in winter, the children spent time outside playing. They had a swing that Dad had hung from an oak tree limb. They had a wagon, puppies, barn kittens, bicycles, and miscellaneous toys. They played exceptionally well together. Their toys

were better than we older three had known. When DeWayne received his first new bicycle, he had a thirty-minute start on us and beat the family home! We looked for him over every hill for ten miles!

As Dad and Mother became more financially stable, they could give them better Christmas and birthday presents. I sent their names to the Children's Hour in Springfield, Missouri, on their birthdays. Their names and birthdays were announced on television, and they were told where their present was hidden. That was a surprise they dearly loved.

My baking skills were zilch. Mother only permitted me to peel potatoes (slowly and thinly), fry them, and bake cornbread. Sometimes, I could open canned vegetables for supper.

On one occasion, we visited our great-aunt—the lady who had delivered me as a baby. She was dying of cancer. Before we left, she, the children, and I knelt and prayed for her to receive God's comfort and encouragement. She sobbed as she prayed on her knees. She thanked us for coming. She graduated to Heaven a few weeks later.

An unusual event occurred one summer afternoon. As I was cleaning the living room, an image of Kenneth, our oldest brother, flashed powerfully in my mind. In the picture, I saw Kenneth fall asleep after he had crossed the railroad tracks driving home from the town of Berryville. He was coming to the culvert below the tracks. There, the picture stopped. Immediately, I told the children, "We have got to pray for Kenneth right now so that he will get home safely tonight." We all knelt on our knees and prayed for Kenneth's safety. That very night, as he drove home, he fell asleep. He remembered crossing

the railroad tracks. As his car approached the culvert, it turned right and steered itself into the creek bed. Kenneth immediately awakened. He restarted the car and drove back to the highway. Kenneth was not a Christian at the time. He had several people praying for him. The Holy Spirit watched over him. The car did not drop off the culvert! Prayer changes circumstances for individuals, communities, parishes, counties, states, nations, and the world. Psalm 91:11–12 (NIV) reminds us of how God has His angels guard us in all our ways. *God cares for those we love! We never stop praying!*

The younger children in our family regularly went to church with me on Sunday evenings and sat in the children's church service. To my surprise, one day, one of the children came to me crying as I worked in the kitchen. I said, "What's wrong?"

The response was, "I want to pray with you so I can live in Heaven."

It touched me to see how the Holy Spirit had touched their heart just as He had touched mine at a young age. We prayed together and embraced. The child went back outside and played in total peace.

Mother's Incredible Dream

December 1955, Mother entered Johnnie Kay's and my bedroom earlier than usual. Her first words were, "Barbara, get up now! I have to talk to you!" My heart skipped a beat with her urgent command! What had I done wrong? What had I forgotten? My mind asked questions as I dressed and went into the living room.

"What did I do wrong, Mother?"

"Oh, you didn't do anything wrong. I had a dream last night. In my dream, you went to hell," she said.

With a sudden gasp of total shock, I said, "Mother! Why did I go to hell?"

She was profoundly serious as she described her dream. "Barbara, I dreamed that you died. Jesus told me He had sent you to hell." She was visibly shaken. She paused and continued to reveal the dream, "I told Jesus that I could not understand why He sent you to hell because I knew you were a Christian. He then told me that you did not continue to live for Him. You went in the opposite direction from God. He said you quit the church and your relationship with Him because I refused to permit you to attend Central Bible College. I want you to

complete whatever papers you must complete to get into college next month! You are going to Central Bible College in January!"

"How can we afford it?" was my next question.

She said, "Don't worry. We'll make it! That was a terrifying dream, Barbara." It took me days to get over the shock of an upcoming change in my life!

First, I cleaned the entire house thoroughly—windows, trim, and quilts, and organized all the dresser drawers and kitchen cupboards. Buttons were put on all the clothes of my brothers and sisters. My clothes were also stitched, patching weak areas where needed, and I prepared for college. Time flew. The hardest part for me was leaving my younger siblings. Would they be able to manage a lot more for themselves? Two of my high school correspondence courses were not completed.

The church surprised me with a shower on the Sunday I left for college. The pastor called me to the front of the church. Different individuals presented me with their tokens of appreciation. One of our seniors gave me a pair of anklets. She said, "Barbara, I didn't know what to give you!" She gave me what I needed—anklets for gym class. One by one, they gave me their tokens of love.

Laura Ray was the neighbor who forded Indian Creek with her husband and two children when the tornado destroyed our home. Lonnie Joe, Roy, and Christine had been in my Sunday evening children's services. Laura handed Lonnie Joe fourteen dollars. He came to the front and handed it to me as her gift. Laura worked at the time. Her house still sat on rocks, and it was small. She had five children inside the tiny house and was an excellent prepper and housekeeper. My heart was so touched. *She gave sacrificially*. Without realizing it, she was filling her heavenly treasure chest. That was more than twenty hours of work for her. Her family had needs. She deeply cared that I succeeded. Strands of love from a neighbor who loved her neighbor's teenager—*me!*

Approximately forty years later, I sent Laura a book of poems. She read the book and sent me a poem she wrote. Her poem was about how we pass our baton of faith on to our family, friends, and neighbors. My friend in San Francisco was a calligraphist. She printed the poem in calligraphy, and I framed it and mailed it to Laura.

On a later visit from California to see Mother, I heard Laura had suffered a stroke. Mother and I went to visit her. Her stroke had left her with a smile. She looked beautiful to me. She knew both of us. On that day, her son, Roy, told me, "Barbara, that poem you sent to Mom came the day we buried Dad. It was here at the house when we arrived from the funeral. It arrived on the right day for us and meant so much to Mom."

The Holy Spirit orchestrated the timetable! We had not heard in California that her husband had graduated to Heaven in Arkansas. The framed poem was forwarded to Laura upon its completion. Nothing escapes the timing of our comforter, the Holy Spirit!

The "choreographed life" is exemplified by the lives of individuals—like you and me—in the Scriptures. They were people who believed that God was who He said He was—would do what He said He would do—regardless of the circumstances encountered.

College Life and the Holy Spirit

College life and classmates traumatized me. My social graces were inadequate; I was emotionally awkward when engaging with peers. After I became a Christian, my closest friends were elderly people and small children in the hillbilly country church I dearly loved. Standing in the college cafeteria line or seated with colleagues at a table was difficult. Even when famished, many meals were skipped. A skin rash covered most of my body by the second week. Eight pounds were lost in the first month. Communication and interactions raged a fierce battle against my future hopes and dreams.

The college was *not* the denominational school my parents would have chosen for me. That made Mother's dream more powerful! She had to be willing to go against her biases. My heart was also skeptical.

For six months before college, I fasted one meal each day to receive Jesus' promise to us—the gift of languages (also called the baptism of the Holy Spirit). My fast was from 12 noon to 6 a.m. the next morning—without liquids. One should always include water when fasting to avoid becoming dehydrated.

As with every true believer, the Holy Spirit entered my heart upon conversion. My fasting was for the gift of languages from the Holy Spirit that Jesus' followers received on the Day of Pentecost. Future believers were also promised the gift. When others in college realized I was seeking the baptism of the Holy Spirit as described in Acts 2, they would congregate around me praying. Though I appreciated their prayers, I requested them to permit me to pray privately. The promised gift was something I wanted to experience between Jesus and me—without anyone's influence. What the Holy Spirit poured into me was most important and personal.

When Jesus ascended to Heaven, *one-hundred-twenty faithful followers* of Jesus did not comprehend His future promise but "believed" what He told them. They "all" returned to Jerusalem and "waited" (as Jesus had commanded) in the Upper Room for His promise—the descension of the Holy Spirit! On the Day of Pentecost, "all" one-hundred-twenty of *His most committed believers* received Jesus' promise—the filling of the Holy Spirit (also called the gift of languages)—including *Mary*, the mother of Jesus. They were Jesus' loyal followers—not new converts! They felt like orphans when they knew Jesus was leaving them! Jesus promised them their advocate in this world—the Spirit of truth (the Holy Spirit)—the world would *not* receive, but Jesus' believers would welcome. (See John 14:15–31, NIV.)

Gabriel had personally visited Mary and told her that the Holy Spirit made Jesus' conception possible within her (Luke 1:35, ESV). *If Mary, the mother of Jesus, felt she needed Jesus' promise of the filling of the Holy Spirit—and followed His command to wait in the Upper Room with the other followers of Jesus—didn't I need His promise too?*

The Holy Spirit's filling of Peter emboldened him! He no longer denied Jesus like he did before Jesus' death—when Jesus needed him most. (See Matthew 26:69–75, KJV.) Only the disciple John had stayed with Jesus through His crucifixion (John 19:26–27, ESV). After Pentecost, however, Peter was changed—courageous without apology! He was fearless, though the same people still controlled the opposing church and government! He was no longer filled with himself and his fear but with the Holy Spirit. In Acts 2:38 (ESV), Peter told the *multitudes* from many countries that if they *repented and were baptized, they would also receive the baptism of the Holy Ghost (Holy Spirit) and their future generations*. Peter's message included me!

After one month in college, with a discouraged heart, I went into the prayer room of the girls' dormitory around 5 p.m. It was during the college dinner hour—another skipped meal! My heart was more desperate for God than food. Alone, I silently wept. It seemed to me that my dream of ever being effective for God in an eternal way was forever extinguished. How could I become truly effective in any ministry God placed me when I was uncomfortable around the students, strangers, and authority figures? In the dark night of my soul, I prayed a prayer similar to the following paraphrased prayer:

"Jesus, I understood You wanted me to come here; I came. If I am where You want me to be and my life is to be given in service for You, why haven't You filled me with Your promised gift of the Holy Spirit as You filled the believers at Pentecost? I know the Holy Spirit lives inside me, but You promised more. You promised that we would have the power to witness—to communicate with others—I want what You promised me!

"College is difficult! You promised the helper to me before You ascended and in Peter's sermon at Pentecost! You promised the gift of languages—communication language with God—which bypasses all this world's darkness, doubt, and evil. You have given the gift to thousands of people in various denominations worldwide. Many hungry hearts had never heard of Your promise! They received Your gift of languages! Why not me?

"I obeyed You and came to college, but it is an enormous burden for my parents to finance my tuition. Guilt overcomes me because, in addition to working full-time, my mother has to do the work I did for the family. Mother says the younger children miss me and want me to return home. They need me to help them prepare for school each day. If You do not fill me this week, I will accept it as Your will to return home where I know I am desperately needed. If You want me to work the rest of my life in my church at home, I will."

My heart emptied before God. One of the most significant decisions in my life was to begin college. Mother's dream had impacted both of our lives! Was it all a mistake? Jesus had promised the gift of the Holy Spirit to "all" His followers. Had I not been a loyal follower, too? My soul was desperately sorrowful as I prayed to God.

Suddenly, a holy presence filled the room. The area around my mouth, including my tongue and lips, grew numb-like with the presence of the Holy Spirit. There was no fear in my heart. Incredible peace filled the prayer room. The Holy Spirit came down upon me in a more powerful way than I could ever have imagined—flooding every cell of my body. The room was filled with His sweet and most amazing presence!

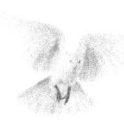

As I continued to pray, a heavenly language took over my speech. Nothing was "pushed" by me! The words I spoke were not in the English language! Heaven's language spoke through my lips—a language I had not learned nor heard. After two hours, I left the room. By that time, the prayer room had filled with classmates—on their knees—praying. A missed meal—the gift of languages from the Holy Spirit—a promise from Jesus received by me.

What a difference the filling of the Holy Spirit made in my life! Was I perfect? *No.* Have I fallen short of Heaven's expectations? *Many times!* Have I been more spiritual than others? Never! *The gift of languages from the Holy Spirit has not been a badge of achievement to wear on my clothing!* Nothing I earned! The Holy Spirit's gift of languages is a gift of grace from Jesus. Every spiritual blessing has come to me through faith, not by any works (Ephesians 2:8–9, NIV). The Holy Spirit desires close communication with us. The Holy Spirit's work always confirms Scripture. *His desire is to immerse us in Jesus. Never does the Holy Spirit, the third person of the Trinity, misrepresent Scripture.*

Significant changes occurred in me. My poverty-level background, fear of failure, and lack of social skills no longer defined me. God's plan for my life was uniquely for me; a purpose-driven life was my gift to Him! It became easier for me to communicate with my peers. Christ-centeredness, not self-centeredness, was the focus of my life.

Does it bother me that many of my dearest friends may not interpret Scripture as I do? *No!* Do I consider myself more spiritual than they? *No!* He knows how to minister to us individually and loves us equally. The Holy Spirit's purpose is first to introduce us to Jesus Christ at salvation and immerse us in Jesus and His gifts as we continue with Christ. He delights that we desire the gifts of the Spirit and that our lives produce the fruit of the Spirit. Gifts and fruit are different. Gifts are freely given to the spiritually hungry. Fruit must mature. Once we have arrived in Heaven, the gifts of the Holy Spirit will no longer be needed as the church of Jesus Christ will be with Him. (See 1 Corinthians 13, KJV.) *The Holy Spirit does not need us to defend His role in the Trinity. He is absolutely capable of defending Himself!*

Each believer will eventually stand before God to answer how we have responded to the Holy Spirit's gifts. Were His gifts appropriately used, or were they ignored and shelved? *Were His gifts misused?* Have we spoken slanderously against His gifts? The Holy Spirit is tender, loving, and sensitive—the most misunderstood person of the Trinity. Ephesians 4:30 (NIV) warns, "And do not grieve the Holy Spirit of God, with whom you were sealed for the day of redemption."

The Sailor Who
Won My Heart

"Who is he?" My heartbeat was a sudden heavy thump! More like an electrical jolt—a heartbeat I had never felt before! The cafeteria line looked like a leveled switchback road on the first Sunday lunch of the 1958–59 school year. He was not even looking my way! Blond, balding, handsome, beautiful teeth, great physique, and expressive light blue eyes. Quickly, I turned and proceeded forward in line. The first guy who made my heart skip a beat! The most handsome guy I had ever seen! Never had I anticipated such a moment!

It was the first week of college in 1958. I casually glanced around for the new freshman for two more weeks but never saw him again. I thought, *Father, why did my heart jump when I saw him? In a special way, I have asked You to reveal the person You know will love me unconditionally for the rest of my life. The heartthrob I felt two weeks ago—was it not from You? If You prefer me to be single, I accept.* The focus of my life would always be on God. The freshman's face was in my memory, but I decided he must have been one of those students who transferred to a different college.

It was my third year of Bible college, and I had not yet taken a foreign language. The thought of a foreign language

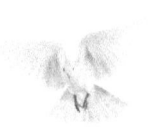

intimidated me. My class load was already full. The courage came to request permission from the dean of women's office to enter the evening Spanish class. She said, "Barbara, you should work this into your schedule. I've never had your feelings. Perhaps the Lord is speaking to you." Another class was not what I wanted!

Hours were spent in the language lab, where I listened to my missed lessons. On my second visit to the lab, I was discouraged. The tape machine would not operate properly, so I sat and studied independently. Suddenly, I heard footsteps. I turned. It was him! The guy from the cafeteria line! He was almost finished with a candy bar, which he kept "on hold" in his mouth! Immediately, I said, "Hi! Do you know anything about tape recorders? I can't make this one work!"

"Don't worry, I'll fix it!" he said. After a few minutes, he said, "My name is Jack Golie."

"Hi, Jack! I'm Barbara McDonald." Less than five minutes later, the tape recorder went up in smoke! I said, "Oh, I'm sorry! Let's report this to the instructor. I'll pay my share." (Any money was made by ironing for fifty cents per hour for the school!)

Jack said, "Oh, don't worry. I will talk to him about this. I don't think you will need to pay anything." Sure enough! The instructor had been told he couldn't get a new one until the old one was gone!

That was our beginning! The following week, I only saw him in class. Later, I discovered he was genuinely concerned about excelling in classes and spent all his time studying—when he wasn't on the football field or basketball court! He had left his 1954 Oldsmobile at home in Whitefish, Montana. Why? He didn't want a girl to date him because he had a nice car!

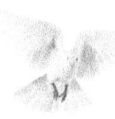

Without my knowledge, the next week, Jack followed me from the cafeteria to the dormitory. He came alongside me and said, "How about going with me to the Friday evening rally?"

My response was, "I don't care." That simple phrase in my Arkansas community meant it was okay with me. Like most people, Jack received my response as "I do not care to go with you." After a minute or two, he suddenly excused himself to leave.

Then I asked, "What time are you coming for me?"

"What? You just said you didn't want to go with me!"

That's when I first discovered that one must understand Arkansans to understand some of our expressions! That was the beginning of our courtship—two dates in October, three in November, and four in December. In January 1959, we started going steady.

In April, the junior-senior banquet was scheduled. One of Jack's friends came to him and said, "Jack, do you mind if I ask Barbara to accompany me to the junior-senior banquet?"

"What? Why are you asking me that question? I'll be the guy taking her to the banquet!"

His friend said, "Jack, only juniors and seniors can attend the banquet—unless you are engaged. You are a freshman!"

Jack said, "I will take Barbara McDonald to the junior-senior banquet!" Our delayed engagement announcement was soon to become official. Jack drove me to my home and requested my parents' permission. He gave me my engagement ring the same day. Jack was my escort at the junior-senior banquet! Because Jack had served his tour in the Navy as a radarman, he was a freshman in the 1958–59 school year.

After our engagement, my friend met me in the dormitory and said, "Barbara, I would give anything if a guy said about me what Jack said about you."

"What did he say about me?"

"Barbara, he said he would be happy in a pigpen with you!"

"In a pigpen?" I gasped! We laughed at his expression and tried hard to imagine why he used that metaphor!

Jack later told me that he knew he would marry me when he saw the back of my long hair in the language lab! He just hoped the face would match the hair!

I said, "Was that why your candy bar went 'on hold' in your mouth?"

Junior-Senior Banquet 1959

From their first meeting in September 1958,
Jack and Barbara never thought of another!
Engagement: April 30, 1959; Wedding: August 7, 1959.

My parents demanded that I spend my summer at home with my family. The surgical technician job I had finished training for was stopped. There was no job at home, but I honored their wishes and worked hard, babysat, deep-cleaned the house, and worked in the yard. While at home that summer, I discovered they were unhappy about my marriage to a Northerner. They preferred a Southerner and for me to live in the South. They had told Jack they would never say yes to me marrying anyone! Jack's ministry had yet to begin. My parents would have preferred me to marry an accomplished speaker!

For most of the summer, I did not reveal my parents' feelings to Jack, who drove from Springfield on weekends. In addition to a full-time college load, he worked full-time as a hospital orderly. Before our marriage, Jack never understood that at that time in history, many Southerners preferred their family to marry Southerners. It was wrong not to tell him about their feelings before our wedding. We drove into the city of Berryville on Saturday afternoon in July. Finally, I mustered the courage and told him about their intense discussions with me about our marriage. Sadly, my expectations were that he would terminate our engagement.

He stopped the car, looked at me, and said, "Darling, I will marry you because I love you. I am not going to marry your family. If you do not have the same commitment, let me know now. You will not marry my family; you will marry me."

He meant every word he spoke. I said, "Jack, I'm marrying you; you are marrying me. Hopefully, they will understand someday." Our conversation was a decision that forever changed our lives. Not once in our marriage did I ever criticize

Jack to my parents. He had the same commitment. Jack never criticized my parents for their reservations about my marriage to him.

The money I needed for a seventy-five-dollar wedding gown was borrowed from Granny. She had a meager three hundred dollars saved for any unknown retirement needs. The money was always pinned into her clothing! Thankfully, she had confidence in me! Mother paid for the material for the bridesmaid dresses. Jack paid for everything else. My father-in-law picked up the tab for my flowers and wedding cake the day before the wedding. Everything was a financial squeeze.

Jack and I made plans to move to the Seattle area. He attended college there. My parents were unhappy, but they accepted it. Perhaps my brothers and sisters had an easier exit from the family nest. It can be challenging for parents to release their first child to anyone. Jack did promise, however, that he would return their daughter to their home for Christmas 1959. Despite being short of money and driving through the snow from Seattle through many states, Jack returned me to Arkansas for Christmas 1959. By then, I had repaid Granny for the wedding gown.

Wedding Picture with Parents

Chester &Veta McDonald, Berryville, Arkansas
Arthur & Martha Golie, Whitefish, Montana
August 7, 1959

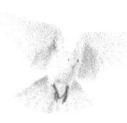

The Warren, Golie, and McDonald Families

Back Row (L-R): Kenneth & DeWayne McDonald (bride's brothers),
Sid Golie & Betty (Golie) Leonard (brother & sister of the groom).
Middle Row (L-R): Edward & Martha Warren
(bride's maternal grandparents),
Chester & Veta McDonald, Bride & Groom, Barbara and Jack,
Art & Martha Golie,
Mrs. Sid Golie (Barbara Jane), & Freeman & Mary McDonald
(bride's paternal grandparents—Granny & Papa)
Front Row (L-R): Johnnie Kay and Lonnie (bride's sister and brother).

Bride and Groom Cut Wedding Cake

The cake was given an extra push when I served Jack.
I was begging Jack not to give me payback!
Jack was contemplating!

Mother and Dad Golie

Martha (Fuhrer) Golie's mother died when she was four. Her growing-up years were difficult. She, her sister, and her brother remained close throughout life.

After her father's second marriage, the family moved to rural Canada. Martha feared that she would miss future opportunities. Her brother lived in Great Falls, Montana. At sixteen, he went to Canada for her. She sneaked away and returned to Montana with him. She supported herself by living in homes and working for them. Martha stayed connected with her father until his death. They visited as often as possible.

With the 1930s Depression and the poor economy in Montana, she could not complete her last two years of high school. Her thirst for learning was never quenched. Initially, German was her first language, but she was fluent in English—an excellent student—and had a brilliant mind. She devoted her life to her family, church, and neighbors.

Vacation in Portland, Oregon.

L-R: Sidney, Betty, Arthur, Martha, and Jack

Martha, my precious mother-in-law, greatly influenced Jack's life through her Christian faith and love. She read the Bible to her children each morning and prayed with them before they left for school in Whitefish, Montana.

Jack was four years old when Art and Martha moved from Havre to Whitefish, Montana. Martha and two other Great Northern Railroad wives began a Sunday school program for their children and others who desired to come. From that small beginning, the Whitefish Assembly of God Church now exists. Arthur helped build the first church.

Martha was more than a mother-in-law to me. She taught me to sew and to cook well. Thank God for a mother- and father-in-law who made me a member of their family. They

took me to Montana's beautiful lakes, fishing, and mountains. They insisted I call them Mother and Dad. Mother Golie was never known to criticize others. She lived her faith. A precious mother-in-law.

Dad Golie grew up speaking Norwegian as his first language. For as long as I can remember, he was still singing in Norwegian—a beautiful voice. He began working on the Great Northern Railroad as a cook. One particular morning, he ran out of milk for the pancakes. He made a quick substitution. One of the guests on the train was the First Lady of the United States (FLOTUS). She loved his pancakes so well that she requested his recipe. He was flattered and said, "Tell FLOTUS I ran out of milk, and I was forced to melt the vanilla ice cream as a substitute." She loved his story!

Dad Golie was eventually elevated to a foreman on the Great Northern—a position he had for many years. He was also a Montana fisherman's guide. Nobody loved Montana more than him. He worked hard for the environmental care of the lakes, rivers, and streams. After his retirement, he helped build the Senior Citizens Center in Whitefish and ensured its maintenance and upkeep. Dad always helped neighbors and invited older men fishing who could no longer drive or go fishing alone. He helped the older citizens with their gardens and picked their fruit and vegetables.

Mother and Dad visited us twice in Bermuda and Hawaii during Jack's military tours. They enjoyed the warmer climates away from Montana winters. Our family has many pictures and beautiful memories of their visits.

Mother Golie told me that her greatest fear in World War II was the fear of being sent to an encampment should neighbors

discover she was of German descent. She only told her children once they were grown. Jack said, "Mother, do you realize how many theology books were written in German? I could have spoken the language and read the books!"

"Jack, you cannot comprehend my fears during the war. I didn't want my three Norwegian-German children taken from me!" was her response—lest we forget!

While visiting us during Jack's four-year Navy tour in Bermuda, we had a photographer come to the house and take their forty-third wedding anniversary picture on December 25, 1973. They were engaged for five years before they could financially afford to get married on December 25, 1930. They had to live with his family for a few months. The photographer chirped, "How about giving her a forty-third-anniversary kiss?" They faithfully loved each other until her death in December 1979—just before their forty-ninth wedding anniversary. Her faith was powerfully strong before her death. Dad's life was forever diminished. He was lost without her. One by one, most of his fishing friends passed. He called us on each of their deaths and expressed his grief. Facing life's sunset alone was difficult for Dad Golie.

Forty-third-Wedding-Anniversary Kiss—Bermuda

December 25, 1973: Special Father and Mother-in-law
Arthur William Golie (06-13-1905/11-30-1988)
and Maria Martha (Fuhrer) Golie (04-13-1908/2-04-1979)

November 27, 1988, was Sunday night. Dad Golie walked outside the church Jack was pastoring in Troy, Montana. Someone said, "Art, why are you standing here?"

He said, "I'm waiting for Martha." Three days later, on November 30, 1988, Dad joined Mother in Heaven as he slept in the church parsonage.

Mother and Dad Mcdonald

The Holy Spirit choreographed Mother and Dad's relationship and lives before becoming Christians. Proverbs 18:22 (NIV) says, "He who finds a wife finds what is good and receives favor from the Lord." A stunning verse is the Holy Spirit-inspired words of Psalm 139:16 (NLT), "You saw me before I was born. Every day of my life was recorded in your book. Every moment was laid out before a single day had passed."

As the reader, you met my parents at the book's onset. On their fiftieth wedding anniversary, January 11, 1986, their children, sons-in-law, and daughters-in-law honored them with their desired fiftieth vow renewal ceremony and reception.

The daughter of the justice of peace was present at their ceremony. She gave an eye-witness report of their marriage day. Dad gave her father one dollar to perform the marriage ceremony. The dollar was given to his daughter for a Bible. She displayed the fifty-year-old Bible.

Fiftieth Wedding Anniversary—January 11, 1986

L-R: Lonnie, DeWayne, Kenneth, Dad, Mother, Barbara, and Johnnie.

Dad and Mother's Cake-Cutting Ceremony

January 11, 1986. Antioch Church, Berryville, Arkansas.

Dad and Mother's Heavenly Graduations

Dad was diagnosed with bone cancer shortly after my parents' vow renewal service. He was the second of our four parents to leave us. In a conversation with Mother, he did not mention that he had been the number-one cheesemaker at Kraft Foods in Berryville. He never talked about their hard economic times nor how many years their suppers consisted only of cornbread and milk. He rehearsed none of their economic setbacks—like when the tornado broke his back in two places. He didn't boast of his musical talents nor how many people loved his tenor voice. Dad mentioned only the deep faith in God he would never lose. He talked about their life journey together—marriage at seventeen and nineteen—and gave the following words to Mother to be told to his family. In his farewell message, Dad remembered Nancy Sue, whom they had cherished for one-hundred-thirty days forty-four years prior (1942).

Dad's Farewell to His Family

- I've never loved people more or been closer to my Lord (*James 4:8, KJV*).
- If the Lord says it is my time to leave, I want His will in my life (*Matthew 6:10, KJV*).
- Just because Jesus did not will to heal me, don't let my death shake your faith (*1 John 5:14–15, KJV*),
- God is able for all things (*John 15:7, KJV*).
- I'm ready to go when the Lord comes for me (*Philippians 1:21, KJV*).
- So, meet me on the "other side" of life (*2 Timothy 4:7–8, KJV*).
- Nancy Sue and I will be waiting in Heaven for you (*1 Thessalonians 4:16–18, KJV*).

Chester McDonald (August 3, 1916 to May 7, 1986)

Dad graduated to Heaven three months short of his seventieth birthday. Emerson Ray, Dad's teenage friend and the "911 neighbor" who had rescued Dad's sons after the tornado, said, "Chester McDonald was the best friend I've ever had." His funeral in the Antioch Church was filled with the people who knew him. For the last decade of his life, he spoke in the community churches that had no pastor. He also pastored in Bonner, Arkansas, where the people loved him dearly.

Mother's life declined after Dad's death. She had never lived alone before and found it unbearable. She departed for Heaven on December 8, 2002, at eighty-four. Years prior, she had asked me to be with her when she left us. I said, "Mother, I live in

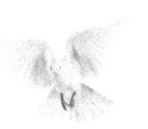
Alaska, but let's pray together that it will happen." We prayed. When I left her the last week of November 2002, she would not open her eyes as we said goodbye. I felt a resignation in her spirit. She told me goodbye and said that she loved me.

She had told Jack earlier, "I am not afraid anymore. Chester and Nancy Sue are waiting for me." He validated her faith and words. They prayed together.

Five days later, I received the call that she was given only a few days to live. The nurse told her we would leave Alaska at midnight. Upon arrival, I reminded Mother of Dad's words. Reportedly, she was in a coma, but she tried to nod and say, "Okay."

Kenneth, her eldest son, graduated to Heaven in October 2001 at sixty-four. Carolynn, his wife, and his entire family were devastated. We felt Mother knew he was gone as she never asked for him again.

After the Sunday night church services, two local ministers, their wives, DeWayne and his wife, Myrna, Johnnie Kay, Jack, and I encircled her bed.

Jack said, "Let's pray the Lord's Prayer together, then I will close in prayer." We held hands in a circle around her bed. Jack touched her aorta, and DeWayne touched her shoulder.

When the prayers were finished, Jack looked at us and said, "She left us as soon as we began the Lord's Prayer." We all thought she had fallen asleep! She looked so peaceful! What an answer to her prayers! She was not alone; three of her children, her daughter-in-law, her son-in-law, and two ministers and their wives surrounded her and prayed as her spirit soared to Heaven. *The Holy Spirit never forgets our requests!* Like her

father's request before leaving for Heaven (see story "Maternal Grandparents—The Warren Family"), Mother's final request was answered as she left for Heaven. *She was not alone! The Holy Spirit had Mother's back! She had trusted Jesus for sixty-four years! He had never failed her! Nine people surrounded her as He lifted her wings to Heaven!*

Johnnie Kay said, "Mom surprised all of us! She decided to sneak away with the angels while we were praying!"

As I authored this book, Johnnie Kay faced her husband's homegoing. Bill's childhood was a lonely orphan's journey that, in time, charted him directly to his heavenly Father. After a bitter battle with COVID-19 and its horrific aftermath, God gave Bill the strength to slowly release his greatest treasures—his wife and children. His farm no longer occupied his thoughts. He no longer mitigated his losses or successes. The Spirit of God within Bill yearned to be unstrapped from his degenerating body—his heavy backpack.

Jana, my daughter, overnighted with them in 2018. She said, "I came down the stairs in the early morning to find Bill reading his Bible. I was so touched by his passion to understand his Bible and commentary. He was running his fingers across the words."

When the church needed extra money for missions, Bill funded the shortage. The spiritual part of Bill matured and anticipated departure. His earthly body—his tent—was broken, but his spirit soared! His planted seeds of trust and faith in God exceed those he planted on his farm. He radiated a spirit of tenderness and forgiveness toward everyone. He was not angry over the chaos of his daily battles with incapacitation. His

faith permitted him to trust God when nothing made sense to him. Johnnie Kay knew that, despite the circumstances, Bill's life was not falling apart, but all was falling into place. He was leaving this world with faith—transitioning out of time into an eternity forever in Heaven. Bill graduated to Heaven at 6 p.m., December 2, 2023.

Making Our House a Home

"Tag this baby 'Golie' and take him to the lab." It was May 1967. Those words lived rent-free in my mind and emotions for years. The doctor never realized how his words impacted me in the Boston hospital. My heart was broken. Jack was out of state receiving his ministerial ordination.

After four days, Jack returned and escorted me to our one-room apartment. At my request, Jack took a picture of my flowers and cards. Our baby boy was carried for eighteen weeks. He was our fourth miscarriage. We named him Jack Karston Golie, Jr. My heart angrily said, "This baby was to be born the first week of October. God, what will You give me in return?" My spirit was bitter; the medical bills were large; we had no baby. The crib was empty. The miscarriage occurred too early for my insurance to help. The expenses were steep.

Early on, the doctors worked diligently to save the baby. Besides food and rent in our one-room apartment—with a shared bathroom—our income went to the hospital and medical bills. The loss of our baby boy plagued my mind. At that time, it appeared God cared nothing about my motherless grieving heart.

We attended adoption classes in Massachusetts. They were terminated when I became pregnant. Losing the baby was emotionally hard for Jack. He immediately began talking about adoption again, and I quietly listened but questioned if I could ever love an adopted child equally to a natural child. Adopted or naturally born, love was the paramount investment in a child— no divided heart. After the miscarriage, a new application was needed. Before it was processed, Jack was called into the Navy chaplaincy on September 18, 1967.

Jack had worked tirelessly to achieve his goal. He carried a full load each semester and worked as a hospital orderly. When he entered the chaplaincy, he had completed his Master of Divinity (MDiv), two years of pastoral ministry, and his Master of Education (MEd), including his high school student teaching requirements.

After Chaplaincy School in Rhode Island, Jack was assigned to the Marine Corps Base in Twentynine Palms, California. Vietnam was the next assignment. Jack did not let his one-year assignment at Twentynine Palms discourage him. Though another miscarriage occurred while we were in California, Jack submitted a California adoption application. Just because he was scheduled to leave for Vietnam did not deter Jack. We wanted to make our house a home.

In July 1968, a call came from the San Bernardino, California, adoption agency. When I picked up the phone, our caseworker said, "Barbara, we have a little girl for you and Jack!" Filled with joy, I said, "When was she born?" The response was, "She was born October 7, 1966!" That week had a quick remembrance for me—*the week that our son was to have been born! I asked God what He*

was going to give us for our loss! He gave us a little girl who was born the same week!

Never underestimate the Holy Spirit at work in your life! Immediately, my mind flashed back to my "sympathy picture" in the backyard of our small one-room apartment in Salem, Massachusetts! Vividly, I visualized the cards and flowers! Someone in Heaven has a perfect memory! Suddenly, I was so ashamed that I had not expected God to turn a painful experience into something extraordinary for Jack and me! *God knew the specific child who needed a home! He had long ago chosen her parents—us!*

When we arrived in San Bernardino, we couldn't distinguish the beautiful face of this nineteen-pound child. She had cried all morning. Why? For less than three months, it had been an unsuccessful adoption. When they packed her clothes, she immediately understood that she was going away again! She knew she was leaving them! She was given up at birth. A loving foster family cared for her until she was seventeen months old. She was then placed in an unsuccessful adoption for less than three months. Nobody from her past had returned to her! More strangers? It is difficult to comprehend her pain at nineteen months and three weeks. Her caseworker had known her since birth and was extremely concerned about a third family. To Jana, it was abandonment! How many rejections and good-byes could she endure?

The Holy Spirit was aware of this child who needed a home! My angry prayer was said in April of 1966 in the apartment's backyard in Salem, Massachusetts—surrounded by our baby boy's grief flowers! Also, in April of 1966, the child to be born for us was in another lady's womb! Both babies were to be born in the first week of October!

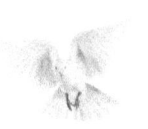
The Holy Spirit is omniscient (all-knowing)! We can *trust* Him! He loves us; He loves children! Matthew 19:14 (ESV), Mark 10:14 (ESV), and Luke 18:16 (ESV) all record Jesus' love for the children. Luke records Jesus' words with a serious warning!

After we had observed Jana's swollen face and eyes and talked for a few minutes, her caseworker said, "Here are your new parents!"

Jana, who refused to look at us, quickly shook her head and said, "No!" Jack and I wondered if an adoption with this young lady was to transpire. She was precocious, and her vocabulary was extensive. We counted more than three hundred words in the first few days.

After five minutes, the caseworker brought her directly to me and said, "Sit down on your mother's lap!" Jana melted in my arms and began inspecting my charm bracelet. God enlarged my heart with love! *I felt she had always been ours!*

We stopped for lunch at a diner on our way home. Jack excused himself to go to the car. Jana immediately cried as she thought he had abandoned us. At that point in her life, everyone had left her! Nobody, except her caseworker, had ever returned. An older couple in the diner looked inquisitively at me. Immediately, I explained that we were her third family, and she had only been with us for one hour. The gentleman immediately took a silver dollar out of his pocket and gave it to her! She understood that money had value and thanked him. However, she wouldn't take her eyes off the door until Jack returned. She pointed to him and excitedly squealed, "Daddy's here! Mommie, Daddy's here!"

When we arrived home, Jana ran from room to room to find her room. It was all set up with her bed and appropriate

decorations. She placed her head against the door frame when she saw her room and sobbed. We couldn't imagine what memories she recalled from her past. She was probably hoping to find the two children in the home she left. She loved them.

In the weeks ahead, we gave her all the attention and love we had in our hearts. Jack would say, "Jana, Daddy's arms hurt because they want to hug you!"

She would run to him and quickly embrace him. Then she would say, "All done, Daddy?"

He would say, "No. Daddy needs more hugs!"

She embraced him until he said his arms no longer hurt.

Jana Kay's Dedication Ceremony
July 2, 1968: Marine Corps Base, Twentynine Palms, California.

After two weeks, the caseworker came to visit our home. Jana and I were making a pie. She was covered in flour as she helped me roll out the crust. The caseworker had been with her since birth. She said, "Barbara, you will never know how happy this scene in your home makes me feel. Jana has lost that worried look in her eyes, and she seems to be at peace with you. Had I not found her doing well, I would have taken her out of your home today! Moving from family to family has repeatedly been a sense of rejection for her. A child cannot continually withstand that kind of pressure. They crumble emotionally."

It took only seconds—not two weeks—to welcome Jana into our hearts forever. We were thrilled with the caseworker's report, who had evaluated her development since birth. God has His angels in many places—protecting, guiding, directing— the little ones that are so pure and vulnerable.

*Jack (Thirty) and Jana (Twenty-Two Months)—Before Vietnam
August 1968 (six weeks before Jack left for Vietnam)*

Vietnam—R&R—Vietnam

Jack left for Vietnam on October 7, Jana's second birthday. He did his best to make sure she remembered him. She did. However, it was another person who walked away from her. She would place her head on the window in Seattle and cry, "Mommie, oin't to pay wif me daddy!" ("Mommie, I want to play with my daddy!") Regardless of how muddy it was, every letter from Vietnam would always have a drawing from Daddy to Jana. She couldn't forget him.

When we anticipated R&R in Hawaii, I worked hard to prepare Jana for their reconciliation. At Sea-Tac Airport, she cried and said, "Dis is not Hawaii. Me daddy is not here!" ("This is not Hawaii! My daddy is not here!")

We arrived in Hawaii the evening before the plane from Vietnam was due. Again, she said, "Dis is not Hawaii! Me daddy is not here!" It was difficult for her to establish trust. The loaded busses finally arrived the next morning; all the marines looked identical! Jana couldn't see her daddy! With her fragile trust factor, she thought she had been tricked! Suddenly, he appeared right in front of us! She was terrified!

We went to our room in the Ilikai Hotel. He spent an hour winning her acceptance. He redrew the pictures of bicycles and helicopters he had sent her from Vietnam. Finally, she said, "Mommie, can me give Daddy me dollar?" The dollar had been placed in her tiny purse. For the remainder of his time, she belonged to him.

The Vietnam era had no cell phone capability. Jack stood in line for hours to make a guarded three-minute call home at Christmas in the middle of the night. Mothers could not wake their young children to hear Daddy's voice.

For the four months of separation after R&R, the pictures Jack drew for her were reminders of Hawaii and what they would do together when he arrived home. Jana excitedly told her picture stories about her and Daddy building sandcastles, digging tunnels, and riding on Daddy's back at Hale Koa Beach.

Hale Koa Beach—Jack and Jana

NAS Jacksonville, Florida—Jack Gregory

NAS Jacksonville, Florida, was Jack's assignment after Vietnam. We immediately began adoption proceedings. We prepped Jana for months for a baby brother. Jack purchased her a wagon as a present from her new brother.

A July morning, at 4 a.m., I quietly packed our car for the three-day venture. We picked Gregory up the next morning and kept him with us all day. It was one of the happiest days of our lives. He had blond, naturally curly hair and a great personality. We focused all of our attention on the bonding of the children. After playing in the pool for hours with Jack, the two children napped in the afternoon.

The minute Jana saw Gregory, her first words were, "He didn't buy that wagon for me! Somebody had to help him!"

Our First Day with Gregory

Gregory Goes to Our "Home"!

The adoption agency required us to return Gregory after his first day with us. We were given custody the next morning. We became nervous as we endured a long wait before their late arrival. Greg still crawled on his hands and feet (no knee crawling). By the time he was one year old, on August 10, 1970, he took his first steps and opened doors. He loved to play with any object that needed to be manipulated with his hands.

The next Sunday, his dedication ceremony was performed at the NAS Jacksonville Chapel.

Jack Gregory's Dedication Ceremony
July 19, 1970: NAS Chapel, Jacksonville, Florida

The dedication ceremony ended with the following poem and rosebud presentation.

Not flesh of my flesh,
Nor bone of my bone,
But in reality, my very own.
Gregory, never forget for
a single minute.
You didn't grow under
my heart, but in it!"

Author Unknown

This rosebud represents you, Gregory.
It is symbolical of your life—which is yet to unfold—to
give glory to God and blessings to others.

Author Unknown

Jack Gregory and Jana Kay Golie
Gregory's First Birthday! (August 10, 1970)

Bermuda 1973—Gregory and Jana

Greg and Shellie's Wedding—Lighting the Unity Candle
Gregory and the love of his life, Shellie, were married in 2001.

July 2, 2005: Alexandra Arrives!

Alexandra, our grandchild, a beautiful gift from God!

Gregory called and said, "Dad, you have to be here the day the baby arrives! Make your plans accordingly!" From Anchorage, Alaska, we arrived the same day she arrived—a few hours later!

Reflections On Our Children

Jana Kay and Jack Gregory—our "chosen" children—made our house a home! Love for them grew inside our hearts—not under our hearts—long before they arrived. Nothing made Jack happier than when others said, "I would have known that was your child even if you hadn't been with them." Jack would say to other questions, "We did better with Jana and Gregory than if we had done it ourselves!"

Our first five babies were left in labs. Heaven has no labs! In 1971, our sixth baby, Janae Kristin, was born in Jacksonville, Florida. After three weeks of hospitalization, she arrived on the first day of the seventh month and lived five minutes. Her lungs needed three more weeks. We did not see her alive as she was rushed to an oxygen tent.

As a family, we went from the hospital to the funeral home and viewed our gorgeous petite baby. She had been gifted with Jack's beautiful eyes, hairline, and facial frame. She had long fingers like mine. *We thanked God we could view our little angel and will hold her in Heaven, along with our other five children!*

As we left the funeral home, Jana immediately asked, "Mommie, Janae came out of your tummy? Gregory did not

come out of your tummy. Did I come out of your tummy?" Adoption questions are asked a parent when least expected! Again, we told her the story of her adoption—being "chosen"— and reminded her of her pictures and the people who cared for her until we brought her home with us. Jack and I assured her that although she and Gregory did not come out of Mommie's tummy, we loved them just as much! They were "chosen" by God—above all other children—to be in our family forever!

The doctors later informed me we had lost Janae due to malnutrition in childhood. The womb was too weak. They sewed the womb to save her. She was active—moving simultaneously with her arms and legs. The tissue was weak; the water broke.

Both Jana and Gregory have brought great joy to our lives. We are most grateful that both of them have deep faith. They have served the church in many capacities. Though he has suffered from multiple sclerosis since twenty years of age, Gregory has faithfully donated over two decades of his skills and time as a church sound technician. Nothing makes Jana happier than giving to others, regardless of their financial capability.

One of our fondest memories was one evening, while Jana and Gregory were in elementary school, they hurriedly ran to Jack with pencil and paper, "Daddy, what do we write on your and Mother's tombstones when you go to Heaven?"

Jack said, "It doesn't matter what you write on mine, but write 'Theophilos' (lover of God) on your mother's!" My tears came quickly. It was not the me I envisioned.

"How do we spell that, Daddy?" Jana asked. Jack calmed all their fears. He told them that if we went to Heaven before them, Uncle Bill and Aunt Lillian promised to keep and love them in

their home. They would always be safe and loved by our best friends. With their strategy session ended, they returned to their rooms and went to sleep.

Unexpected Diagnosis

Our Forty-Eighth Wedding Anniversary
Anchorage, Alaska (08-07-2007)

"The doctor has no appointments available!" the receptionist told my husband. Jack refused no for an answer.

"I need an appointment for my wife! This is an emergency!" Two of my lymph nodes were the size of large marbles and had been extremely sore for several days.

Jack was scheduled to travel seven hours to the church in Tok, Alaska. He canceled the trip until after the biopsy. The doctor's words, "Follicular low-grade non-Hodgkins lymphoma." That name meant nothing to me. It was October 2007.

The consultation jolted me into reality. The lymphoma was already in stage four. We were told that no treatment was available for this specific lymphoma. When a tumor became aggressive, I would have four to six weeks to live. As we left the hospital to return to work, Jack's first words were, "Angel, whatever this means for us, please know that I am with you every step of the way." Maybe my time to graduate to Heaven had come? My body felt in shock for a few days. My brother, Kenneth—sixteen months older than me—had died with the same diagnosis in 2001. He was sixty-four; I was sixty-nine.

Our outstanding Engineering Manager, Patrick McDevitt, to whom I was secretary, gave me a beautiful goodbye luncheon and gift. It was most difficult to say farewell to the Alaska friends I had worked with for seven years. The realization that I would never see them again was daunting.

We moved to Decatur, Alabama, where we had purchased a home. The medical referral was to the lymphoma specialist at the University of Alabama. Three labs—Anchorage, Seattle, and UAB—gave the same diagnosis.

Jack accepted the pastorate of a struggling church in Alabama. We did not tell the church or the neighbors about the cancer. I desired quality days with my family. We prayed for my healing. My body had no pain—only tiredness. We improved the new residence, painted the entire house inside, and painted the wrap-around porch with its many pillars. Jack built

me raised gardens, and the vegetables and fruit were lush—tomatoes, cucumbers, peppers, strawberries, blackberries, and blueberries.

CAT scans were scheduled every three months for almost two years. Tumors were measured. The doctor was terrific! He loved my optimism and asked me "to keep doing whatever I was doing. Don't forget to rest when you feel tired!"

On August 7, 2009, Gregory, Shellie, Alexandra from California, and Jana from Alaska joined us at Hale Koa Hotel in Hawaii for our fiftieth wedding anniversary. *God permitted me to see my children as adults (added Shellie and Alexandra to our family) and blessed Jack and me with our golden wedding anniversary. My heart overflowed with thankfulness that I lived to see the two life-long prayers answered. God had been a wonderful Father to me!*

Valentine's Day 2010

Monday night, February 1, 2010, pains began in my chest. To inform Jack was like saying I would die in four to six weeks. Many times since the diagnosis, I awakened with his hand on my back, silently praying for me. He loved me unconditionally. On Sunday, February 7, my courage failed on our forty-minute drive to church. The pain continued. Sunday, February 14, on the way to church, I said, "Jack, I must discuss something with you."

With an inquisitive look, he said, "Yes?"

"Jack, I am having pains in my chest." His face grew pale. I said, "It is hard to tell you that the pain has been waking me for two weeks—just as the doctor said it would."

Taking my hand, he said, "We're together in this, Angel." After a prayer, he looked at me and said, "Would you sing a solo in church today?"

"Yes," I said. Then, with both our hearts in silent communion, I felt the Holy Spirit nudge me to tell the church—before the solo—that I had been living with a cancer diagnosis for two and one-half years. As the minister's wife, that was a giant challenge for me!

When Jack called me for the solo, I sat at the piano and turned the microphone toward the congregation. "Church,

I have something to tell you. In September of 2007, I was diagnosed with follicular low-grade non-Hodgkin's lymphoma.

"When they told me the diagnosis, I didn't understand, but it is a cancer that attacks the lymph nodes. My body has been full of tumors—stage four. The doctors do not know how many years they have been inside me. I have not been in pain—tired often. We were told there was no cure for this specific cancer. However, I know God can heal all kinds of diseases. He created me; He can recreate me.

"Please don't fear my presence with you; I am not contagious. That is why I haven't told you; I didn't want you to be afraid. Don't bother to ask how the cancer is doing. Cancer always does fine unless the Lord removes it!

"God's plan for my life is unknown to me. Whatever it is, it is the best plan for me. If it is for Heaven, I am ready to leave. Long ago, I asked God to let me see my children become adults before He called me. They are grown. Then I asked Him to let me celebrate my fiftieth wedding anniversary with Jack. He answered that prayer last August.

"However, if He wants me to stay, I want to stay. I have loved being Jack's bride for almost fifty-one years. Jack and I have prayed for my healing, but we don't badger God. We paraphrase a portion of the prayer Jesus taught us to pray: 'Thy kingdom come; thy will be done on earth (in my life) as it is in Heaven.' (See Matthew 6:10, KJV.)

"Since my diagnosis, I have prayed my paraphrased version of Isaiah 43:1–3 as follows,

Do not fear, Barbara, for I have redeemed you.
I have personally invited you by name.
You are Mine!
When you pass through the waters,
I will be with you!
When you pass through the rivers,
I will not permit them to sweep over you!
When you walk through the fire,
you will not be burned.
The flames will not set you ablaze!
Barbara, I am the Lord your God,
The Holy One of Israel, your Saviour!

"The solo is 'Hide Me, Rock of Ages.' This song is a prayer, so I will not look toward you. I will look toward Heaven. Please pray with me as I sing. Don't look at me; look toward Heaven with me."

My country-music voice flowed smoothly through the verses. The third verse started with the following words, "When my journey is completed, and there's no more work to do. Savior, guide my weary spirit to that happy land beyond the blue."

When I said "journey" in the third verse, a gentle upward surge began halfway between my knees and ankles—at the exact location in each leg. To describe the surge, it was like an ocean's gentle wave flowing slowly over a sandy beach. As the Holy Spirit surge came up through my body, it felt like a "holy" scrub cleaned each cell. How one describes an inside cleansing, I do not know, but I felt like the Holy Spirit surge cleaned and recreated me on the inside! It was an incredible experience to

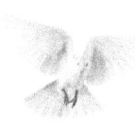

have the Holy Spirit escalating through my body in a dynamic way.

That surge continued through my body as I finished the verse and the song's chorus. As I sang the last word of the song, the surge went out at the top of my head! I felt physically purged; my strength was zero—like a rag doll—weak and wobbly! My quick prayer was, "Lord, get me to the front seat without falling!"

I relayed the story to Jack when we began our journey back home. He was overjoyed and said, "Do not give any of this information to your doctor when you see him on Tuesday's (February 16) appointment. Do the usual blood work and CAT scan. Let's see what his report says."

Two days later, I followed Jack's protocol all the way. My appointment with the doctor was at 2 p.m., February 16, 2010. We began the regular tests at 7:30 a.m. Finally, after 4 p.m., the doctor came into the room. He gave Jack and me his usual bear hugs and sat down on the bench by Jack. He thumbed through a thick binder and said, "Well, Barbara, whatever you are doing, you must keep doing! There is no cancer in the kidneys, no cancer in the liver, no cancer in the stomach, no cancer in the lungs, etc. There are no cancer cells or tumors in your body!"

Jack said, "Excuse me, doctor, did I hear you say there are no cancer cells in Barbara's body?"

The doctor said, "That is correct, Jack! Whatever she is doing, she should keep doing!"

Then I spoke up and said, "Well, doctor, I have tried to tell you twice that a few people were praying for me."

The doctor interrupted me and said, "Now, now, Barbara! If I give you a good report, God gets the credit! If I give you a bad report, I get the credit! I'll see you again in three months. Those cancer cells must be hiding in there somewhere!"

We both loved my doctor and understood in advance that he did not believe in divine healing. He did love his patients and was very honest with me. From the beginning, he told me that after I began hurting, he would give me radiation to relieve the extreme nausea I would suffer in the last days of my life. Personally, I preferred nausea rather than the loss of my hair. Once one tumor became aggressive, he said I would only live four to six weeks.

In 2015, on my fifth annual visit to him, the doctor I saw before seeing him said, "Barbara, may I ask why you are here today?"

Surprised, I said, "This is my annual visit since my healing in 2010 when I was in my third year of the diagnosis. He has asked me to come back for a full ten years."

The doctor said, "I believe in divine healing. Tell him of your healing today! It must come from you!"

I said, "I have tried three times, but he doesn't let me finish. I will try again!"

"Make it happen!" were the doctor's words.

My doctor entered the room, hugged us, and sat down. "Well, let's look at Barbara's report."

"Why, doctor? You haven't found anything wrong with me since February 16, 2010. Doctor, I have never told you what happened on February 14, 2010."

Immediately, his eyes stared into mine. "What happened on *that* date?"

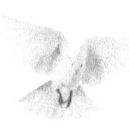

"Yes. Something happened on that date."

"Tell me what happened."

The story was told of what happened as I was singing. He sat quietly—never releasing his stare into my eyes! When I finished, he took his hand and gave me a big smile and a high five.

As we left, I said, "Doctor, do I need to keep returning for ten years?"

He said, "Barbara, you are my most optimistic patient. I need your optimism!" Jack encouraged me to return to him as long as he wanted me to come.

I was in Houston with Jack the following year and could not keep the appointment. In 2017 and 2018, I returned. It was in 2018 that he referred me to someone else as he was transferring. As I pen these words to this book, it has been fourteen years! Two other doctors responded to my healing by defining it medically as "instantaneous recession."

Against all odds, God healed me of cancer on February 14, 2010. It was a beautiful, unexpected surprise! Other doctors say it was an "instantaneous recession." I accept both! All I can say is I sensed God's power in my body! All scans have been fine since that time! Jack and I felt God said to me that day, "*Happy Valentine's Day, Barbara!*"

Through My Valley of Why

Jack Golie, My Hero

Jack, my extremely ill husband, lay asleep in the passenger seat of our 2000 Tundra. July 2017—and our forty-fourth trip to MD Anderson Hospital in Houston from Decatur, Alabama. Jack insisted I wake him when we exited Interstate 65 onto Highway 20 West. He knew my fear of the treacherous construction traffic in Birmingham. Once I finished the exit maneuver, Jack was asleep and lifeless-like again. A long and lonely drive

to Houston. How I missed his humor and camaraderie! The silence was deafening. My heart reflected on our beautiful life together and our painful, unknown future.

Jack K. Golie, my hero. His charisma was captivating. "Wind Beneath My Wings," our favorite love song, described my heart. Our drive to Houston twice each month was not a sacrifice for me. Could I face life without him?

"Now Is the Hour" was the song that birthed our tears as he left R&R in Hawaii (1969). At midnight, he and a plane-load of Marines returned to the Vietnam War Zone. More muddy love letters from him to tease my fears.

Before Jack boarded the plane to return to Vietnam
from R&R in Hawaii (May 1969—12 Midnight)

Vietnam Reflections

As the plane engines roared, Jana, our two-year-old daughter, screamed, "Dat plane is gonna hurt me (my) daddy!" Jack saw Jana from the plane's window as she cried and reached for his plane. He rushed off the airplane and talked to her through the tall fence that separated us. She calmed down when she saw he was safe. Some men returned to Vietnam from a beautiful R&R vacation and never saw their wives or children again. *Lest we forget!*

When Jana and I went to the military base in Seattle, she would wrap her arms around the knees of each serviceman she saw in uniform, tilt her head back so she could look straight up at him, and say, "Me daddy in Upnam!" They understood, picked her up, gave her bear hugs, and talked to her about her daddy, who loved her and would return to her and Mother. Servicemen and women understand the pain of separation. *Our brave-hearted military personnel are exceptional in every way!*

Each night while Jack was in Vietnam, Jana knelt by her chair, pressed her palms together, closed her eyes, and said, "God, oin't to pay (play) wif (with) me (my) daddy." She kissed his picture and went to sleep.

"God, please, no disappointment for this little one; she belongs to You!" was my prayer.

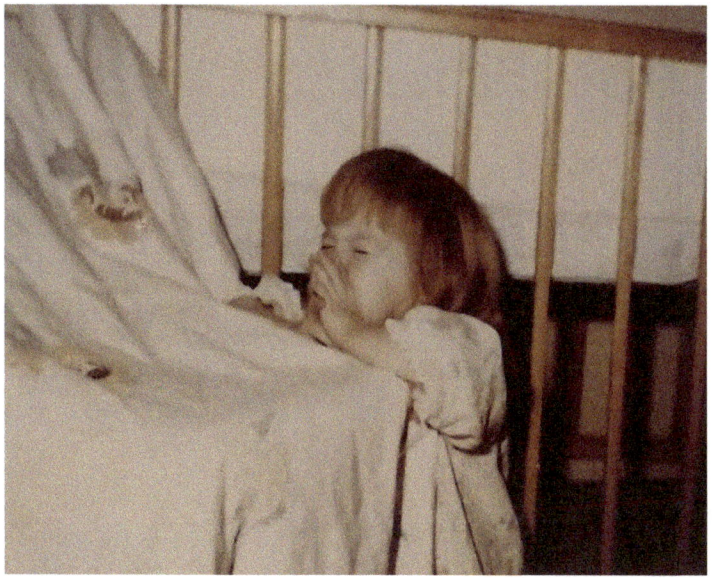

"God, oin't to pay (play) wif (with) me (my) daddy."

Jack left for Vietnam in October 1968—on Jana's birthday—less than three months after we adopted her at almost twenty-one months. We were her third family since birth. Goodbyes were intensely painful and unexplainable to her. How many goodbyes can a child under two years suffer? She wept uncontrollably when he left us in 1968 at SeaTac Airport. Her doctor said Jack's return would be emotionally healing for her—the first person in her life to return. *"We will deal with the aftermath if he does not return. She has to believe he will come back to her."* Jack kept himself alive in her heart in letters with his love notes and sketches of her favorite animals, military vehicles, and Vietnamese bicycles.

Reflections on Jack's Ministry

My thoughts drifted back to the drive. Why did Jack have to battle death instead of me? He spent his entire life serving others. He was still needed! For almost fifty-eight years, I have honored Jack as my special gift from God—my husband, lover, forever best friend, and confidant. His personality was enviable. Regardless of the tension in any room, *Jack was non-pretentious.* People relaxed in his presence.

"Barbara, I love Jack. He's the strongest man I've ever met!" were the words of Jack's doctor—a world-renowned MDS leukemia specialist! Jack never complained of pain. Puzzled, I questioned the doctor. He said, "Barbara, Jack is in terrible pain. He is concerned for you!" Jack was silently suffering so that my pain was lessened! Once a dedicated US Marine, always a US Marine! Others always came first! *Life without Jack would be too difficult to imagine.* His lifelong, effervescent, non-judgmental personality could never be replaced.

Never will I forget when Jack was stationed at Camp Pendleton Marine Corps Base in California. The Marines were on a massive exercise in Twentynine Palms, California. Waiting for him to return home a few days later, I fell asleep.

Awakened by the Holy Spirit, I knew Jack was in trouble. He should have been home by 11 p.m. I prayed. Feeling a need for further prayer, the only place I knew to call after midnight was the Prayer Tower in Tulsa, Oklahoma. Someone answered, and I expressed my concern, "My husband is on military exercises, and I am worried. He should have called me by now. Please pray."

Around 4 a.m., Jack walked through our front door. Except for the whites of his eyes, he was pasted with dust! Immediately, I rushed to him and said, "Jack, what happened?"

As I buried my face in his dusty clothes, he wrapped his strong arms around me and softly said, "Angel, be thankful I came home. We left Twentynine Palms on schedule. While seated in one of the vehicles, a fluid emptied all over me from the ceiling. I ran and informed the pilot. He was aware and was turning the plane to go back. Everyone prepared for a crash landing. All possible emergency vehicles waited on the ground for us! God landed us safely!"

Thank You, Holy Spirit, our omnipresent life choreographer!

The heavenly Father, Jesus Christ, His Son, and the Holy Spirit have spoken to individuals throughout history in thousands of life-threatening situations. God loves you and me! Heaven *unconditionally cares for those you love! Believe it! Be expectant daily! He has your back! Be comforted in the fact that He loves those you love more than you love them!*

On another occasion, I worked for a prestigious law firm in San Francisco. My extraordinary boss offered Jack and me his Tahoe condo for a mini-vacation. In the late afternoon of our first day in Tahoe, a flash picture of our son, Gregory, came into my mind. The picture showed his scooter crashing on a specific stretch of highway. We prayed. When we arrived home the next day, Gregory said, "Well, you guys will never guess what happened to me on the highway yesterday!"

"Did it happen around 5:20–5:30 p.m.?" I asked.

Stunned, he said, "Yes."

Our Father loves our children! Jesus died for them! The Holy Spirit canopies their lives as we pray!

"Gregory. The Holy Spirit prompted us to pray for you. We knew something was wrong. The Holy Spirit knows your whereabouts when we don't know."

He had been on his scooter with a friend. They had crashed as they returned to Pleasanton, California—on the stretch of road I envisioned. They suffered only slight bruises. It could have been so different except for the Holy Spirit, the revelator!

When Jack was in Vietnam with the Marines, the Holy Spirit often prompted me to pray. In Vietnam, helicopters brought in mail quickly and tried to escape harm. On one occasion, Jack and his friend walked to the helicopter to mail letters to their families. Enemy fire opened up on them. Jack's dear friend was killed immediately. Jack said to himself, "Why not me?" Upon reflection of the incident, Jack said, "I realized nobody was going to die before their number was called. In the meantime, we trust God."

As a child, one young daughter informed her father she was worried about dying. Her father reminded her that he only gave her the train ticket before she would get on the train. He told her that our heavenly Father knows when we need our ticket. When the call comes for us to graduate to God's home,

our hearts will be infused by our Father with strength for the journey. *As a follower of Jesus, He will gladly validate our ticket!*

It was in 1975 when the Holy Spirit awakened me around 2 a.m. to pray. Jack and I were living at Camp Pendleton, California. Quietly, I slipped out of bed, entered our living room, and knelt by the sofa. My spirit sensed a problem with a member of my family in Arkansas. The Holy Spirit directed me to Psalm 91:15–16. After I felt at peace about the situation, I returned to bed.

Early the next morning, I received a call from my brother, DeWayne, and his wife, Myrna. DeWayne said, "Barbara, I have called you to pray for me. The doctor told me I needed surgery immediately. The cancer biopsy is extremely bad. Surgery is scheduled."

I said, "DeWayne, the Holy Spirit woke me up last night, and I want to quote the following two verses from Psalm 91:15–16 (KJV), 'He shall call upon me, and I will answer him: I will be with him in trouble; I will deliver him, and honour him. With long life will I satisfy him, and shew him my salvation.'"

Myrna, DeWayne's wife, fasted and prayed until after the surgery. The doctor had said he had little hope for DeWayne. They had two young sons. The aggressive cancer was contained and did not spread. DeWayne is now a grandfather. The work of the Holy Spirit is never ending in a Christian's life. In a world that hurts emotionally, spiritually, and physically, the Holy Spirit desires to be the comforter, the counselor, and the healer. *The Holy Spirit can perfectly reset our life situations!*

A young girl in one of the congregations Jack served had recurring dreams that she would die at twenty-eight. My compassionate husband could not tell her that she would not

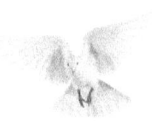

die at twenty-eight. Only God knew the time of her future demise.

Jack took a chalkboard. He drew a line down the center of the board. He titled the two columns "Before Death" and "After Death." He asked what currently worried her. A constant fear was that her father would be killed in Vietnam. Jack wrote her fear in the "Before Death" column. She named all her worries and concerns with tears streaming down her face.

Then Jack said, "Now, let's look at what it will be like for you after death." He transferred each concern from the "Before Death" column to the "After Death" column. For the first fear, he wrote, "There will be no more wars to worry you because you'll be with God." One by one, Jack eradicated all her fears in the "Before Death" column.

She looked at us and said, "Are you saying I'm all worried about going to a place where nothing bad will happen? It's crazy for me to fear going to a place like that!" She began laughing! Her haunting death dreams ceased! Her father, a marine, returned from Vietnam.

Jack said, "Barbara, the Holy Spirit gave me those thoughts. They were not mine." What heavy burdens our children carry! The Father, His Son, Jesus Christ, and the Holy Spirit love our families with everlasting love! *The Holy Spirit has our back!*

Life Without Jack?

Against all odds—on this July 2017 trip—for twenty-five and one-half months, Jack has bravely fought his cancer battle. Friends have admired his courage, especially Colonel (Ret.) Rufus Bowers, Jack's close friend.

Lately, however, he silently changed. He has been extremely weak and slept most of the time—just like now, sitting beside me. Jack's spirit is directed from "a life well-lived" to Heaven— *from mortality to immortality*. His thoughts are seized away from those he loves most—his family—to Heaven, his eternal home. Jack's expressive soft blue eyes reveal a "moving up higher" or "graduating" soon look—*stepping out of time into eternity—to Heaven, God's majestic home!*

Every cell in my body feels the sting of life without him! How long will Jack and I have the same address? "Father, have I passed Your tests?" Tears dripped from my face. Cement-like walls encircled me. Jack has always said that God's shoulders were big enough to manage our emotions toward Him—good and bad. I prayed, "Where are You, God? I feel death's relentless iron-clad grip on Jack! *In our brokenness, is a miracle coming from You?*"

On our drives to Houston, I always harmonized with gospel tapes. On that drive, I felt no music within my soul. My heart burst with pain. Tears blurred the drive as the miles ticked away. Silent, deep sadness from Jack's imminent death crushed my diminished courage, as well as my spiritual and physical strength. Grief, a natural killer, made a determined push for my demise. It was a deadly poison that my heart innocently sipped. Self-pity had to go; my faith needed restoration. Jack needed me desperately—at my best—not drowned in self-pity.

Our fifty-eighth anniversary was imminent. Would Jack be with me? We were grateful for a long and beautiful marriage. Many military marriages received far too few anniversaries. The families of fallen servicemen and women suffer every Father's Day, wedding anniversary, birthday, and holiday. Jack never forgot their sacrifices for our nation. Our days are numbered by God. "Please, God, give us our fifty-eighth anniversary less than one month away!" was my desperate prayer.

Jack completely trusted the sovereignty of God in his crippled, abated body. "Angel, I believe, and I pray the prayer of Jesus, 'Your kingdom come, your will be done' (Matthew 6:10, ESV)." In personal prayer, Jack always paraphrased his prayer, "Your kingdom come; your will be done in my life as it is in Heaven."

My heart cried, "Lord, grant me the trust in You that Jack has steadfastly maintained—regardless of how this uncharted journey ends."

Revisited Memories— Yakutat, Alaska

As the miles ticked off our journey, precious, fresh, and painful memories resurfaced. From January to June 2015, Jack accepted an interim pastorate in Yakutat, Alaska. It was a wintry morning in January 2015 when we arrived. As we stepped into the Yakutat airport, two community leaders met us.

Their first words were, "Pastor Golie, we need you to officiate at the funeral of one of our citizens. We have no minister in the city this week." Jack's introduction to Yakutat.

A few weeks later, ninety-year-old Siguard ("Sig") Edwards's funeral was conducted. Sig was the only remaining soldier from the Territory of Alaska Volunteers who fought in the World War II battle in the Aleutians. He also served in Cuba, Myanmar (Burma), and India. A recipient of distinguished state and national military awards. All Yakutat celebrated Sig's patriotic life with deep love and respect.

After the funeral, the burial ceremony was so cold that Jack couldn't turn the pages of his Bible. A congregant gave him heated gloves to finish the burial service. The funeral introduced Jack to the whole village. They graciously accepted him. He felt privileged to be there for an honorable military hero.

As May approached, the church asked Jack to accept a permanent position. Jack was seventy-eight, and I was less than two years younger. We loved Alaska. Jack especially loved a church filled with ambitious young people. His spirit never knew a birthday! One of his statements, "These wrinkles on my face say I have birthdays! Wrinkles are deceptive! My spirit's forever young! I challenge any of you to a game or two of H-O-R-S-E, ping pong, handball, or horseshoes!"

Jack seriously considered the permanent pastor invitation. After prayer, he said, "Angel, I want this election to be about Jesus Christ—not me. He knows our future. I have prepared a two-page ballot. We are beginning the sunset years of our lives. We want to be in God's perfect will for each remaining day. Like the Marines, we want to die with our boots on—being right where He desires us to be. If there is one negative ballot, I will not accept the position."

Each voting member received a two-page ballot. A one-hundred percent vote without one adverse comment was the result. Jack had asked every question he could think of about our influence and ministry in Yakutat. We both were confident we were where God wanted us to be. Jack excitedly made plans for an active ministry once we returned to Yakutat.

The permanent pastor position became official in June 2015. Jack said, "Angel, you go home two weeks early. Pack what you feel we need to pastor here in Yakutat. In two weeks, I'll drive us back through."

Our excitement level was high. Jack was anxious to grow closer to the members and the community. As their interim pastor, one family generously loaned us a car. As a long-term

pastor, our 2000 Tundra would be boarded on the ferry in Washington State for Yakutat.

When Jack arrived home, the Tundra was packed and ready to leave immediately. Excitedly, I met him at Huntsville airport. He said, "Angel, I cannot kiss you. I have a sore throat." The second sore throat in a month—a critical issue for Jack's doctor. After two days of tests, Jack was diagnosed with MDS leukemia. Jack was told, "Twenty-four-year-old men with your diagnosis die within three to six months." Wow! A curve ball we did not see coming!

"God, did we miss Your will?"

Our Yakutat Goodbye

It was natural for Jack to pray, "Jesus, not my will, but Thine be done was Your prayer. I want Your will, Sovereign Lord. You know what is best for me." Since his tour in Vietnam with the Marines, Jack considered each day a gift from God. It was difficult for me to pray *that* prayer. Life without Jack was not worth living. We refused to permit the diagnosis to overwhelm us. We kept the truck packed for Yakutat. A miracle was expected.

After treatment at the University of Alabama (Kirklin Clinic), we transferred to the MD Anderson Hospital in late August 2015. A new therapy was accepted. When we arrived at MD Anderson in Houston, we planned to continue onward to Alaska.

Sadly, Jack's doctor strongly emphasized that Alaska was no longer in our future. It was a long drive back home—an Alaska-packed truck going east! Slowly, we emptied its contents. *That was one of the many turnarounds in our over twenty-six-month journey. My heart began to expect the unexpected.* For Jack's future, it would be twice monthly treatments in Houston. Approximately 1,440 miles were driven on the shortest trips.

To the amazement of the doctors, Jack's mobility and energy stayed at a moderate level. Eight months later, in December

2015, we flew to Yakutat to say goodbye to the congregation and take our items from the parsonage. We were privileged to enjoy Heidi and Heather Holcomb's beautiful Christmas program for the children in the new church building. The church was almost completed by capable volunteer laborers. It was Jack's joy to have participated. Tok church members also flew to Yakutat and donated time.

My heart was broken as I packed our personal belongings from the parsonage. Jack lay on the sofa and greeted the members who stopped by to say goodbye personally. One of Yakutat's young adults spent one hour with him. The visit emotionally touched Jack. It was difficult as we walked away from what we thought was God's will for us.

Jack's piercing light blue eyes followed my every move as I filled the boxes. They expressed *"what might have been."* Clearly, I remembered his words after the pastoral election, "Angel, I love these people. Will God keep me here for my final years of ministry?" He and I cherished each memory in the closing chapter of Jack's ministry in Yakutat. We loved the hidden village, charming people, physical landscape, and the world-class surfing beach.

One of my favorite memories was shortly after our arrival in Yakutat. Jack said, "Angel, come for a drive with me! I want to show you the future church!" He took me to the ocean beach.

"Jack! I thought the church was to be built near the parsonage?" I said.

Jack laughed, "Oh, it will be, Angel! Look at those gorgeous logs in the bay! Those logs drifted up on their own. God sends us free logs to build the church! Isn't that exciting! Think of

the money every church we've helped to renovate has spent on lumber! God floats free logs to this isolated village! It's a miracle—God floating logs for the needed lumber! He floats logs for their homes! Think what it would cost to ship lumber into this village!"

Lying quietly on the sofa, Jack was silent about any discouragement he may have felt. There were no complaints about pain, his apparent weakness, nor any remarks questioning God's turnaround of what we thought was His plan. His reflections were broken only by Herb and Curt Holcomb's quick stops as they picked up our boxes. Each stop was a fun-filled conversation for Jack. *He desperately needed that!*

To say goodbye to anyone was difficult. The time came too swiftly to leave the parsonage for the last time. We departed from memories of church families at our table, visiting, laughing, children playing around us—even under the table—and Jack teaching two weekly Bible studies. We loved the sweet camaraderie!

Before our farewell at the small airport, we were escorted to Herb and Heidi Holcomb's home. Suddenly, the congregation arrived and gathered around us. They stood Jack and me in the group's center and prayed goodbye prayers. The children gathered closely to Jack. When I felt movement during the prayer, I peeked. Jacquelyn Holcomb, a junior high student, had both arms extended around Jack. As she walked round and round him, she prayed. She and many others wrote to him throughout his illness. Never had we felt more loved by a congregation of people. Everyone prayed for a miracle! *Their encouragement helped us cling to hope.*

We hugged the people at the house who could not go to the airport. At the airport, final goodbyes were said. As the small plane lifted off the ground, the people caught their last glimpse of Jack. The youth waved goodbyes from the airport window. Jack soberly gazed at his last view of them. He sat quietly back in the seat as the plane turned toward Cordova and Anchorage. My heart tried to absorb all the memories of Jack and our unrealized dreams in this tiny coastal Alaskan town. In such a soft and tender moment, *Jack squeezed my hand twice—his usual pattern all our marriage years.* As we absorbed our memories of Yakutat for the last time, *holding hands was easier than talking through our tears.*

Once we arrived in Anchorage, Jack was hospitalized due to extreme weakness. Emotionally and physically, he had silently internalized the final goodbye to the Yakutat church family. Leukemia hit him hard. The doctor said he could not be released until he could fly without expiring in the plane—*another unexpected event.* After three days in the hospital, he was dismissed with orders to fly directly to Houston Airport.

The Yakutat church sent Jack checks throughout his leukemia battle. A few visited us, including Herb and Heidi's son, Caleb. Youth letters encouraged Jack to survive his test of the unexpected chapter of our lives.

On a previous trip to Houston, Velvet Ivers called Jack to remind him that the church continually prayed for him. He had an enjoyable conversation until she stated how much he was missed by the Yakutat church family. Jack quickly concluded the conversation; I looked toward him. Tears flowed down his face. He said nothing more. Going for cancer treatments

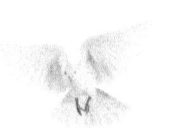

instead of pastoring at Yakutat was God's mystery—"*Not my will, but Thine be done.*"

"Not my will, but Thine be done" prayers were easy for Jack. Not me. Now that he is in Heaven, I have often prayed the prayer. Recently, I asked Clifford Christensen a prayer question my daughter had asked me. His reply:

"We pray not to inform God but to express our love and faith in Him. Jesus prayed that the cup of suffering be removed only if the Father willed it. We pray to express our desires to the Lord while trusting that in every situation, He knows best. Children ask their parents for things they cannot have, not because their parents don't love them, but because they know what is best for them. Jesus is our best friend, and it is right that we be honest with Him. He always loves us with perfect love."

Crushed Dreams

MDS leukemia had waged its war against Jack's body for over twenty-five months. His longevity was lauded at doctor's conferences worldwide. They were stunned by his lengthy and relentless battle. "Father God, what is Your plan for Jack? Heaven?" Sadly, my prayers were mostly to get God to do what I wanted Him to do! By comparison, Jack's prayers were aligned with God's will and plan for his life!

When I asked Jack why I was healed, he said, "Angel, I couldn't have gone through this without you!" Hearing him say he needed me as he fought life's final battle with pain touched me deeply. Brave-hearted Jack had never emotionally removed his Marine combat boots!

The Bible verses most commonly quoted for those who need healing are Matthew 21:22, John 15:7, and 1 John 5:14–15. Prayer is unlimited in scope. However, those powerful verses have specific *three-fold* conditions: *first*, faith (belief); *second*, according to God's Word; and *third*, according to God's will.

In a letter after our 1959 engagement, my precious and saintly mother-in-law-to-be wrote, "Jack's never still. He's had 'ants in his pants' since he was born. Each non-school morning, he walked outside our Whitefish, Montana, home. Suddenly,

all the neighborhood children joined in on ventures with Jack! A dozen boys went to the lake, the city dump, snow sledding, and fishing. Jack was born on the move! My kitchen filled unexpectedly with boys! Understand you'll never have a dull moment after you marry Jack!"

How right she was! We lived in thirteen states plus Bermuda! No dull moments in our life and marriage! His parents visited us in every location for as long as they lived.

Mother Golie would be aghast at her son's silence and weight of fewer than 130 pounds. At four years of age, Jack had driven their car off the golf course hill in Havre, Montana. He couldn't reach the gas pedal or brakes! He couldn't see through the windshield! Her same son, whose energy had never diminished, had become extremely tired and silent.

The favorite story of Jack's parents was when he, a ten-year-old, and his brother, Sid, brought their "treasure-filled" wagon from the Whitefish city dump. Disgusted, Dad poured the junk into the living room's potbellied stove. Jack tried to tell him that some of their "good stuff" was dangerous! He had found something special he wanted to give to Dad. Dad was too tired of their dump junk to listen! Jack and Sid quickly ran to the barn. After a loud boom, they returned to the house to check on their parents. The lid of the stove had blown off! Dad Golie removed his belt because they had not told him of the dangerous shell! To Jack's surprise, Mother Golie, a submissive wife, stepped between them and said, "No, Art! He tried to tell you! You wouldn't listen!"

If she could observe her son now, Mother Golie would brokenheartedly agree with me that God was saying, "Jack, I want

you to come home. Heaven is where you now belong." *Jack's angel escorts were prepared to descend. How much longer would he be with me?*

Jack's First Tour
in the Navy

Jack was at the ice skating rink, a high school graduate at seventeen years old. His friend said, "Jack, why not go with me to Missoula tomorrow and join the Navy?"

Jack's response, "Why not?"

Jack returned home and knocked on his parents' bedroom door, "Dad and Mother, I'm joining the Navy tomorrow!"

Simultaneously, they sat up in bed! Who is this son we raised? They were still in shock the next day after the Great Northern granted him a leave of absence, and he drove away with the recruiter! The recruiter promised him a corpsman position, but after testing, the Navy said that they needed him as a radarman.

Jack left family, friends, the railroad, his Tri-Valley Ice-Skating Championship, and six years of Tri-Valley Boxing to join the Navy. He said, "It was one of the quickest and best decisions of my life!"

After training at Treasure Island, Jack served on the USS Badoeng Strait ("Bing Ding"), one of the lead ships at one of the Eniwetok detonations. The Bing Ding remained longer than other ships in the operation. Jack was among the few who witnessed an incredible event—a hydrogen bomb explosion. He was in awe of its magnitude!

Jack—Nineteen Years

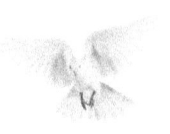

Jack Loved People and Life

After finishing his enlistment, Jack completed college and seminary. He was then commissioned into the Navy chaplaincy. After retirement from the military, Jack stayed active in church ministry in California, Montana, and Alaska. In 1997, he completed his Doctor of Ministry (Dmin) degree from Fuller Theological Seminary, Pasadena, California. He loved "mining" the richness of Scripture in Greek and Hebrew. Educational degrees did not awe him. He rarely mentioned any title. When he was asked what he would like to be called, he always said, "My name is Jack. You may call me Jack, Pastor Jack, or Chaplain Jack."

Colonel Rufus Bower, USMC (Ret.), said of Jack, "He was a 'Navy man,' but a 'Marine's Marine.' Physically and spiritually, he was always at the right place and at the right time. Other than Jesus, no better friend. Jack spent the dash between his years well. Never have I seen a man who was more like Jesus Christ."

At his funeral, Reverend Robert Angles reminded us that "Jack was a minister who served with a towel, not a title." Jack always affirmed, "Extensive education, prestigious doctorates,

or military rank cannot impress or satisfy a soul's search for God. Only the Holy Spirit—the wind, the breath, the Spirit of God Himself! His Cross (not my will, but Thine be done) must be active in our lives to be used by Him. When we see individuals as God sees them, they will know that God loves them and that we love them."

In Bible Studies, Jack often said, "We want every person to know that God is who He says He is; He will do what His Word says He will do—regardless of the circumstances in our lives!"

After military retirement, Jack remained active in the ministry and in sports! He loved basketball, handball, and tennis. As he grew older, he would usually be chosen last on his first visit. After two or three games, he was among the first three chosen. The team loved his friendship. When the players used God's name as a curse word, Jack calmly said, "Why are you blaming Him? You did that foul all by yourself!" They called him "bro" (brother)—permitting Jack to introduce them to their best friend—Jesus Christ.

On one occasion, Jack's nose was broken in a basketball game. After a long wait at the doctor's office, he attempted to straighten it himself. On his way to another game, I said, "You must get your nose straightened."

With a burst of laughter, he flirtatiously said, "Angel, I straightened it! What you see is what you get—a bit crooked! I'm no longer your handsome husband?"

Exiting the car to return to my San Francisco office, I looked upward and said, "Okay, God, did You hear that?" Still laughing, Jack heard me. When he returned from the game, his nose was perfectly straight! Shocked, I said, "What happened?"

Jack said, "Well, God must have heard your prayer! The first hit I received was an elbow to my nose! I went into the men's room and discovered it was straight!" He recited that story dozens of times! *A rare ability to laugh at himself!*

A medical mystery was how Jack was highly active and athletic, yet his white blood count dropped unacceptably low over the years. *Medical doctors advised him to go to the emergency room immediately with a sore throat or cold to prevent pneumonia. We did that repeatedly.*

Communion on Our Knees

Two weeks after Jack's diagnosis in June 2015, we attended the Redstone Arsenal Chapel in Huntsville, Alabama. When communion was served, the congregation could kneel at the altar or receive communion seated. Jack said, "Let's go to the altar, Angel." Along with several others, we received communion on our knees. Jack silently prayed at the altar until the last ones were served. Together, we returned to the pew.

Jack took my hand as we left the church and said, "Angel, the Lord spoke to me during our communion at the altar." Jack had never been more serious. We both stopped walking; Jack held my hands. While we stood alone on the hill above the Redstone Arsenal Chapel, my husband, a humble servant of God—who had requested to pastor only struggling churches—looked at me and said, "He told me to understand that my broken body is a representation of what His church is like to Him—*broken*." My heart ached as he mournfully spoke the truth from his heart.

"Shut-Mouth" Conversations

My thoughts snapped back to the drive. So many turnarounds in the twenty-five-plus months we had fought leukemia. With my eyes on Interstate 20, I said, "God, will there be a fifty-eighth anniversary? I am not ready for You to take Jack. He is not a burden to me! Life would not be life without him! Christians have prayed each day for Jack. Time is no longer a friend. His body has wasted away. Are You going to heal him or take him, Lord?"

Tears flooded my face as we continued the long, straight stretch of Highway 20. Jack awakened. Shocked at my tears, he looked at me and said, "Angel, what is wrong?"

Immediately, I blurted, "What is wrong? You don't know? I thought God would heal you! You have lived twenty-five and one-half months since your diagnosis. Twenty-four-year-old men die within three to six months. You have lived longer than anyone before you! However, the miracle has not yet occurred, Jack. Please do not ask me if I count this all joy because I do not count this all joy!"

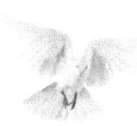

Jack understood my broken heart. Slowly, he turned his head and looked straight ahead. After a long pause, he quietly said, "Angel, do you know what I don't understand?"

In a mumbled response, I said, "What do you not understand?"

Jack was silent for a few moments. In a broken voice, he said, "I can't understand why He loves me so much!"

Ouch! Jack looked death straight in the face with sincere gratefulness. He was willing to accept all the chipping, buffing, and sanding he needed in preparation for his final "well done" from Jesus. Death held no grip—no victory over his faith and confidence in God! He would be released to God's home and be free of leukemia! The complaints came from me! Since the beginning of his illness, Jack reminded me that God was sovereign and Jesus had taught us to pray, "Thy kingdom come. Thy will be done" (Matthew 6:10, KJV). Yes, this earth is only the womb of Heaven—*a preparation place*—a *cocoon* we all live in until we are called to live forever in Heaven! *Can we call this world our nine-month residence?* Why do we laboriously *strive* to be so comfortable here? Even Abraham kept looking for that city whose builder and maker was God! *Yes, Barbara, focus on the enduring riches; this life is extra-temporary!*

My Arkansas hillbilly heritage described a powerfully effective direct response that caused all talk to cease as "shut mouth." Jack's grateful statement—filled with faith and confidence in God—gave me an instant "shut mouth." He never complained; he never blamed God. "Father, as Jack's wife, what is Your message to me? May I not miss, ignore, or fail the lessons. Father, I am broken. Please teach me tenderly how to plow *Through My Valley of Why.*"

"Angel, Let's Learn from This Experience!"

Jack always taught that Heaven would be the most creative place imaginable! He once said, "Married couples worry about intimacy in Heaven. When will we realize that God never gives any of His children a diminished exchange? In Heaven, we have glorified bodies! We cannot imagine Heaven's majesty! We will know as we are known. You will be known as Barbara and as my wife, Mrs. Jack K. Golie!"

Since his diagnosis, Jack said, "Angel, we want to receive all from this experience that God intends. We do not want to ignore the lessons God planned for us." *Jack knew strength was not born in weakness!* Tenacious faith encountered the bitter waters of Marah and moved on! Faith boldly combats the life-threatening stormy winds and waters of our Lake Gennesaret—Jack's leukemia! Saint Paul declared, "Where, O death, is your victory? Where, O death, is your sting?" (1 Corinthians 15:55, NIV).

As Jack grew weaker, I watched his faith surge! He was no longer thinking of physical healing for his body. He was "enduring to the end" (Matthew 24:13, KJV), waiting for his eternal reward. We took communion together daily. I served the wafer; he served the communion juice. As his illness progressed—

never knowing when it would be our last communion—I could no longer do my part without breaking into tears. On one occasion, Jack said, "Angel, it is quite difficult for you to count this all joy, isn't it?"

I quickly responded, "Jack, I do not count this all joy!" Through my tears, I said, "Do you?"

"Not perfectly, but almost always. Someday you will too, my darling," he said.

The Holy Spirit's presence filled the room. Another teachable moment for me. The precious Holy Spirit—the Spirit of truth—the Spirit of holiness! The comforter—the paraclete—the one who comes alongside us—when we desperately need Him! I needed Him—desperately!

During one of the times Jack served communion, his face transformed into a heavenly radiance as he prayed over the communion juice for the seven people in the room. Jana, our daughter, also witnessed the marked radiance in his appearance. It was a never-to-be-forgotten experience! *A sacred, holy moment we never wanted to end.*

Suddenly, Jackson, Mississippi, came into my view! We always stopped at the Baskin-Robbins on the many trips to and from MD Anderson Hospital. Jack never turned down his favorite black cherry milkshake—one of the few food choices he always consumed. The energy in the milkshake usually kept him awake for twenty minutes. The medical team encouraged me to give him whatever he desired to eat. He needed energy to live. Lately, his food intake has been feeble.

We continued our drive on Interstate 20 and eagerly anticipated a restful stay at Barksdale Air Force Base in Shreveport, Louisiana. Barksdale was an overnight stay where I did not

have to disinfect the room before Jack entered—doorknobs, TV clickers, toilets, showers, headboards, chair arms, and tables. We packed our disinfectants, linens, pillows, and blankets for other hotels. Jack's feet never touched the carpet. His immunity was dangerously low.

The Air Force Runner

At 5:05 p.m., we finally reached Barksdale Air Force Base. For wheelchair access and overnight parking, we parked at the back of the building. Immediately, I lifted his wheelchair from the Tundra. In his weakness, Jack found it too difficult to help me maneuver him into the wheelchair. He slowly slid down on the cement with both his legs in an excruciating position. My arms filled with goose pimples from his awkward position. Quickly, I tried to pick him up—without success—my biggest fear in our travels. Jack said, "Angel, you cannot lift me! Get help!"

Quickly, I ran and knocked on two doors—locked! In a nearby park, I saw a couple. They could not hear my call for help or understand my wild emotions. As I ran back to Jack, between sobs, I cried, "God, I need Your help right now, please. Give me the strength to lift Jack!" Suddenly, around the back corner of the building, a tall, handsome, strong serviceman appeared doing his daily run!

"Please," I said through my tears, "please, lift my husband for me!"

He slowed down, quickly picked up Jack, and sat him in his wheelchair. He stamped himself in my memory, but I failed

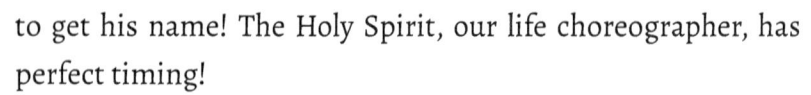

to get his name! The Holy Spirit, our life choreographer, has perfect timing!

On every medical trip, the Holy Spirit was our faithful choreographer! He positioned strangers in our lives at precisely the needed moment! What a friend and helper! Our 2000 Tundra—Jack's most comfortable ride—never broke down! My heart cried, "Holy Spirit, why do I fear when You have never failed us?"

A Servant Heart

Years ago, I vividly recalled asking Jack what he wanted to hear Jesus say to him upon his arrival in Heaven. His quick answer, "I want to hear only five words: 'Jack, you have been faithful.'"

The Holy Spirit revealed the Father's love to Jack. In turn, Jack loved the people. Jana had once commented to me, "Mother, I visualize the Holy Spirit as the looking glasses of God and Jesus!" How right she was! The Holy Spirit is the administrator for the Father and the Son in this world. He is the member of Trinity that we all meet first! Yes, He is the person who first tugs at our hearts to accept Jesus Christ!

Jack often said, "The ground is level at the foot of the cross. Nobody sits on a stump!" There was no one that he would not reach out to—he saw in them what they failed to see in themselves—the image of God! Regardless of hygiene, status in life, or how they responded to him, they were created in God's image. Jesus Christ had died for them! He wanted to see them dare to dream and see the potential God had placed inside them. Jack believed every person with whom our lives intersected had a divine purpose! Obstacles could become stepping stones to God and life turnarounds!

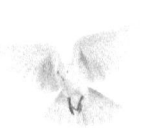

Jack said, "How can I tell anyone that God loves them if I do not love them? If I do not show love to the person for whom Jesus loved and died, how does that make Jesus feel about me? If I do not love others, I am not His true disciple. Jesus said that others would know we were His disciples by one simple test— that we love one another (John 13:34–35, NIV)! That is walking our talk! No other alternative! His commandment! What do we show if we do not love one another? Love cannot be negotiated! Jesus set the parameters for love!"

In college, Jack volunteered in downtown missions of various cities. In Seattle, he drove me to a couple's dirt-floor shack. They had a yellow tiger cat for company. They had chest colds. Jack gave them groceries and got an agency to help them. He had been a professional boxer until his strength was gone. As I gave her a Christmas gift, with tears, she said, "This is the first Christmas my niece, Barbara, has forgotten me. God sent me another Barbara!" *Only the Holy Spirit can choreograph such a heartwarming, predestined moment.*

Another couple Jack took me to meet lived in a dumpy hotel near the downtown mission. They had a newborn baby. Their only food was from the mission. The man was a cook. They had moved from California to Seattle and fell upon challenging times. We gave them groceries and food for the baby. Jack helped the husband find a job as a cook. The couple soon became self-sufficient and volunteered their time and talents in the mission. Their setbacks did not destroy them because the Holy Spirit used someone to thread a strand of love that opened a path forward for them! (Jack called it Holy Spirit net fishing.)

Jesus also said, "My command is this: Love each other as I have loved you" (John 15:12, NIV). Jesus' non-compromising,

riveting command challenges all Christians! There are untold opportunities for us to love others as Jesus commands. We are left without excuses! Jesus—knowing our hearts—precisely warned us about only loving the people who loved us! See Luke 6:32–36 (NIV). *That's an awesome warning.*

Because Jack cared for people, they relaxed in his presence. He never broadcasted his profession nor exhibited a "holier than thou" attitude. Yet, everyone seemed to weave "What do you do?" or "What is your profession?" into a conversation with him. In 1964, I remember a nursing instructor in Boston was overcome with grief over her mother's death. She said, "Barbara, I met your husband and felt so relaxed in his presence." The Holy Spirit orchestrates opportunities. *It is not how much of the Holy Spirit we have. It is how much the Holy Spirit has of us!*

Even as I author this book, our daughter's former manager in Alaska called her. He was deeply saddened over the death of a friend. As he remembered the death of Jack, he said, "Remember when you introduced your dad to me at breakfast? I can't explain my feelings when your dad hugged me goodbye." That encounter happened in December 2016, eight months before Jack's death. Jack's inner peace and warmth were contagious throughout his bout with leukemia. *When we love as Jesus loved, the Holy Spirit can reach others through us!*

The Holy Spirit was the silent leading character in the following stories. These events occurred in the ordinary schedule of Jack's daily life as he battled MDS leukemia. He could have excused himself as too tired. He never thought of himself first. He knew his time was short. He told me, "As long as we both have breath, we can be used by God. Let's keep our Marine boots on! Angel, you and I will never take our boots off!"

The following stories illustrate how the Holy Spirit touches the lives of others even as his body was wasting away with leukemia. As an executor and administrator, the Holy Spirit purposely choreographs our schedules and interactions to bring us closer to Jesus. There is one caveat—we must have our hearts tuned in to listen to His voice. Be inspired! Be encouraged! Be expectant! *Through your valley of why*, the Holy Spirit has your back!

Our Special Pharmacist

My heart has often reflected on the lives Jack touched at the MD Anderson Hospital. One of the principal pharmacists was so gracious. When three of Jack's vertebrates broke, he came to Jack's room and encouraged us to call his personal phone at the hospital, while traveling, or when he was home. His cordialness was shocking!

One day, he told me, "Barbara, you and Jack got something beautiful in your marriage. I would love to be married if I could find a companion to create a marriage like yours. You two have something special." In the loneliness of our suffering, his words to our weary hearts were like "apples of gold in pictures of silver" (Proverbs 25:11, KJV). Yes, God had gifted us with a beautiful marriage—one I did not want to lose!

Our marriage was beautiful. We both tried to keep it that way. Mothers can get too busy. One evening after work, I had Jana on the piano and Gregory on the guitar. Dinner was being cooked. Jack was talking to me as I whizzed by him. I did not bother to stop or make conversation. He said, "Barbara, you are too good of a person to act like that!" His was a correction with such loving, affirming words I have never forgotten!

Jack had accepted that if his health did not improve, God would lift him out of time into eternity. Lovingly, it was as though God had whispered to my husband, "Jack, this earth is not your final residence. It is only the womb of Heaven. You have reached maturity; you will soon exit this world for your eternal home. I'll give you a few more days with your family." *Our special pharmacist was the Holy Spirit's thread of love to validate and lift my weakened wings.*

Jack's Hour with the Doctor

In the spring of 2017, they checked to see if the leukemia had gone into Jack's spine. They were concerned it could go to his brain. When the doctor entered the room, I said, "This is one time I must leave the room. This is too much for me to watch!" She understood and told me to return in an hour.

As I walked back into the room, Jack said, "Barbara, please tell the doctor about your healing from cancer."

Shocked, I said, "You want to hear, doctor?"

"Yes, please tell me." After communicating my miracle story, she thanked me and went on to her next patient. Jack had not expected to see her again.

Gracefully, she entered Jack's room the following morning before reporting for work. "Jack, thank you for our conversation yesterday. Last night I had all my family in my home. I told them everything that you said to me yesterday. Thank you for answering my questions. I understand everything so much better now."

Jack's words thundered in my memory, *"Barbara, we never take our boots off until God calls us home!"*

The Graduating Nurse

The Holy Spirit continually guided Jack's conversations and interactions at MD Anderson Hospital. One by one, the Holy Spirit sent individuals to his room. It was a divine orchestration when a student nurse entered his room one morning. I witnessed the following conversation.

"Jack, what have you done as a profession?" she asked.

Jack said, "For several years, I have pastored small churches in Alaska that faced challenges. When I was seventeen, I entered the Navy as a radarman. After four years, I left the Navy, attended college, married Barbara, and went to seminary. I returned to the Navy as a chaplain. During the chaplaincy years, my career was quite evenly divided between the Navy and the Marines. The military has been a major part of my life. No complaints. Barbara and I have enjoyed a wonderful life."

Without any coercion on Jack's part, she immediately began to ask him questions about the problems she faced. She shared that her parents had moved to Houston to live with her and her children until she completed her nursing training.

Jack answered all her heartfelt questions. He then asked her permission to pray for her. He always prayed simple, uncomplicated prayers—childlike familiarity with God. He

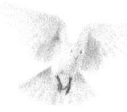

prayed a loving prayer for her career, children, and parents. Disappointment had presented her with challenges.

She said, "Jack, this is amazing! My last hour of school was with you!" *Her face glowed with peace and a dogged determination to enable her broken heart to go forward!*

Perfect Timing

It was April 2016 when Jack became extremely ill while at the hospital. One of our most prolonged stays in the hospital—twenty days. Jack could not stand while having his blood pressure taken without a backward fall on the bed. His legs and arms were swollen to twice their normal size. His condition baffled the doctors. There were whispers that his time had come to depart. His six months of projected longevity had ended in December 2015.

A couple of cardiologists walked into the room. They said, "Jack, you have got to have a pacemaker inserted into your chest."

Jack answered, "If my arms swell twice their normal size from a simple PICC inserted into them, what would a pacemaker do to my chest? No. I respectfully refuse a pacemaker. For my entire life, doctors have told me that I have the heart of a twenty-four-year-old."

The experienced doctors were not too happy with him, but they understood his rationalization. As they left the room, the senior doctor said, "Okay, Jack, be aware, you will not leave this hospital until you can walk around this nursing ward twice on your own."

Jack looked inquisitively at me and said, "Angel, I do not want the pacemaker! How can I manage pacemaker surgery with my legs and arms swollen twice their size? How do you feel about the situation?"

With a boldness that was not me, I said, "Jack, we must rely totally on God. We will not call anyone for special prayer; we will talk to God. He will talk to specific people to pray." We took communion and prayed. We agreed that we would wait for God to move in His unique way.

The next day, Jack was the same—swollen terribly! The largest compression socks on his legs caused the skin to break in seven places. One night remained before the heart doctor returned to address the pacemaker.

Morning came; Jack's legs were the same. The therapist came to the room. Later, the nurse arrived, "Are you going to stand for us today, Jack?" At that moment, Jack's phone rang. With hesitation, I answered it, though I wanted to wait and see if Jack stood.

A lady was on the phone, "Hello! My name is Mary (alternative name), and I am calling from Florida. I want to pray for Jack Golie right now." She spoke with urgency.

As I left Jack's room, I said, "Mary, if Jack ever needed prayer, he desperately needs it now." (Approximately five weeks before, I had submitted a prayer request for Jack's healing to their prayer center.) Mary prayed for three minutes, talked to me for a couple of minutes, and then asked me if she could pray one more time. After the prayer, I returned to Jack's room.

To everyone's surprise, the senior cardiologist walked into the room behind me. Both of us were shocked at what we saw!

Jack stood alone! He independently checked his own blood pressure and said, "Nurse, are you sure this works correctly? You said this was a new one!"

The doctor looked at me and asked, "What's happening here?"

I said, "I just arrived too! Why don't you ask the nurse?"

The doctor asked, "Nurse, what's going on here?"

The nurse responded, "Doctor, I don't understand this! He fainted backward yesterday. Today, I have taken his blood pressure three times. He stood one minute between each pressure measurement! He's been standing the entire time! His blood pressure is 110/90!"

The doctor looked at me, stroked his chin, and said, "Incredible! Incredible!" He was the doctor who had told Jack he would be given a pacemaker if he didn't stand. They all left the room.

Jack gave me an astonished look, and I said, "Would you like to know what happened?" He was amazed at Mary's phone call and prayer. Mary's prayer started when Jack stood. The third blood pressure test finished when I returned to his room. Jack did not feel faint, though it was the first time he had stood in many days. The blood pressure scenario took six minutes—the approximate time Mary prayed.

Imagine the precise choreography of the Holy Spirit when He lifted Jack out of his hospital bed that April morning of 2016! Mary—a lady we did not know—called from Florida! She was in the office for four hours each week. They were not always the same—*her volunteer hours were based on whether she received a ride to the Prayer Center! The Holy Spirit orchestrated the entire scenario!* As if on cue, the doctor saw Jack on his feet after he finished

three blood pressure tests within six minutes! Who—other than the Holy Spirit—the "wind" of God—could have timed such amazing choreography?

In a hospital room at MD Anderson—located in front of the nurses' station—the Holy Spirit physically restored Jack's strength and stability! He used different people in several states. No one knew the timing of the blood pressure evaluation or Mary's call. As the grand finale, the Holy Spirit brought the senior cardiologist from his upstairs office to Jack's room at that specific moment to witness the result of three blood pressure tests! The same cardiologist who had told Jack he would not leave the hospital until he could walk around the nursing area twice unassisted! *The Holy Spirit has perfect timing!*

Only the Holy Spirit—the helper—the Spirit of truth—can execute such choreography! His presence in our lives is not limited to time, people, or places. The Holy Spirit can be everywhere at once! Jesus' ministry was geographically limited, but the Holy Spirit can be everywhere simultaneously. That is why Jesus said it was expedient for Him to leave for Heaven so the Holy Spirit could descend from Heaven and live inside us! (See John 14:16–18, NIV.)

We stayed one more night at MD Anderson Hospital in April 2016. Jack walked around the entire ward twice without assistance! He drove most of the 700-mile trip back home. Jack called the pastor of the Spanish Church, Selby DeLeon, as he had invited him to speak at the Spanish Church the next morning! *Seated in a chair, he focused only on Christ. He did not mention his prior twenty days!*

Monday, his arms and legs were almost normal. Unbelievable recovery! The Holy Spirit, this world's resident representative

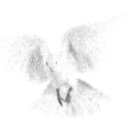

for the Trinity, orchestrated everything in detail! The Holy Spirit's ministry is limitless! *He immerses us in Jesus.* There is no competition with the three persons of the Trinity!

Jack and I felt sure this miracle was the one we had prayed for—happening ten months after the doctors had diagnosed his leukemia. Not all storms destroy us. Some clear our path! *We were refreshed to be on cloud nine, if only for a limited time.*

It would be great to tell you that my husband was healed! He experienced a "life-extension miracle." Jack was not to have lived past three to six months after his diagnosis. He kept faithful each day to God. He studied the Scriptures at least twenty hours per week, enjoyed weekly Bible studies with Tim, preached as often as he was home on Sundays, and encouraged his family. *When Christians hinted that Jack's faith needed to be stronger or that he should pray harder for healing, he took no offense.*

One day, Jack said, "Angel, why is it that Christians always talk about the beauty of Heaven, but nobody wants to leave? It is God's will for us to go there! Do we not believe what we say? Do we not believe that our heavenly Father has a perfect plan for us in Heaven?" The Holy Spirit, our life choreographer, has planned our entire life! See Jeremiah 1:5 (NIV). *The creator of the universe has planned our eternity! Imagine!*

Jack loved one-on-one ministry more than standing in front of a congregation. Servicemen who had ministered with him did not forget him in his illness.

Ken Jaeger, an Indiana and Texas friend, physically and musically supported the religious services aboard the ship. Wherever they live, Ken and Pam, his wife, serve Christ. Jack never made phone conversations about himself. When

Ken called to speak to Jack again—and heard that he was in Heaven—he broke into tears.

John Whitson of Hawaii experienced a spiritual transformation while on the DESRON 35 cruise. Since his conversion in December 1978, John has faithfully served Christ. He and Jessie, his wife, have sacrificially and consistently assisted ministries in Hawaii for decades. Commitment!

Chase Musick, a serviceman from Montana, met Jack in Tok, Alaska. Jack was Stacey's pastor for years. He performed their marriage ceremony. Now an Army chaplain, Chase was Jack's last visitor before he entered the hospital for the last time. A *"Little Jack Musick"* now resides in their home.

Jack did not grieve over the negatives of his illness. His attitude was thankfulness. His words still resound in my memory, "Angel, isn't it amazing? God took two dumb kids who loved Him—you and me—and used us to bless a few people."

Goodbye to Our Church Family in Tok, Alaska

In August 2016, Jack was beating the odds. His life extension miracle in April 2016—ten months after his diagnosis—gave me an expectancy. We flew to Alaska to pick up our daughter's car. After arriving in Anchorage, we drove to Tok, Alaska, as we exited the state. Jack preached his last sermon there on Sunday morning. As he spoke to the congregation we had grown to love as our family, his final sermon was, "Finish Your Race Well."

He taught a Bible study on Sunday evening and said final goodbyes. It was not an easy goodbye for him. He treasured everyone's comments. His face and eyes were swollen; his spirit was undaunted. At 3 a.m., Monday morning, he made his final drive out of Alaska.

The love of the Tok congregation deeply touched Jack. He was their pastor for almost ten years—a congregation we both dearly loved. The Tok congregation individually dug deep wells of love in our hearts. Without any solicitation on our part, the Tok and Yakutat churches sent love offerings that assisted with heavy medical and travel expenses.

As I am editing this book today, it is Jack and my sixty-fourth wedding anniversary. It helped ease the pain when I

spoke recently with two of our Tok friends, Chuck and Juliet Churchill. We both shed tears when he spoke of Jack. Chuck, an Alaskan native, said, "You will never know how much I miss that guy! I could ask him questions, and he would never get defensive. He made Bible study fun when we answered the questions. I loved his remarks like, 'That dog won't hunt!' or 'That dog's not going to lift his head!'"

In a separate conversation, Juliet said, "He was so patient with me. He was like a father! He always said, 'Juliet, let's go over this again. I want to make sure you understand.' He was the first minister to invite us to lunch or dinner. We couldn't believe it!"

Their story was so like Jack! It made him feel close to me. It was not just another day of the week. It was our wedding anniversary! We were miles apart! He was in Heaven; I was in Virginia!

Then I secretly said, "Father, I'm here today. Jack is with You! We have no communication whatsoever! Could You let me know that this day in my life is still unique and special? You took Jack from me. Please show me that You care about my wedding anniversary!"

After a few hours, Jana, my daughter, called me from downstairs and said, "Mother, you received a gift! It is on the table!" A few weeks before, Jana and I had crossed the street and welcomed our new neighbors, Jesse and Beth Paule. On August 7, 2023, Jesse, a fantastic gardener, and Beth, his wife, felt it in their hearts to purchase me a beautiful tall orchid in my favorite color. When? On my sixty-fourth wedding anniversary!

My thank you card said, "You did not know today was my wedding anniversary. The Holy Spirit knew and used your kind hearts to show He cared."

With tears in his eyes, Jesse came to my porch and said, "It is hard to believe the Holy Spirit used us! We had no idea!" The Holy Spirit, the administrator for the Trinity! He used *"listening hearts"*—Jesse and Beth!

Goodbye to Sid— Jack's Brother

We drove from Alaska through Canada and visited Jack's brother in Whitefish, Montana. Both knew Jack was weak, but they did not know that Sid, his only brother, would leave before Jack. During the visit, we shared love and special memories of the past. Before saying goodnight, we prayed with Sid and his invalid wife, Barbara Jane. A stroke had disabled her for eight years. She and I prayed together three times before we separated. She must have sensed that we would never meet again. As she gripped my hands in tears, I told her how I wished I could take her disability and pain from her to give her a much-needed rest. It was an unforgettable visit. *We did not know we would never see them again.*

Jack was deeply saddened when Sid died suddenly on December 1, 2016. Jack and Sid had always been remarkably close, especially as children. Due to a weakened body and plane connections, Jack could not attend the funeral. He wrote Sid's eulogy. He had previously called Sid at least once each week. Sadly, he removed Sid's name from his phone because he instinctively called his number. *Jack was the only surviving member of his original family.*

Jack's favorite story of him and Sid involved three junior high bullies. Jack heard they planned to attack him on the viaduct as he walked home from school. He gathered about twenty young friends to ward off the younger two of the three bullies. Jack was going to fight the oldest one. When they began their march over the viaduct, the bullies stepped out from hiding. As Jack approached them, he realized the noise behind him had subsided. Only Sid, his brother, remained with him. Jack said, "Sid, I don't want them to hurt you. Go with the others."

Sid said, "No, Jack. I won't leave you! *You're my brother!*" Jack begged him to go with the others. Sid refused.

Jack said, "Sid, cover your head with your arms and run as fast as possible! I will try and keep them away from you!"

Jack never forgot Sid's moving remark. After that day on the Whitefish viaduct, the bullying ceased.

For his remaining months, Jack missed Sid terribly and longed to see him in Heaven. Sadly, in October 2018, Sid's lovely wife, Barbara Jane, also passed. Dad and Mom Golie's family are together again.

Goodbye to Joe— Pennsylvania Trip

Thanksgiving 2016, we were in Houston. On that specific trip, Jack asked his doctor, "What is your current diagnosis for me?"

His outstanding doctor touched Jack's knee and said, "Jack, you should have been gone last April." His doctor was visibly moved.

In stunned silence, I walked out with Jack. It would have been good to hear that his health had improved because Jack was supposed to have died within three to six months after his diagnosis. It had now been eighteen months. The doctor was right! Jack was dying in April of 2016, but God had extended his life. We both knew in April that because of a stranger's prayer call, he did not die—his life was extended. As we quietly walked, my heart cried, "Okay, God, is the life extension almost over?" Jack had already broken the records and become the topic of conference discussions.

Jack seemed to be reading my thoughts. He reached for my hand and said, "Doesn't sound so great, does it, Angel?"

Choking back the tears, I said, "No, Jack, it doesn't."

Jack was kept in the hospital for five days. Joe Hicks, Jack's college and seminary friend, called him, "Jack, I would like to see you again. The doctors tell me that I will soon leave for Heaven. Could you and Barbara come to Pennsylvania and visit Wanda and me?" How could Jack refuse the request of his life-long friend?

We arrived back in Decatur, Alabama, on November 30th. Jack said, "Angel, keep enough of our clothes in the suitcases to leave for Pennsylvania tomorrow morning. We need to get a good night's sleep." Jack's eyes were puffy; his face was swollen. He was pushing his strength to its limit.

I asked, "Are you confident we should make this trip?"

He replied, "Joe's last request of me—I wouldn't think of not going!" Yes, I should have remembered. Jack would never take off those Marine boots! Necessary clothes and his medical PICC needs were packed—a daily routine.

"God, why can't I move on from the bitter waters of Marah? Jack keeps a direct focus on the promised land! I stop too long at the Marah's bitter waters and rehearse the pain with You." (See Exodus 15:23–24, NIV.)

In 2 Samuel 24:24 (NIV), when offered the thrashing floor for free, David said, "No, I insist on paying for it. I will not sacrifice to the Lord my God burnt offerings that cost me nothing." A final goodbye to Joe, who wanted to see him again, was a small sacrifice—a nothing burger—to Jack. Five days in the hospital, a swollen face, a medical PICC in his arm, puffy eyes, a charged-up credit card, and a diagnosis of impending death are nothing compared to the love of a friend dying within a few days.

We left early Thursday morning for Mt. Morris, Pennsylvania. Jack drove half of the trip. On Sunday, our last day, Joe, Wanda,

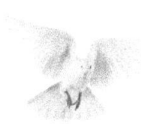

Jack, and I celebrated Joe's eighty-first birthday (Monday the fifth) and Jack's eightieth birthday (Wednesday the seventh). Jack and Joe reflected on past and current events related to Scripture. God gifted all four of us with beautiful memories of the past. Laughter came easy and refreshed us despite Jack and Joe's unpredictable future.

We left their home late Sunday night to return to our hotel; Joe wanted us to stay longer. He said, "Jack, if I am in Heaven before you, I'll be waiting for you to arrive!"

Jack said, "Joe, if I reach Heaven before you, I'll be among the first to greet you!"

Joe then turned to Wanda and me, "Remember, Jack, and I will join that great cloud of witnesses in Heaven. We'll be praying for you two until you arrive!" Jack and Joe embraced.

Jack enjoyed his and Joe's hours together. Their life ministry, their love of the Scriptures, and the faithfulness of God throughout their life's journey—those conversations—had fed their spirit. Sickness and death could not conquer their faith, joy, and expectations of Heaven. They had both lived deeply committed lives to Jesus Christ. Their lives had been dedicated to others—often sacrificially—without the love of self, money, and pleasures. (See 2 Timothy 3:1–5, NIV.)

Jack and Joe didn't mention IRAs, savings and checking accounts, or accumulated possessions—they only talked of their treasures in Heaven. They had filled their heavenly treasure chests with "enduring riches" that outlast life and satisfy one's heart eternally. They did discuss 1 Corinthians 2:9 (KJV, Open Bible), "But as it is written, Eye hath not seen, nor ear heard, neither have entered into the heart of man, the things which God hath prepared for them that love him."

As faithful and dedicated pastors and ex-military, *death held no grip on Jack and Joe*. Neither did they offer complaints about their degenerating bodies. They both realized that Christians suffered pain in the Bible's "Hall of Fame and Faith" (Hebrews 11, KJV). *Eighteen days later, Joe, a servant pastor for his entire career, was in Heaven.*

Years before, Jack had told me that when he closed his eyes at night, he would often see a panoramic scene of faces—sons, husbands, and fathers—Americans—your neighbors and mine—who died in Vietnam. One hillside memorial service honored eighty-eight courageous marines. Upon his return from Vietnam, Jack said, "I consider each remaining day of my life a special gift from God. Because I am still here, I want to make each day count for eternity."

Jack and Joe looked at death as a step out of time into the eternal arms of their Lord and Savior, Jesus Christ! It held no fear—no clutch—over them! They lived forgiveness—no grudges or unforgiveness captured and imprisoned them! They were volunteer captives of Jesus Christ! *As they neared death, Jesus was all that mattered. Their spirits soared as they neared their eternal home!*

Chaplain Jack K. Golie—Vietnam (1968–69)

Goodbye Sermon to Church in Hartselle, Alabama

July 2017: Jack affirmed, "Jesus is my healer!"

Pedro Romero, the interpreter, was a former gang member. He experienced a spiritual transformation that changed his life

forever. He gives all the praise to Jesus Christ and to his mother, who never stopped praying for him.

In the early summer of 2017, Jack was home from the MD Anderson Hospital. The Spanish Church in Hartselle, Alabama, had invited Jack to speak to them again. After his sermon, he gave question/answer time to the small congregation.

One of the questions was, "In the Scriptures, all the people who came to Jesus were healed. How does it make you feel that you have not been healed?"

As seen in the above picture, Jack raised both hands toward Heaven and said, "Jesus is my healer. He is my Sovereign Lord. The moment I leave this earth, I will be healed forever!" (See Revelation 21:4–5, NIV.) *Thankfully, Pedro's wife, Maria, caught that memorable moment with her phone!*

Jack and Tim's Bible Studies

Bible studies were conducted between Jack's scheduled appointments in the hospital. In one study, he chose a back area in one of the coffee shops. A nurse came to one of the nearby tables. It was apparent that she was listening, though her back was toward us. After the study finished, she walked over to Jack and said, "You'll never know how much your Bible study meant to me today. Thank you." She then excused herself and returned to her job.

Jack and Tim studied the Bible together in the early 1980s in Troy, Montana. Each morning, they met for Bible study and prayer before Tim left for work. When the doctor first diagnosed Jack, he told me, "I need to find another minister to study the Bible with during this time." He picked up his phone, "I know; I'll call Tim!"

Excerpts below from their communications show Tim's support and intentional encouragement over their years of friendship.

Dear Pastor Jack,

You have exhorted me in every possible way about the importance of the church. I see Christian life in a different way. If the church is strengthened, then I am strengthened. We maintain spiritual health as part of the church. God's grace takes us beyond ourselves and makes us more like Jesus.

Your relationship with church members was especially notable toward two distinct groups—children and outcasts. You cared for the hurt ones in the church; you did not discard the difficult ones. All of us loved to be around you because we felt loved. There was always a warmth, which, by the way, is a quality not found in the world. Sadly enough, rarely in the church. I can't describe it any other way except as a "warmth" that nourished.

In commitment, you never counted the cost when the opportunity to minister presented itself. You lived as if your life was not your own. Certainly, you have given yourself on behalf of the church. Hours of prayer, study, planning, and work have been invested.

Your integrity has been a breath of fresh air. No traits are more essential to a church leader than integrity and purity. Leaders must have outward integrity and inward integrity.

God's Word has affected my life. In our *study of Jonah*, I learned that God would spare nothing but move Heaven and this entire world to bring me to Himself.

The *book of John* brought me increased faith in the Son of God. When I pray in Jesus' name, I have a firmer grasp of what that name makes available to me.

The *book of Romans* reproved me as it moved from "they," "you," "me," and "I" in the accusation of guilt. It taught me not to put people down but to value all people and see them through God's eyes—to treat people with care and dignity with a view to the power of the cross. My life has grown in thankfulness. I see myself as a product of God's mercy, not of any righteousness on my own.

Nehemiah taught me how to respond when a Christian falls or when the people of God are in desperate condition. It is not a time to blame. Nehemiah asked nothing for himself; he asked only for God's people. I learned in Nehemiah that real maturity weeps and never points the finger of blame. It is my responsibility to help build identity in the lives of God's people.

Our study in Ephesians, chapter 4, showed me how to avoid the terrifying process that begins with futile thinking and ends with an uncontrolled indulgence in evil of every kind. My personal life, home, and church need an atmosphere welcoming to the Holy Spirit and His work. I can avoid throwing water on the fire of God's Spirit by avoiding talk that tears down what God is building up. I will be free from bitterness, anger, combative spirit, and slander.

From Genesis, I learned that my wife, children, friends, church, job, property, etc., are gifts from God. As a good steward of these gifts, they can be a Garden of Eden in my life. I learned that God's Spirit broods over the formlessness of an unbeliever's life—giving me hope for my friends.

Much love, Tim.

The above picture was Jack's next to the last Bible study with Tim. Jack asked to wait in a side office for his medical appointment. He was under 130 pounds; his arms were black. When Jack was wheeled from his appointment, his grieving doctor said, "Barbara, Jack is dying!"

Their final Bible study was on August 19, twelve days before Jack's death. The topic: "The Proper Understanding of the Nature of Temptation" (James 1:13–15, KJV). Tim was unaware that Jack could not turn the pages of his Bible or notes. His strength was limited to holding his phone. He mentioned nothing to Tim about his physical difficulties.

As I turned the pages for him, I realized that one more study time together—though very weak—was Jack's way of saying his final goodbye to his long-time friend, Tim. No sad farewells or mention of his incapacitation—just his usual goodbye, "Catch you down the road, Tim!" (A phrase I placed on the dedication of this book to Jack.)

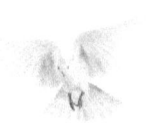

Final Reflections— On Our Forty-Fourth Houston Trip

For so long, I looked at the strings on the back side of the needlepoint of Jack's and my life. God had not given him the miracle I had prayed for, but he had given Jack a life-extension miracle that surprised all the doctors. At the best estimate, Jack was not to have lived past September-December 2015. As we traveled on our last trip to MD Anderson Hospital—Jack had already lived twenty-five-plus months. His competent doctor had done his best—not only medically—but as a friend to both of us.

How my heart knew we were on our last trip to MD Anderson, I do not know. Jack's body could no longer take the weariness of the journey. That is when his doctor at MD Anderson, an MDS leukemia specialist Jack dearly loved, transferred him to Vanderbilt University Hospital. That would be approximately one hundred miles from our home. Nurses said goodbye for the last time. They loved Jack's optimistic attitude despite the many needles. Several expressed their faith in God to him.

Their final goodbyes were realistically saying, "We will see you again in Heaven."

Jack's strong back had suffered three broken vertebrates due to medications. Surgery had tediously repaired them. In the last two weeks of his life, I personally heard two more vertebrates break. I cried out, "Jack!" Jack said nothing—he didn't even moan. He could then no longer help us get him out of bed.

Jack, a strong individual who had taken six years of boxing as a child, looked at me and said, "Angel, you do realize I cannot lie on my back forever?" Thankfully, the cracked and broken vertebrates never affected his spine—giving him feeling for the duration of his illness. The first three were repaired. Jack hoped his life extension miracle would help doctors learn more about the effects of the disease—his personal gift to others who would make the same journey. He had miraculously broken length-of-life records.

When Jack had walked, we consistently entered the hospital hand in hand. He always said, "Angel, we've been holding hands for a long, long time. Holding your hand today is just as exciting as the first time!" He usually said "wong, wong" time as a memory of our son's baby words. We did not hold hands as we departed from January to July; I pushed his wheelchair. He had never had a negative disposition toward me through his long, drawn-out battle with leukemia. Even in his diminished strength, he loved and encouraged me. Jana and I, who were with him continually, were amazed.

Once, when he called me in the night, my body was so stiff and sore that it took me five minutes to get to his side of the bed. In tears, I broke, "Jack, I am so sorry!"

He apologized.

My voice choked, "Jack, please never apologize. I'm so thankful we are together. You have been so tender and patient. You make me feel like I am caring for Jesus' special child when I help you!"

Tears filled his eyes. Emotional and physical unspoken pain—and the unknown events of each day often stole our words. Our silent thoughts were understood.

It was 2017, and our fifty-eighth anniversary would be August 7th. Jack knew my thoughts and said, "I promise to still be with you for our fifty-eighth, Angel!"

"You have never broken a promise to me, Jack Golie," was my guarded response.

Two weeks later, on August 7, our fifty-eighth anniversary came. We were so thankful God gave us one more! I gave Jack two profoundly serious cards, one not so serious. Jana approached me, "Mother, Dad kept reading your cards repeatedly for thirty minutes." *When the ones we love know they have to leave us, they need assurance of how much they are loved. They need to know our hearts will grieve because of their absence.*

Throughout his illness, Jack kept telling me, "Angel, we've had a wonderful life." Jack realized I needed help to plow "through my valley of why." He tried to soften my heartache a thousand ways before he left. *What a gift from God he was to me!*

Through Jack's extended challenge, one Bible verse literally became a visible experience. Saint Paul described the body's "wasting away" as graduating from mortality to immortality. The emphasis is on the "inner self" or the Spirit of God within us that is renewed daily.

So we do not lose heart. Though our outer self is wasting away, our inner self is being renewed day by day. For this light momentary affliction is preparing for us an eternal weight of glory beyond all comparison, as we look not to things that are seen but to the things that are unseen. For the things that are seen are transient, but the things that are unseen are eternal.

Second Corinthians 4:16–18 (ESV)

His many quotes I committed to memory. I needed to remember the times and the laughter we had enjoyed. One quote everyone recalls was Jack's greeting over the phone, "Is this the (_____insert your name_____) that the Lord hath made?" Jack said, "People need to be reminded that they are made in the image of God. There are so many who would tell us differently." Other favorite quotes were:

- "It's a *great, great* day!"
- "Angel, this is the day the Lord hath made for you and me!"
- He loved Col. Rufus Bower's phrase, "If life gets any better, I just can't stand it!"
- "What does the Scripture say?"
- "Don't you *love* God's Word? I *love* God's Word!"
- If a Bible study answer was not on target, "That dog won't hunt!" (or) "That dog won't even get up!"
- "*If* God says it is good, it is good!"
- "*Trust* God; He is sovereign."

- "Don't think we'll need to ask questions in Heaven."
- "Thy will be done—in my life—as it is done in Heaven."
- *"Obedience* = Thankfulness
- *"Thankfulness* = 'Well done, My good and faithful servant.'"
- *"All things work together for our good—when we love Him!"*

"Angel, not just some things—*all things*—even death!" (See Romans 8:28, KJV.)

Jack's Final Sermon— August 20, 2017

After several visits to Vanderbilt in July, Jack was extremely weak. He asked me to call Pastor Selbey DeLeon. When I handed him the phone, he asked, "Pastor Selbey, are you ready for the second part of the last sermon?" Pastor Selbey and his wife Dannie had invited Jack to speak at their Spanish Church in Decatur, Alabama.

Pastor Selbey said, "Yes, Jack. When can you come?"

Jack knew his time was short for worshiping with the Spanish congregation he dearly loved. He answered, "Is Sunday okay for you?"

It was Sunday, August 20, 2017 (eleven days before Jack's death). When we arrived at the Spanish Church, several men graciously rushed out and unloaded Jack's wheelchair. They placed him into the chair and pushed him to the steps. Then they picked up the chair and took him to the landing. He was so glad to see everyone. He needed to feel wanted, missed, and loved by other Christians.

Jack's weight was down even more. Both his arms had severely blackened. For comfort, he wore his Hawaiian dress

shirt. He couldn't bear the weight of my hand to lay on his arm without feeling the pressure.

The second part of his sermon, "Let's Go to the Other Side," was delivered. (See Luke 8:22–39, KJV.) Members of the congregation cried as he spoke. When he finished, there were few dry eyes.

Heaven opened Jack's loving heart to me, revealing his deep love for Christ. Jack clearly expressed Jesus' journey of love. He left the crowded area where there were many needs and searched for one person, an isolated demoniac named Legion. Jesus calmed the largest obstacle on the journey, the raging Lake Gennesaret storm. *All His efforts were to deliver healing to an outcast husband and father living in a cemetery!*

He then expressed how the healed man wanted to go with Jesus, but Jesus commissioned him to go home and tell his family of his miracle. The congregation understood how Jesus sacrificed to reach one person—even them! Jesus left the multitudes, crossed a stormy Lake Gennesaret, and walked on the water to increase the faith of His disciples to reach one tormented soul.

In my mind, I saw the stark contrast between Jack and the healed man. Jesus told the healed man to return to his family. However, with my husband, Jesus seemed to be telling Jack to leave his earthly family and come to his heavenly home. My heart cried, "God, give me the strength to release him to You! I cannot release him without Your help!"

After he finished the sermon, he gave them time to participate. He said, "To you who want to respond, please tell me how the Holy Spirit spoke personally to you today." (Jack did not mention his physical condition in his sermon.)

One lady's paraphrased response was, "I appreciate you coming when you are going through so much physically. I want to love people like Jesus loved people."

The Holy Spirit's presence was in the room. Even the youth explained what they had understood from the sermon about the love of Jesus. They comprehended that Jesus Christ would always be with them in their Lake Gennesaret's of life.

Suddenly, the inaudible voice of the Holy Spirit whispered to me that I had heard Jack's last sermon. He once said, "I have prayed, 'Not my will, but Thine be done.' Throughout this ordeal, Angel, I have sacrificed my broken body to God. Since January, I have only been able to move a little. You know that I live my life flat on my back. I have asked God to heal or take me in His time and sovereign plan. My days were numbered before I was born. I know that suffering is never for nothing." (See Psalm 90:12 and 139:16, NIV.) Jack had no blame toward God—only total surrender to His plan.

Jack's Last Sermon—August 20, 2017; Pastor Selbey DeLeon, Interpreter.

Jana Questions Prayers for Healing

Tears flooded Jana's face as she approached her father a few days before he left for Heaven. With a broken voice, she said, "Dad, tell me how you suffer so bravely—never once have you complained of your horrific pain? I can't understand! What's suffering like for you, Dad? What's it like to be dying? I'm so sorry! I've prayed for your healing. Those Bible verses I've prayed for have not come true. Dad, I'm not sure I believe them anymore! Listen to these verses, Dad." In heart-wrenching transparency, she laid her typed verses all over his bedside and read them to him.

At that moment, Jack fast-tracked down memory lane and visualized the twenty-month-old daughter he first embraced. She was removed from her first adoptive family. She didn't know why she left. Her eyes were swollen from crying! He recalled when he forced her into my arms as he boarded a plane twice to leave for Vietnam. Her crying had not kept him with us. Jack was the first person who ever returned to her. As only a father's heart can understand his daughter's feelings of rejection, Jack said,

"Daughter, you continue to pray for everyone's healing. Those verses are one hundred percent effective. I'm thankful you've prayed for my healing. God says, 'I've got a greater plan for Jack.' I don't want to leave my family, Jana, but I've responded to God with the words of Jesus' prayer, 'Not my will, but Yours be done—in my life—as it is in Heaven.' Trust Him!

"Jana, I'm nearing death. I can't tell you exactly what death is like because I've never died before! I do know what the Scriptures say. As I told your mother, 'When I close my eyes in death, I'll open them up in Heaven.' Then, I am healed forever! My back will not have three repaired and two more broken vertebrates. I will have a new body! This is your first time observing one of your parents dying. It's difficult for you! Trust God!

"I'm not concerned about my final test with pain. The only question I keep repeating to God is, 'Have I loved every person in the churches I've pastored as You love them? I've tried. If I failed, please forgive me.'" (Jack felt that Ezekiel 34 was the unconditional love that he, as a pastor, should always seek to achieve.)

"Jana, Jesus could lean over to the Father this morning and say, 'Dad, let's heal Jack today!' Instead, He told His Father, 'Dad, give Jack the strength to talk to Jana when she goes into his room with a broken heart.' That's how much God loves you and me, Jana!"

Jack spoke in awe of the "role reversals" of the rich man and Lazarus, the two men in Jesus' parable. He described the sumptuous scene at the rich man's home where Lazarus was the beggar. He then described the scene in Heaven where Lazarus was celebrated, and the rich man was the beggar. Jack said,

"Angel, when we leave this world, we are escorted by angels! What a concept!" (See Luke 16:19–31, KJV.)

Goodbye Indicators

Sunday, August 27, 2017, Jack was too weak to attend church. When he was first diagnosed, they had told him he had to stay away from people as much as possible. The first Sunday, he stayed away from the church as suggested by the doctors.

The next Sunday, he said, "No more! Even though my immunity is deficient, I will not stay isolated. I can't hurt anyone. It is me who's vulnerable. God has numbered my days." During his entire illness, he never once caught a cold. Even though he was surrounded by hundreds of seriously ill patients in the hospitals, he was never sick except with his own diagnosis.

After his treatment at Vanderbilt on August 24th, Jack received no strength. His weight had gone down to 125 pounds. The nurse said, "You've got to wake him as we are closing the ward. The doors have already been locked."

With his eyes closed, Jack said, "Angel, tell the nurse to go home. It's okay. I'm really tired." My heart sank. The nurses at MD Anderson had told me the end would come when the blood transfusions no longer gave him energy. For sure, his energy was gone. It hurt to dissipate it with a long ride home and the energy it took from him to be placed in bed.

On Saturday, August 26th, I called Vanderbilt Hospital and told them he was extremely weak. The blood transfusions on Thursday were ineffective. They gave me the option of hospitalization or remaining home until Monday. That was the saddest weekend of our lives. Jana and I did everything possible to express love to him—his last two days at home. He spoke for a few minutes with Gregory, Shellie, and Alexandra.

Arrangements were made to have him taken by ambulance to Vanderbilt on Monday. Jack refused. He said, "Pastor Selbey will help you get me to the car. I am not going by ambulance. I will sit in the passenger seat of Jana's car."

Pastor Selbey came to help us lift Jack into the passenger seat. As we drove away, Pastor Selbey gave Jack an exceptionally long look. Jack saluted him! Later, Pastor Selbey told me he knew he would never see Jack again.

After testing and another blood transfusion at Vanderbilt, they planned to take him to the ICU, and I asked, "Why?"

They said, "We can keep him alive with all the machines and trained staff."

"No," I said. "My husband has suffered five broken vertebrae. His body cannot sustain someone pounding on his chest."

One of the three doctors walked around to my side of the bed. He softly said, "Mrs. Golie, if he were my father, I would not take him there either. We can place him in palliative care for his remaining hours."

In a broken voice, I asked, "How many hours does Jack have left with us?"

He said, "Up to seventy-six hours."

Then I faintly mumbled, "We will go to palliative care."

Jack was asleep while the doctors were in the room. After they left, I said, "Please wake up, Jack. I must talk to you."

He opened his eyes and looked at me.

Softly, I said, "Jack, you and I have never had secrets from one another, have we?"

His eyes were questioning, "No, Angel. Why do you ask me that?"

In a low voice, I said, "Well, I will not keep any secret from you now." His eyes looked at me curiously! I continued, "Jack, the doctors told me you are to be taken to palliative care."

Jack had been an orderly through college and seminary. He knew hospitals and procedures. He knew the seriousness of the situation. His soft reply was, "How much time do I have left, Angel?"

Struggling to keep my composure, I answered, "You have up to seventy-six hours—maybe a few more, maybe less."

He appeared peacefully relieved and said, "Oh, okay. I need to go back to sleep; I am so tired. I'm sorry, angel, but talking hurts my chest."

The first admission that he was suffering! Jack's diligent Bible studies, prayers, and sermons were finished. His life of ministry was completed. God's ministering angels were now orchestrating his departure. Jack so willingly submitted. His seabag was tied tightly. He was ready for the master of the seas to anchor his ship into Heaven's eternal harbor. He would finally hear his long-awaited words from Jesus, "Jack, you have been faithful!"

Tuesday afternoon arrived. The staff came to move him to palliative care. The transfer to the palliative care unit was

through an underground tunnel. They had to run down the previous hill to push the bed to the top of the next hill. Jana ran with them. My feet were severely swollen from lack of sleep. Jana ran to Jack; she knew he did not understand the fast race. She was the first to reach him and said, "How are you doing, Dad?"

He said, "Wow! What was that all about?"

In the late afternoon, Jack looked at us peacefully for several minutes. He could no longer speak as it was too painful. Jana raised his arm to rest on her head for the picture below. We did not realize this was the last time his expressive blue eyes would give us a long and loving gaze while they silently said, "Goodbye. I love you!"

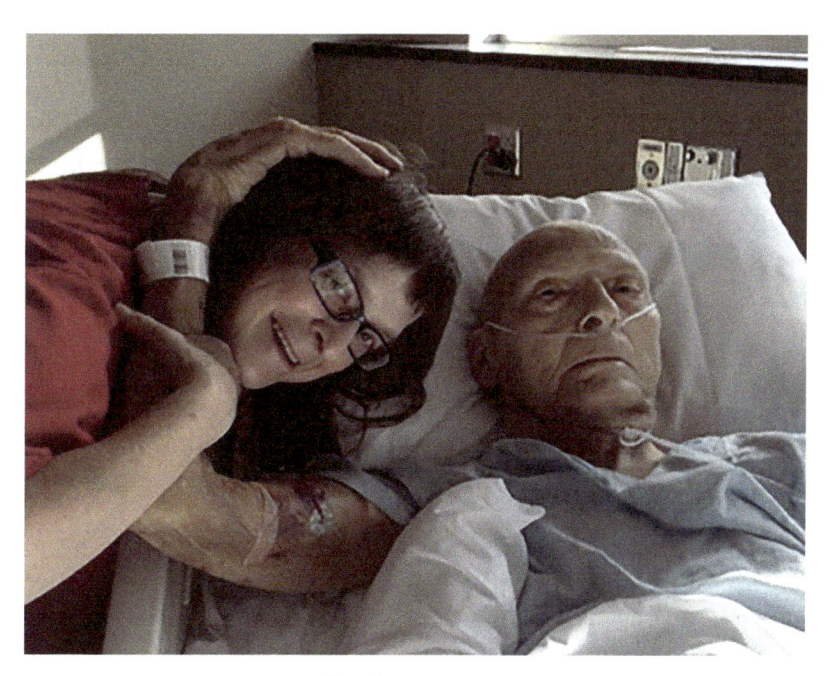

Jana and Jack—August 28, 2017
"Goodbye. I love you."

When I took the picture of Jana with Jack, his eyes never left me. Jana leaned close to him, and I took a good picture of him looking straight at the camera. He then looked straight into my eyes for a few minutes. I walked to the right side of the bed and took his hand. He closed his eyes, opening them for only a few seconds at 5 p.m. Once he closed his eyes again, they were closed forever.

The unread newspaper Jana had bought him earlier lay on the window shelf. His last spoken words were, "Thanks, Jana. Put it on the window shelf, and I will read it later." He always read the newspaper. That day was the exception.

Reflections on our life scrolled in my mind as I stayed by his bedside and held his hand Tuesday night, Wednesday, and Wednesday night. One of the hospital chaplains and the ward nurse supervisor (a seminarian) celebrated communion with Jack, Jana, and me at 4 p.m. on Wednesday afternoon. The ministers prayed. Jack was fully aware as I served him grape juice on a cotton swab for communion. The moments were sacred. Both ministers had already spent time with us during the day.

The ministers left the room. Jana and I were alone with Jack for the remainder of the night. We thanked God for Jack's life— for such a wonderful husband and father. We prayed that angels would continually minister to him *as his spirit soared home*. With angel escorts, we prayed for a peaceful and painless exit to Heaven. Jack had not opened his eyes since Tuesday afternoon when we took his last picture with Jana.

When Heaven's Escorts Came

August 30, 2017, at 10:30 p.m., I prayed silently from my heart and said, "Father, it would have been wonderful to have been able to say goodbye to Jack. I didn't know he would not open his eyes again." My heart was devastated that there had not been a goodbye. Jack squeezed my hand twice as I finished that silent prayer (his usual pattern)! Then he *held* the squeeze on my hand!

In shock, I said, "Jana, please turn on my phone and take a picture of our hands." Jack held the squeeze until the phone came on, and Jana took the picture. He then released the squeeze. To Jana and me, it was a miracle!

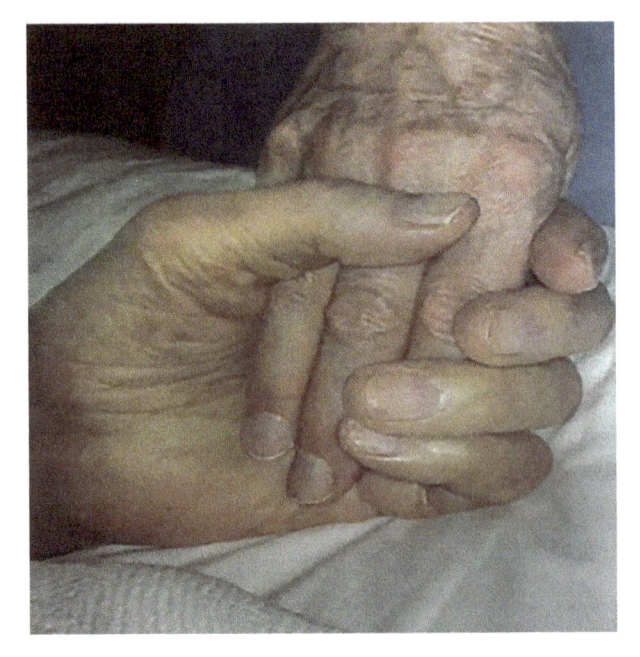

Jack's "Hand-Hold"—His Final Goodbye—10:30 p.m.,
August 30, 2017.

Jana said, "Mother, how could he squeeze your hand like that? He had no strength! That had to be an angel holding that squeeze!" Hopefully, Jack's white knuckles can be seen holding tightly to my hand. God hears prayers that are not voiced—prayers from the depths of our hearts. There are no limits to the omniscience (all-knowing) and omnipresence (everywhere present) of the one who walks alongside us—the Holy Spirit!

The Holy Spirit's presence was so real throughout the evening. When Jack's heart flatlined around 1:30 a.m., I lost it. Immediately, I pressed my face against his and said, "Jack, I'm not ready to let you go!" As I kept talking, his heart started beating again. The heaviest sense of guilt overcame me to think that his hesitation was for my sake. Then, I apologized to Jack and God for my utter selfishness.

Why wouldn't I want him to leave his wrecked body of pain to be forever healed and be with our Lord? Jack's words had always been, "I don't care if Heaven is black as long as Jesus is there! It is not the streets of gold that impress me; it is Jesus I want to see!"

My lips were against Jack's left ear, and I began praying for angels to escort him. Over and over, I quoted Psalm 23. At 1:45 a.m., August 31, 2017, Jack's heart flatlined forever. Nobody can understand what it is to lose a loving companion unless they have experienced that deep loss. It is the bottom depth of sorrow. It is as though ninety-nine percent of all that is you has departed with them.

As I continued to sob with my face against his, I heard his voice. He was saying, "Angel, I'm not there anymore. Look up!"

It was so real that I immediately stood and said, "Jana! Jack told us to look up!"

From the window, Jana and I looked up into the skies and waved goodbye to him! The occurrence was an absolute reality to me! While we waved toward the skies, a lightning bolt popped outside the window. *We both saw the brilliant lightning as the thunder clapped.**

The doctor arrived at the room around 2:15 a.m. Jack's death was documented at 2:22 a.m. However, Jana and I were there at 1:45 a.m. when Jack exited his body of pain and illness. We remained in the room for two more hours. Though Jack's earthly body was still lying in the bed, the husband and father

---

* According to weather.gov, three tornadoes touched down in TN on the Golie family's memorable night of August 31, 2017. Up until 11:30–12:00 midnight, tree limbs were broken by the winds. There was flooding in specific areas. From the information, there was no more damage after midnight.

we knew had departed. Only Jack's empty shell (tent or outer earthly covering) remained on the bed.

The Jack we knew and loved had safely anchored in God's safe harbor—Heaven. The husband I treasured for fifty-eight-plus years was waiting for his family! He had heard the words he longed to hear, "Jack, you have been faithful." *See Matthew 25:23, (KJV)*.

As I reflect on how resolute Jack was through his suffering, his doctoral thesis on 1 Peter surfaces in my mind. He memorized the book in English and Greek. His absorption of that powerful book gave him steel-like faith.

Jack's thesis gives insight into his spiritual strength in submission to the suffering he gracefully endured (1 Peter 1:6–7, NIV). Jack's words:

"My goal is to view suffering in every form as a gift from God to refine my faith. Continually, I remind myself that suffering is a privilege and a high honor. Never again will I focus on gold because it perishes as time ticks away. However, my refined faith will continue forever. *I am determined to allow its message to penetrate my spirit so that my whole being will be filled with that inexpressible and glorious joy*."

My Open Vision of Jack

Our home overlooking beautiful Chula Vista Lake was for sale. Jack wanted me to move into a retirement village. After his funeral, I plunged into the final stages of another move.

In April, I attended an Alaska memorial service for the ministers of our denomination. Simple memorials for Jack were also conducted in Tok and Yakutat, Alaska.

June 2018 approached. A potential buyer offered me far below the price for our home. No money would be committed before September. My answer was no. One hundred thousand dollars of renovations were made to the home. An extra lot was added. National home sale statistics were grim.

After a disappointing late-night call, I poured my soul out to God, "God, You promised to care for me when You took Jack. He made a covenant with You. I need Your help selling this house where You permit me to live. Everything we have is Yours. Send Your buyer." I pressed my face into the pillow with tears flowing. For the first time in my life, I fell asleep sobbing.

In my deep sleep, I experienced an open vision. As Jack walked into our bedroom, I was awakened. He had on his Marine khakis with the sleeves rolled above his elbows. He wore his combat boots! (I should have expected that!) I quickly

jumped from the bed to greet and tell him about our problem. Before I uttered a word, I covered my face with my hands and buried my head into his chest—tears flowed uncontrollably.

Jack put his strong arms around me (no longer weak and black from illness), laid his head over the top of my head, and stroked the length of my hair. He slowly repeated the following sentence three times, "Angel, everything is going to be okay. Angel, everything is going to be okay. Angel, everything is going to be okay." Then he was gone, and I sat on the side edge of the bed.

Within three days, the house was sold to a Christian engineer and businessman who loved the house and paid the asking price. God had affirmed His promise in Proverbs 15:25 (ESV), "The Lord tears down the house of the proud but maintains the widow's boundaries."

As a Christian, I look at the death of my companion optimistically—*Jack is in Christ, and I am in Christ—we cannot be far apart!* Those were Jack's words to me!

When our anniversary came in 2018, it devastated me to face the day. Our daughter Jana came into the bedroom and told me that Jack's picture had fallen over during the night. It was on our piano. I rushed in to see what had happened. Instead, I found Jack's secret fifty-ninth-anniversary card! Before he left us, he had dictated the card—not to be given to me until our next wedding anniversary. Shocked, I quickly opened the card. He concluded his note with, "Angel, you were a great trooper! I've given you enough memories to last for your lifetime! We'll be together again soon!"

"Together Again Soon" = Heaven!

August 7, 2009: Our Fiftieth Wedding Anniversary
Hale Koa Hotel Beach, Hawaii
Heaven = Together Forever!

Epilogue

Embrace the Wind of the Holy Spirit traces the beginnings of the author's Ozark hillbilly heritage. If you love inspirational stories, this book is a must-read!** As the author revisits vulnerable, raw, and sacred emotions throughout the book, the Holy Spirit will gracefully speak to you. Grace is not hoarded for life's emergencies but dispensed by your heavenly Father as needed.

Jack's noble and faith-based approach to death in "Through My Valley of Why" encouraged all who knew him to dig their deep well of faith.

In one of his many goodbye conversations, Jack told Barbara, *"Scripture takes us behind the scenes to reveal the news before the news. Since Israel became a nation in 1948, the events of the world have spiraled on a fast crescendo, flowering smack-dab into the book of Revelation. Israel is God's time clock. Be alert to how the nations of the world deny her existence. It is not a time to be afraid. It is time to look up!"* (See Luke 21:28, KJV.)

Jack and Barbara's beautiful life together was intricately connected with the ocean. Jack's family repeatedly said goodbye to him as he sailed on Navy ships.

** For the term of this contract, the author's proceeds from this book will be donated to the most needy Christian missions internationally.

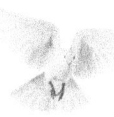

Barbara and Jana reside in Virginia, a few miles from the ocean. They enjoy close interactions with military families. Gregory's family has always resided in California.

"God's Word ~ Your Safe Harbor" is the upcoming *free* newsletter of Jack's Bible Studies. If interested, submit your request to jkbe1959@gmail.com.

Printed in the USA
CPSIA information can be obtained
at www.ICGtesting.com
LVHW010150130624
783008LV00001B/2